CP   1st 10⁴

Inside
East Germany

Inside
East Germany
The state that came in from the cold

Jonathan Steele

URIZEN BOOKS
NEW YORK

ISBN 0-916354-73-3 hardcover

First published in the United States by Urizen Books,
Inc. 66 West Broadway, New York, N.Y. 10007

Printed in Great Britain

Contents

Preface

Powerful Communist parties have become an unmistakable landmark on the political map of Western Europe. In France and Italy where they used to be on the sidelines and in Portugal and Spain where they spent decades underground, Communists have broken on to the central political stage. Although the parties themselves are old, their reappearance has come to many people as a shock. A philosophy whose appeal seemed outdated or discredited has suddenly been resurrected as a living force. A new generation of European voters, raised since the end of the Cold War, is prepared to give Communism a second chance.

To anyone who would listen, the parties have repeatedly asserted that they have changed. Now the audience is bigger. Questions about the Communist parties' character, allegiance, motives and goals are no longer academic. They have become a central theme for political discussion in Washington and throughout the West. Are the Western European parties truly independent of Moscow as the French, Italian and Spanish Communists say they are? How far are they prepared to go in compromising revolutionary principles for the sake of joining coalitions with non-Communists? What indeed is their revolutionary blueprint? Do they accept a form of political pluralism and has the concept of the 'dictatorship of the proletariat' been discarded by the French and Italians as a temporary expedient or a permanent amputation?

Are parties that come to power through the ballot-box ready to let the electorate change its mind and vote them out again?

Is the arrival of Communists on the political stage in a few Western countries already an 'irreversible' phenomenon, and is it likely to lead – as Dr Henry Kissinger has suggested – to a 'domino' process in which Communist parties in other European countries will gain respectability, grow in strength, and eventually become a major, perhaps the major, political force? Above all, what are the Soviet Union's intentions towards Western Europe? Does it favour the rise of Communist parties as a step towards a neutralist and in the long run a pro-Soviet Western Europe, or does it fear it as the beginning of an unknown road which might lead to a third centre of independent Communism, as troublesome to Moscow in the end as Maoism has been for more than a decade and a half? In his warnings about European Communism Dr Kissinger expressed the view that the rise of the French and Italian parties could cause as many headaches in Moscow as in Washington.

Political memories tend to be notoriously short. Many of the questions that are being raised about European Communist parties now were also asked before the Second World War, particularly in Germany. In the late 1920s Germany had the largest Communist party in Europe outside the Soviet Union. In 1932 it won almost 17 per cent of the vote, a percentage as high as the French or Portuguese Communist parties have today. The debate about its motives and loyalty was considerably fiercer than any of the current discussions in Europe now. Of course the debate was not resolved by the party's advent to power and an examination of its behaviour in office. Backed by a majority of German non-Communist and anti-Communist politicians who were not prepared to take the risk, Hitler swept into power and crippled the party with a wave of arrests and executions.

Driven underground and into exile, the party managed to survive Hitler's terror and an almost equally damaging purge by Stalin a few years later. When German Communists re-emerged at the end of the war, circumstances were very different. Germany was ravaged, desperate, and partly under Soviet military occupation. German Communists were no longer operating within the framework of the pre-war political debate. Nevertheless, many of the themes which had been alive in the Weimar Republic and which are being revived with the return of the Western Communist parties today were discussed in the early post-war years. German Communists in the Soviet Zone were never in total agreement with Stalin or among themselves. Like the French or Italian Communist party programmes now, the first post-war German programme did not talk of the 'dictatorship of the proletariat'. It called for a broad alliance of democratic forces behind reforms in agriculture, the economy, and education, and assumed that the transition to socialism was a long way off. Six months later the party published an article, 'Is there a separate German road to socialism?', which pointed out the differences between Germany and Russia. At times, before and after the war, German Communists went into a tactical alliance with Social Democrats as the French party does now, and then later tried to ignore them as the Italians have done.

The German Communist party provides the deepest and longest store of experience of how Communists in Europe have adjusted to the possibilities of power in a sophisticated urban political system, where civil liberties and the rights of free assembly had long been accepted. With the partial exception of the much smaller Czechoslovak Communist party, the other ruling parties which emerged in Europe were installed to power – in Poland, Hungary, and the Balkans – in countries whose economy was largely rural and which had never enjoyed a Western political tradition.

Some may say that the later development of the Soviet zone into a Stalinist satellite proves an inherent Communist drive towards totalitarian forms of Government. This is precisely why they suspect the sincerity of Italian and French Communists who promise now to adhere to the prevailing rules of the game. But it is equally arguable that the pressures for a hard and undemocratic line in the Soviet zone came mainly from Stalin's perception of Russia's security needs. In a war-torn Europe and at a time when the ideological conflict between East and West was at its highest he judged the Soviet Union to be economically and militarily inferior to the United States. An open system in the Soviet zone would be too risky.

The geo-political framework within which Western European Communism operates today has changed. But the themes for debate are similar. It is also worth pointing out that in spite of overwhelming Soviet control in East Germany the country has remained faithful to some national traditions and evolved in a number of ways which are more European than Russian. If German Communists were able to do that in the face of Soviet military occupation, how much more independent could or would Italian and French Communists be?

For many years East Germany has been looked at in broad terms as a carbon copy of the Soviet system. But as the rise of Western Communist parties begins to focus urgent, new light on to European Communism, the differences between Communist parties are arousing as much interest as their similarities. This study aims at satisfying that interest. It examines the pre- and post-war debates between Communists and non-Communists in Germany to see how their results later bore fruit in the development of the German Democratic Republic and of the unique society which it has become. The revived discussion about Western Communism is unfortunately short on hard experience and historical data. But where clearly comparable situations do not exist, skewed evidence is better than none at all. If its specific features can be distinguished from what is of general significance in European Communism, the history of the German Democratic Republic provides one of the few test-beds that we have.

Washington, 1976   J.S.

Acknowledgments

Many people have helped to germinate the ideas in this book. Others have generously given information. My thanks go out for scores of conversations on everyday issues with too many residents of the German Democratic Republic to name, but I should particularly like to thank those who talked about the country's past. They include Werner Goldstein, Otto Gotsche, Robert Havemann, Stefan Heym, Walter Janka, Kurt Kohn, Jurgen Kuczynski, John Peet, Elli Schmidt and Fritz Selbmann.

Among West Germans I owe a special debt to the following people who generously made material available: Jörg Mettke, the first correspondent of *Der Spiegel* in the GDR, Doris Cornelsen and Manfred Melzer of the Deutsches Institut für Wirtschaftsforschung, Berlin-Dahlem, and Hartmut Zimmermann of the Free University, West Berlin.

Boundless thanks, too, to Ian Wright, the Foreign Editor of the *Guardian*, who gave me time off in the last stages of writing, and to my wife, Ruth, and the numerous friends who read parts of the manuscript and made suggestions.

Abbreviations

BPO	Betriebsparteiorganisation (Factory Party Organisation)
CDU	Christian Democratic Union
Comecon	The Council for Mutual Economic Assistance
DBD	Demokratischer Bauernbund Deutschlands (Democratic German Farmers' Party)
DDR	Deutsche Demokratische Republik
DFD	Demokratischer Frauenbund Deutschlands (Democratic German League of Women)
DIW	Deutsches Institut für Wirtschaftsforschung (West German Institute for Economic Research)
FDGB	Freier Deutscher Gewerkschaftsbund (Federation of Free German Trade Unions)
FDJ	Freie Deutsche Jugend (Free German Youth)
FRG	Federal Republic of Germany
GDR	German Democratic Republic
GNP	Gross National Product
KAP	Kooperative Abteilungen der Pflanzenproduktion (Co-operative crop departments)
KPD	Kommunistische Partei Deutschlands (German Communist Party)
LDPD	Liberal-Demokratische Partei Deutschlands (Liberal Democratic Party of Germany)
LPG	Landwirtschaftliche Produktionsgenossenschaft (Agricultural production co-operative)
NDPD	National-Demokratische Partei Deutschlands (National Democratic Party of Germany)

NES	New Economic System
NKVD	Narodny Komityet Vnutrennikh Dyel (People's Committee for Internal Affairs)
NVA	Nationale Volksarmee (National People's Army)
RIAS	Radio in the American Sector
SED	Sozialistische Einheitspartei Deutschlands (Socialist Unity Party of Germany)
SPD	Sozialdemokratische Partei Deutschlands (Social Democratic Party of Germany)
UNESCO	United Nations Educational, Scientific and Cultural Organisation
VEB	Volkseigener Betrieb (Nationalised Enterprise)
VVB	Vereinigung Volkseigener Betriebe (Association of Socialist Enterprises)

NOTE ON EXCHANGE RATES

At the beginning of April 1977:
£1 = 4.12 – 4.08 East German Marks
$1 = 2.39 – 2.36 East German Marks

Introduction

On October 18 1973 a short elderly man with a bald head and metal-rimmed glasses mounted the podium of the United Nations General Assembly in New York. His name had been unknown to most delegates a few weeks earlier. Otto Winzer was Foreign Minister of the German Democratic Republic, and at the age of seventy-one it was a triumphal moment for him and his country. Once the Soviet zone of Germany, more commonly known as East Germany, the GDR had finally broken through a long international boycott to become the one hundred and thirty-third member of the United Nations.

On the same day the General Assembly accepted the Federal Republic of Germany and the Bahamas as its other new members. West Germany had been a member of several UN agencies, including the World Health Organisation, and the United Nations Educational, Scientific, and Cultural Organisation (UNESCO) for more than twenty years. It joined them in the early 1950s when Western influence was paramount at the UN. Its allies felt some qualms about giving the Federal Republic full membership so soon after the war which had given rise to the United Nations, and West Germany remained outside the General Assembly. But its absence from the annual forum in New York had little effect on West Germany's self-esteem. From its foundation in 1949 the country was a recognised member of the international community and enjoyed full diplomatic relations with most states in the world.

Its speaker in the General Assembly that October of 1973 was Willy Brandt, Federal Chancellor, Nobel Peace Prize winner and statesman of international renown. To many people around the world he personified 'the good German', a man who had fought the Nazi regime in his country and then gone into exile rather than collaborate with a dictatorship which was to wreak unparalleled destruction on the European continent.

Yet in what way did his record differ from that of little-known, apparently insignificant Otto Winzer? In April 1933, two months after Hitler came to power, Brandt, then nineteen, had fled in a fishing boat from Germany to Norway. He was a member of the Socialist Labour Party, a small left-wing splinter group, and carried in his briefcase the first volume of Karl Marx's *Das Kapital*. For the next fourteen years he lived in Scandinavia, working against the Nazis. He spent most of his time in Norway, but had two secret resistance missions to Germany to his credit. After the war he stayed two more years in Norway, then renounced the Norwegian citizenship which he had taken out, and went back to a ruined Germany.

Otto Winzer was thirty-one when Hitler became Chancellor. He had been a member of the German Communist Party (die Kommunistische Partei Deutschlands) since 1919 and was later put in charge of the Young Communist International publishing house. A conspicuous member of the party which was Hitler's first target in 1933, Winzer went underground in Berlin as soon as the Nazi drive against the Communists began. In 1935 he went into exile in the Soviet Union. During the war he was active in the National Committee for a Free Germany which was based in Russia and tried to persuade German prisoners of war to turn against Hitler. Shortly before the war ended Winzer became one of the first German anti-Fascists to return to Berlin. His job was to organise the de-Nazification of schools in the German capital.

Like Willy Brandt, Otto Winzer was a 'good German'. Most of his senior colleagues in the GDR also suffered under Hitler, and tried to organise resistance during the war. Walter Ulbricht, who died as the GDR's Head of State two months before it joined the United Nations, spent most of the pre-war Nazi years in Western Europe keeping up underground party cells. He too lived in Russia during the war. Erich Honecker, the present first secretary of the ruling Sozialistische Einheitspartei

2

Deutschlands (SED), spent ten years in Brandenburg prison in Berlin after a Nazi trial for high treason.

The trouble was that these 'good Germans' helped to found the 'bad' German state, the 'other Germany', the German Democratic Republic. For more than twenty years West Germany and its allies in the North Atlantic Treaty Organisation refused to have any dealings with it. In the Western world it was considered a bastard state, an artificial satellite of the Soviet Union. The building of the Berlin Wall in August 1961 fixed the stereotype of the GDR's illegitimacy in many people's minds. Under the so-called Hallstein doctrine, devised by one of its state secretaries, Walter Hallstein (who later became president of the Common Market Commission), the Federal Republic declared it would cut off aid and break relations with any state that recognised East Germany. Throughout the 1960s the ban had considerable effect in the Third World among states who felt too poor to resist this financial threat. The Hallstein doctrine was the diplomatic arm of a consistent West German policy of trying to prevent the Communists in the GDR from consolidating their rule. It was backed by a variety of means, including direct economic and political pressure, a campaign to encourage a brain drain of skilled people from the GDR, massive radio and television propaganda, and in some instances outright sabotage and subversion by Western agents working in the GDR. Only with Willy Brandt's accession to power in October 1969 did senior West German politicians first accept the existence of a second German state. Even then it took almost five more years of hard negotiations before the two states exchanged permanent missions and officially recognised each other.

Although the Western boycott was the most aggravating international issue for the GDR, its relations with its allies in Eastern Europe were not without problems. In spite of the GDR's official integration into the Warsaw Pact and Comecon, they also took a long time to give up the feeling that it was an artificial state. The GDR had to achieve legitimacy in the eyes of its friends as well as its enemies. For the first years after the war Stalin saw the country primarily as a strategic buffer for the Soviet Union and a source of reparations payments. The interests of the small minority of Communists in the Soviet zone took second place. Three times, first under Stalin, then under Malenkov and Beria, and finally under Khrushchev, the Soviet Union toyed with the idea of withdrawing from the country in return for the neutralisation of all Germany. Although the Russians hoped, at least in the first years after the war, that a neutral Germany would be leftward-leaning they were more concerned to ensure it had a safe foreign policy than a Communist political system. In 1955 to the chagrin of the East German leadership the Soviet Union recognised the Federal Republic without demanding a diplomatic *quid pro quo* for the GDR. It was not until 1974, almost exactly a year after the GDR's entry into the United Nations that reciprocity came and the major Western power, the United States, recognised the GDR.

Poles and Czechs who had suffered much at the hands of Germans were in no hurry to be convinced that the 'good-ness' of the GDR outweighed its 'German-ness'. The GDR was German. To them that was enough. In accepting the GDR as a separate state, the Polish and Czech Governments saw it mainly as a way of keeping Germany divided rather than out of respect for East Germany as such. Poland and Czechoslovakia delayed the GDR's entry into the Warsaw Pact until after their own. They were against the formation of an East German army until the country signed treaties which guaranteed their new post-war borders.

For two and a half decades the GDR's leadership had to live in diplomatic purdah. Its foreign policy was almost entirely dominated by the struggle to come in from the cold. Most of the credit for finally succeeding must go to Walter Ulbricht who was effectively the real power among German Communists from the end of the war. His faults were many and even his close colleagues never found him an easy or likeable man. With his stubbornness and stern personality he was not unlike Konrad Adenauer, the first Chancellor of the Federal Republic. But Ulbricht's effort in creating the GDR against the wishes of the West and in spite of some reluctance in the East was the greater personal achievement. He was arguably the most successful German statesman since Bismarck, although Bismarck's achievement was the unification of Germany and Ulbricht presided over its division.

This was not his original intention. Until the end of the war

4

neither he nor any other German Communist wanted, let alone foresaw, that Germany would later become two separate states. They never meant the division of Germany into occupation zones to be permanent. Only as the general split between East and West developed did Ulbricht's strategy focus increasingly on the preservation of Communist rule in the Soviet zone. To him this meant above all the consolidation of state power in Communist hands. Opposed on several occasions by his party colleagues, and subjected to a continual barrage of hostile and derisory propaganda from the West, Ulbricht went doggedly on. He was never the stereotype 'Kremlin puppet' which his detractors sometimes like to claim. He frequently showed great tactical skill in moulding Moscow's German policy and preventing some of the deals with the West which threatened to go over his head. He retired in 1971 as first secretary of the party shortly before the GDR achieved widespread recognition but he remained Head of State until his death. Although his health was failing, his departure from the top party job was largely engineered by a firm but gentle push. His domestic policies were arousing growing criticism from his colleagues, and the Russians found him too inflexible once the process of negotiations with West Germany began. Nevertheless, it was Ulbricht who laid the ground for making the GDR too strong to ignore.

Ulbricht and his German Communist comrades also had to win legitimacy for their rule in the eyes of their own citizens. International recognition would mean little if the society's internal stability was in doubt. And that stability could not be based on compulsion alone. There had to be something of a voluntary consensus behind it. Throughout the 1950s and 1960s the GDR leadership's dilemma was this: it wanted international recognition in order to justify and sanction the party's rule, but that recognition was likely to bring pressures for a relaxation in that rule. Ulbricht decided that the key was economic development. The stronger East Germany's economy became, the more indispensable it would be to the Russians who would be less tempted to give it up. Its allies and its enemies would respect it more. And so would its people. In Eastern Europe for the first years after the war economic development meant the installation and expansion of heavy industry. Wages were kept low. The shops contained little to buy. In the GDR it took the workers' riots of June 1953 to persuade the leadership of the necessity to provide people with a bigger immediate return for their labour.

Eight years later it became clear that still more had to be done. No other East European Government has faced the enormous challenge of having a sister nation with a common language just across the frontier which constantly sought to denigrate it and woo its people, and to which they could simply transfer — at least until the Berlin wall was built in 1961. The decision taken then to shut out the reality of West Germany was accompanied by an equally important decision to shut out the myth as well. Ulbricht resolved to go all-out for development in consumers' interests and thus prove that with its own 'economic miracle' people in the GDR could live as well as their West German neighbours, and ultimately better.

East Berlin now has two effective city centres. They symbolise the change of emphasis. The old pre-Wall centre which is still the political hub is the Marx-Engels-Platz, scene of May Day military parades long after the rest of Eastern Europe gave them up. Around it stand the headquarters of the Council of State and of the Socialist Unity Party. Nearby, alongside the Cathedral which is under restoration, stand the brand-new Palace of the Republic and the white egg-box of the Ministry of Foreign Affairs, two triumphant statements of the GDR's successful drive for recognition. Less than half a mile away from these unpeopled open spaces are the future monuments of the GDR of the 1970s — the new ten-pin bowling alleys and discothèques of the town hall arcades, the cafés round the foot of the television tower and the shopping centre on the Alexanderplatz. A red neon sign advertising the national savings bank faces customers streaming out of the Centrum department store, the most modern and best-stocked in Eastern Europe. The building nearby with the coloured mosaic on the façade is the teachers' headquarters, the 'House of the Teacher'. Beyond that from another sign put up by the state advertising agency there winks one of the key phrases of this save-spend-and-learn society — 'Advertise for a purpose'. No other East European society is quite as purposive as East Germany. The marriage of German traditions to the goal-directed philosophy of a Communist state

6

has produced a particularly intense, disciplined, and orderly society.

Collectively and individually the goal is high mass consumption and universal welfare services. It has become a truism to point out that all over Eastern Europe since the early 1970s governments have been trying to fashion a new consensus, based on their ability to provide a reasonable and steadily growing standard of living. Consumer satisfaction now has a high priority. The Alexanderplatz with its concrete affluence is the symbolic result. In the years since the Wall went up the supply of every kind of consumer durable has increased considerably. By its economic results the GDR has assured its position. It is the world's eighth industrial nation according to output per head, and it has the highest standard of living in Eastern Europe. By whatever indicator you want to measure it, whether it is the percentage of families with cars, the size of people's flats, or the amount of meat they eat, the average family in the GDR is better off than in the rest of Eastern Europe. Its Eastern neighbours respect the GDR now as a full partner; perhaps even fear it a little. Its Western neighbours are beginning to look for lucrative business deals.

The World Bank has calculated that in 1974 the GDR's *per capita* income overtook that of Britain.[1] At $3,710 per person it was ahead of Britain's $3,590. The fact that East Germany has drawn ahead may have some psychological importance. West Germany's economic advance was hard for some people to accept, but is now a recognised reality. For the other Germany to catch up with Britain has a different meaning. The complacent assumption that whatever Western Europe's economic troubles might be there was always a part of Europe where things are irredeemably worse has become out of date. Remember the Cold War clichés? Life there is 'drab'. The people's 'lot' is hard. The standard of living is not everything and there are many aspects of life in the GDR which anyone will want to criticise. But it is no longer possible to argue that the system is both politically unacceptable and anyway economically inefficient.

The years since the Wall was built have produced a kind of 'GDR-consciousness' in East Germany. Its undoubted air of permanence convinced most East Germans that the GDR is a viable state, and willy-nilly 'their' state. One West German academic researcher found that already by 1966 as compared with 1962 the number of people describing themselves as 'loyal' to the existing system had increased from 37 per cent to 71 per cent.[2] The stubborn West German attitude of officially pretending that East Germany did not exist went on so long that it became counter-productive in the end. Whatever they thought of their own state, many East Germans became tired of being pitied or patronised by West Germany. The younger generation born since 1940 who now form around two-thirds of the population understandably cannot fathom the argument that East Germany ought never to have been created. To them it seems a ludicrous abstraction. The GDR is the place they know. The country's astonishing successes in the Olympic Games created widespread satisfaction at home, and forced hundreds of millions of television-watchers around the world to come to terms with the GDR's existence. In 1976 its athletes won 40 gold, 25 silver and 25 bronze medals, more first prizes than any other country except the Soviet Union, which has more than thirteen times its population.

The GDR is recognisably both German and socialist. Germanness is of course a notoriously hard concept to define. It takes one into the realm of trying to characterise nations, which always runs the risk of prejudice. One factor in mitigation is that all over Eastern Europe much the same prejudices about Germans abound as in the West. They are known for their hard work, efficiency, intensity, respect for authority, and that well-concealed sense of humour. At an anecdotal level one could give example after example of the German-ness of the GDR – the cleanness of its streets, the fondness for uniforms, the need to show your papers before you go into any office building. In the Museum of German History in Berlin they display a photograph of the Duke and Duchess of Windsor's visit to Hitler in Berchtesgaden in 1937. The Duke was forced to abdicate, says the caption, 'because of his pro-Fascist views'. No nonsense about love for a commoner, divorce, or other personal trivia. In some East German newspapers Sunday is the day for the 'lonely hearts' advertisements. 'Am active scientist, practical, reliable. Seek husband, between 43 and 50, with Marxist-Leninist world outlook'. Further down the column there was this one: 'Capable pensioner seeks similar companion. Interested in gardening. Ordinary worker preferred, not a drinker.' What could be more direct, more explicit, more purposeful?

Discipline and hard work were obvious factors behind the country's economic growth from the 1960s onwards. In contrast to the rest of Eastern Europe, with the exception of Czechoslovakia, East Germany is at least one generation ahead in its experience of industrialisation. Its labour force is more sophisticated and better trained. Early on, Ulbricht accepted the need for the 'scientific-technical revolution'. Germans respect skilled work and technical achievement and they are well rewarded in the GDR. In East German factories a whole variety of encouragement and incentives is offered to workers to go in for trade training and attend night school. The idea of self-advancement through study and application is generally accepted. The hierarchy of academic and professional titles is now almost as rigid as before the war. Instead of 'Herr Professor' people nowadays are more likely to be 'Kollege Diplom-Ingenieur', but the status of titles has not changed. In the 1950s their revival had a specific purpose. The GDR authorities knew that they could never match professional salaries in the West. They hoped to compensate the middle class and dissuade them from leaving by restoring the system of titles. Because scores of doctors were deserting, the medical profession was given more than any other. Since then the mania for titles has become part of the whole GDR system.

Another characteristic of the GDR which is part of a long German tradition is the way authority runs from top to bottom. In its modern guise it is described as 'democratic centralism' and 'the leading role of the party', but it has the effect that lower-level cells within the party obey higher ones without question, and that social bodies outside the party take the lead from it. The phenomenon is remarkable when compared with Poland which tempers Communist rule with a tradition of anarchy and romanticism. The 'good' side of the coin is German respect for the law. In many Eastern European countries, including Poland, there is a high incidence of small-scale corruption which is a relatively common feature in rapidly industrialising countries with a new bureaucracy. In the GDR it is less pervasive, though not absent altogether. The 'bad' side of the coin is submissiveness to authority. People do not stand up to be counted. They lie down in order to be ignored. As the unkind saying goes, Germans find any instruction better than none – 'besser ein Befehl als kein Befehl'. Talking with German officials from the Free German Youth, the trade unions, or the SED, one notices how often the phrase begins 'Our task is to ... '

Laws in the GDR have a different connotation from those in the West. They are often not so much a list of rights, regulations and prohibitions as a general catalogue of pious statements and vague instructions in a long preamble. The 1974 Youth Law, for example, begins 'The main task in the formation of the developed socialist society is to educate young people as citizens to be loyal to the ideas of socialism.' It goes on in paragraph 30 to say that 'local councils together with the leadership of the Free German Youth are duty-bound to support a higher level of qualifications on the part of amateur dance bands as well as club managers and disc jockeys'. Some Western observers have made the mistake of interpreting this didactic tendency of 'laying down the law' in every walk of life as a survival of Fascist attitudes under a different ideology. That is crude and inaccurate. Feelings of racial superiority, of chauvinism and of national self-pity are conspicuously rare in the GDR, and are combated fiercely by the authorities. Attitudes of 'beggar-my-neighbour' and philistinism, or the feeling that weaker members of society must look after themselves, are also not prevalent. 'Red Prussia' is a label that is closer to the mark, although that too smacks of a militarism which is not there any more in the GDR. Much of pre-war Prussia is in the GDR today, but neither of the GDR's two party leaders were Prussians. Ulbricht was a Saxon. Honecker is from the Saarland.

In its superficial appearance East Germany has probably changed less than the Federal Republic. In the small towns and villages which were not too badly damaged in the war life still seems much as one imagines it was in the 1930s. Where bombs and artillery shells did not fall, the demolitioners' bulldozer and the motorway and parking-lot have not brought their chaos either. In Halle the old-fashioned chimney sweep with top hat and square-cut tail-coat still plys his trade. In Leipzig young couples are driven to their wedding reception in a covered horse-drawn carriage complete with coachman. Visitors from West Germany or elsewhere who knew the area forty or more years ago often go back now to revisit a home town, a childhood sea-side resort, or student digs. Amazed and delighted, they find the pub is still on the corner and the sea-front boarding house has not been replaced. West Germany has changed greatly. Many observers have remarked that the Federal Republic with its materialism, its brashness, its competitive and energetic business climate, the style of its suburban life, its non-ideological trade unions, and its worship of gadgetry, has become the most American country in Europe. East Germany remains perhaps more German than West Germany.

Its system certainly represents socialism of a kind, 'socialism with a German face'. It has some features common to all in-dustrial societies, but in its basic structure it is different from any Western capitalist society. The state owns the means of pro-duction. Agriculture has been collectivised, and the economy is centrally planned. In this, East Germany differs both from West Germany and from pre-war Germany. A revolution has been imposed. The old ruling-class has completely disappeared from power. In its place society is now managed by a broadly based and increasingly well-trained elite. Its membership is still relatively open, and the ticket of admission is professional expertise as much as loyalty to the SED's ideology. Political power is centred exclusively in the party, but status and privi-lege are not confined to the political managers. It is a society which has achieved a certain homogeneity between interest groups and an undoubted levelling-out of differences in income. With its universal ten-year schools the educational system is fairer than the old pre-war system of selection. Women have won a more equal place in society than ever before in Germany or in West Germany now. In 1974 84 per cent of women of working age had jobs, one of the highest ratios in the world.[3] The GDR's working mothers have more pre-school facilities for children than any of their Eastern or Western neighbours. Three-quarters of all pre-schoolchildren have places in crèches or kindergartens.

In many ways the GDR has succeeded in providing its people with stability and security. Streets are clean and pedestrians wait for the green light before crossing. The German bogy of inflation is under tight restraint with state control of prices and wages. Consumer prices are subsidised more generously than elsewhere in Eastern Europe. In 1974 as a result of the Government's determination to prevent worldwide inflation from affecting prices in the shops, subsidies for retail price maintenance accounted for as much as 9·3 per cent of the budget. It is idle to speculate on how the GDR would have turned out under any leader other than Ulbricht. The present system has the stamp of his personality. If he had a philosophy, it was to create a state in which the door to a revival of Fascism would be firmly closed and in which German virtues would be combined with a socialist order. The working class would have a higher standard of living and greater possibilities for self-fulfilment than ever before. Sitting in his suburban Berlin garden in Niederschönhausen, next door to the house of Ulbricht's widow Lotte, and not far from several of the villas that have now been turned over to newly arrived Western diplomats, Otto Gotsche who was Ulbricht's secretary for more than twenty years echoes his master's voice: 'We have created a state which is clean and decent, where orderliness reigns and people are hard-working, and in which we have built up cultural opportunities that Germany has never had before.'

Since Ulbricht's retirement his former colleagues have made some adjustments to his policies. Ulbricht was criticised for concentrating too much in his later years on 'Strukturpolitik' – the idea that it was enough to change the structures of the economy and of society in order to build socialism. He had been brought up in the old German tradition of seeing power as something that was embodied in the state. 'Staatlichkeit', the state's legitimacy and weight were closely bound up with the extent of its territory. Socialist power meant socialist flags on the map. His colleagues found this concept remote and uncompromising. They wanted a closer attention to the detail and day-to-day content of socialist society. They modified the schoolmasterly and rather puritanical tone of Ulbricht's policies. In the early 1970s the SED made it clear that there was nothing shameful, immoral, or unsocialist in citizens wanting more of a private life and more private property, provided that that property gave them no unfair control over their fellow-citizens.

One of the many paradoxes of the GDR was that it allowed a substantial sector of private enterprise to remain long after comparable industries had been nationalised elsewhere in Eastern Europe. In 1971 private enterprise still accounted for one-sixth of the country's industrial output. Several private entrepreneurs – 'red millionaires' – owned factories with a turn-over of more than a million marks. In the spring of 1972 the party finally forced them to sell their holdings to the state. At the same time it encouraged private shopkeepers and craftsmen to continue, and it gave a new boost to the private citizen as consumer. It was made easier for people to build bungalows around Berlin and other cities. Magazines dealing with home improvements, fashion, and leisure activities were promoted.

'Consumer revolution' has become the pat phrase for the current trend in Eastern Europe. The new prosperity is easily visible. What is less visible but is no less real is the country's social system. In spite of the move towards more consumer benefits, East Germany is still very different from Western Europe. The reactions of East Germans who have come West as pensioners or defectors agree with the views of most outsiders who spend some time in the GDR. The country's collectivist ideology, implanted now for more than a generation and backed by a substantial narrowing of income differentials has had an effect. The state takes on the responsibility for providing almost everything, from stable consumer prices to a job for every school-leaver. People expect the state's promises to be kept. They make higher claims on it than most people do in the West. The collecti-vist ideology has spread at a second level. All citizens are mem-bers of 'brigades' or 'collectives' in their factories, offices or places of residence. These are more than production teams. They have a social role in arranging some leisure activities, in helping members' families in cases of illness or bereavement, and in electing representatives to the lay courts which deal with petty crime and neighbourhood disputes. In the West it is fashionable to deride these collectives as sinister, or else phoney on the grounds that they do not work. Thirty years of experi-ence in the GDR seem to have ironed out the hard edges. The so-called 'Wohngemeinschaften' or 'house collectives' are in-deed often little more than paper organisations. In line with the general trend towards more private life at home, fewer people bother to keep them going. In the workplace where the need for collective action is clearer they function better.

East German society has its contradictions and inner tensions. The basic problem is that the leadership's defensive attitude, built up over the long years of confrontation with the West, makes it excessively distrustful of its own people. Nowhere is this more true than on the issue of travel to the West, which is more restrictive than in nearby Poland or Hungary. Western radio broadcasts can be heard anywhere in the GDR. Western television can be seen in most places. Occasionally one hears stories of conservative party members who refuse to watch Western television in the presence of their children, not because they are afraid to (it is not illegal), but because they do not want to create a conflict of loyalties. Such people are getting rarer. It is openly admitted that most East Germans get much of their information and entertainment from the West. The West exerts a fascination, because it is so near and yet so far, and because the party has painted a devil's image of it for so long. Hardly anyone of working age is allowed to travel to the West. The party's policy rests on the notion that as family links between East and West Germans die away the pressure for travel will lessen. History is on the party's side. Of course the notion is naive. A young East German wants a trip to the West not because he has an uncle in Stuttgart but because he has seen Paris or Italy on the TV screen and like most normally inquisitive people in Warsaw, Budapest, or London, wants to see them in real life.

A sizeable group near the top of the party realises this, and would like to innovate. They are aware that economic progress has brought a substantial popular consensus in favour of some form of socialism. Few people would want a return to capitalism. But that does not mean they are satisfied with the *status quo*. There is a demand for some kind of new opening both to the outside world and towards a wider internal debate. People want fewer taboos on discussion of controversial issues. They expect a maturer, more self-confident attitude at the top and a greater willingness to take risks and learn from mistakes. Stefan Heym, one of the GDR's most respected and loyal writers, has written: 'Any politically sensitive informed person can feel that underneath the calm surface of life in the GDR a struggle is being waged over the direction in which the Republic is to develop: is socialism here to be a bureaucratic homunculus, estranged from the people, or a living movement vibrant with ideas that men everywhere will want to make their own?'[4] By early 1977 it was obvious that this would be the key issue for the next few years. Emboldened by the Helsinki Agreement, with its provisions for easier re-unification of families, and disappointed by the slow pace of change since East and West Germany recognised each other in 1973, hundreds of people applied officially to emigrate. The authorities' reaction was to stiffen up. The new tension reflected another victory for the most cautious elements in the leadership, who proceeded to exile the country's best-known folk-singer and balladist, Wolf Biermann, and launch reprisals against other intellectual dissidents. But their victory is likely to be only temporary, for the underlying problem will not be solved so easily.

The GDR is Europe's youngest state, diplomatically accepted throughout the world. It has a high standard of living. But its politics still have a cramped and bureaucratic feel. What it needs is greater political openness and a new intellectual stimulus. As Heym puts it, 'this would give the Republic an image with a sparkle'.[5] It has conspicuously lacked that until now.

I

Splits and Wounds on the German Left

In its internal policies as well as in its attitude to the West, the party leadership in East Germany has always been tougher and more uncompromising than its counterparts in the rest of Eastern Europe. Not even the Soviet Union has shown such firmness of ideological principle. With the coming of East–West *détente* in the early 1970s when other Communist parties soft-pedalled their public criticisms of Western imperialism, the East Germans carried on largely as before. While *Pravda* kept an almost total silence on the Watergate affair, the main party paper in East Germany, *Neues Deutschland*, carried frequent and accurate criticisms of President Nixon. It gave continually prominent coverage to the triumphant North Vietnamese sweep towards Saigon in March and April of 1975. An apparently embarrassed *Pravda* never once put the news on its front page.

Earlier, when Willy Brandt as Chancellor of West Germany had approached Eastern Europe with his Ostpolitik, the East Germans maintained the frostiest front. They expressed the strongest suspicions of the 1968 reform movement in Czechoslovakia. When the armies of Bulgaria, Hungary, Poland and East Germany withdrew after the Soviet-led invasion, the East Germans were brazen enough to hold public rallies of 'thanksgiving' for the returning troops.

The GDR's stance is commonly explained as 'conservatism'. In order to defend itself and screen its people from the attractions of West Germany, the party leadership over-compensated. It set out, so the argument continues, on a twin policy of confrontation with the West and ideological orthodoxy at home as a barrier behind which to shelter. Although this functional explanation has some truth in it, it is too flat. There are important psychological and historical reasons for East Germany's distinctive stance. Some of them go back beyond Hitler to the days of the Weimar Republic when the German Communist Party was one of the strongest forces on the German Left.

The Party has a long collective memory. Founded in the aftermath of Germany's defeat in the First World War, growing into adolescence during the crises and retreats of the 1920s, the party saw the flower of its membership torn asunder first by the Nazis' terror machine and later by Stalin's silent purges. Those that survived the war could not help but brood over the past and remember the bewildering range of moral, political and physical pressures they had been forced to face. To them caution and defensiveness were almost second nature.

When Hitler came to power on January 30 1933 the Kommunistische Partei Deutschlands (KPD) had an estimated membership of 300,000.[1] Apart from the Communist Party of the Soviet Union, no other party in Eastern or Western Europe was so large. In the last free parliamentary elections on November 6 1932 the KPD won almost six million votes, giving them 16·9 per cent of the total and some one hundred members in the Reichstag. The Social Democrats, the SPD, had seven and a quarter million votes. In some cities, including Berlin, Düsseldorf and Halle, the Communists came out ahead of the SPD and the Nazis with the largest single vote.

A month after becoming Chancellor Hitler used the pretext of the Reichstag fire to start mass arrests of Communists. Hundreds of members were rounded up. Others escaped abroad or went underground. Many left the party. In 1935 Wilhelm Pieck, who later became the GDR's first president, revealed that out of 422 leading KPD officials 52 per cent had been arrested, 5 per cent had been murdered, and 10 per cent had left the party.[2] Scores of those arrested died later in prison or concentration camp. Many who went to the Soviet Union were killed during Stalin's purges. But those who survived became the core of East Germany's post-war elite. None of the new post-war Communist states had as relatively large a group of seasoned party cadres as the GDR.

They were to become known as 'activists of the first hour'

and were held up in the new society as its leading heroes. Fritz Selbmann, a former KPD deputy in the Reichstag and after the war a deputy minister of industry, described them in his book *The First Hour* as 'the people who in the days when Germany had suffered total military defeat and the complete collapse of its economic, political, and social order after the darkest night in German history, took over the task of leading the German people out of the misery into which they had been thrown by the crimes of Nazism'.[3]

Many of these activists had had their commitment to the party and their vision of a future Communist Germany sharpened by long years of exile or detention in Nazi prisons and concentration camps. Apart from Walter Ulbricht and Erich Honecker, there were men like Hermann Axen, now a member of the SED Politbüro, who spent three years in Zwickau prison, emigrated to France, was interned in 1940 and later was deported to Auschwitz; Franz Dahlem, a member of the Politbüro from 1928 until 1952, who was a veteran of the International Brigade in the Spanish civil war, moved to France after 1940 and in 1943 was sent to Mauthausen concentration camp; Hermann Matern, a post-war Politbüro member who escaped from prison after a year under Nazi interrogation, and then worked all over Europe in the resistance.

With their long history of suffering for the cause, these men formed a powerful basis for the new party after the war. They had the backing of hundreds of lesser known Communists who managed to survive the Nazi period. In the years after 1945 they were joined by a new generation of young Communists. Throughout Eastern Europe after the war thousands of people joined the local Communist parties. In Hungary, Czechoslovakia, Bulgaria, Poland, Romania and Yugoslavia, party membership soared. Some joined out of genuine idealism and enthusiasm. Once it was clear that Communist rule was there to stay, many others took out a party card because they saw it as the ticket to a good career. From the beginning there was an element of cynicism in the party's midst. But with Stalin's new purges in the 1950s and the shattering revelations in Khrushchev's denunciation of the dead dictator in 1956 the ranks of the cynics grew. Some of the original idealists lost faith, but stayed in the party out of habit, apathy, or opportunism.

In East Germany there was a vital difference. Until 1961 the border to the West was open. For the price of a rail ticket on the S-Bahn in Berlin careerists and the disillusioned could always leave. Thousands did. By a process of natural selection the party in East Germany was left with the most militant and dedicated of the new generation. Together these Young Believers and the old KPD survivors formed a party that was inevitably more 'ideological' than the parties of its Eastern European neighbours where pragmatism, not to say opportunism, was stronger. The East German party, the SED, also felt itself heir to a long and proud tradition. After all, Karl Marx and Friedrich Engels were Germans. Germany was the country where Lenin had expected the revolution to come first. This sense of belonging to the potential revolutionary core of Europe gave an added note of seriousness and purpose to the German Left.

A crucial element in the tradition was the split between Communists and Socialists, and between Marxists and revisionists at the end of the nineteenth century. If Karl Marx was German, so too was Eduard Bernstein, the 'father of revisionism'. It is not too fanciful to see the seeds of Germany's later division after 1945 in the bitter debate between Bernstein and the orthodox Marxists half a century earlier, and in the continuing clashes between Communists and Social Democrats throughout the Weimar Republic. A follower of Engels, Bernstein published a number of articles between 1896 and 1898 which criticised the principles of Marxism. He argued that the new social conditions in Germany made it essential to revise Marx. For two decades the German working class had enjoyed a slow but steady improvement in living standards. The SPD's parliamentary strength was growing, and the trade unions and the co-operative movement were becoming stronger. A trend towards reformist gradualism was gathering pace.

Bernstein's main opponent was Rosa Luxemburg, a native of Poland who moved to Germany in 1898 and later became a co-founder of the KPD. She argued that the contradictions within capitalism were getting sharper. Whereas Bernstein saw trade unions as a weapon weakening capitalism, Luxemburg said that by themselves they could not overthrow the wages system. All they could do was affect the level of wages. A revolutionary party was needed. Luxemburg rejected Parliament which

Bernstein believed was an institute 'above the classes' and an embodiment of society's will. She wrote: 'Parliament is not a directly socialist element gradually impregnating the whole of capitalist society. On the contrary, it is a specific form of the bourgeois class state.'[4] Two practical issues loomed as continual dilemmas before the German Left. What attitudes should it take towards coalition Government and revolutionary violence? Luxemburg was against coalitions. Socialists should only use Parliament, she believed, in order to have a wider and more effective platform for waging the fight against capitalism. 'In bourgeois society', she wrote, 'the role of social democracy is that of an opposition party. As a ruling party it is only allowed to rise on the ruins of the bourgeois state.'[5] She believed that legislative reform had a useful place, but should never be allowed to replace or rule out the need for revolutionary violence in certain conditions. Thirty years before the collapse of the Weimar Republic and the rise of Hitler, Luxemburg dealt with the issues that were later to exercise the German Left in their starkest form. In 1902 she commented: 'If social democracy were to accept the opportunist standpoint, renounce the use of violence, and pledge the working class never to diverge from the path of bourgeois legalism, then its whole parliamentary and other activity would sooner or later collapse miserably and leave the field to the untrammelled dominance of revolutionary violence.'[6]

These quotations from Rosa Luxemburg are necessary reminders of the political split that was to grow and widen on the German Left. Fierce recriminations and antagonism between Communists and Social Democrats were the bread on which many of the future leaders of both East and West Germany were nurtured, including Willy Brandt and Walter Ulbricht. A heroine now in East Germany, Luxemburg would have found much to criticise in its centralised authoritarian structure. (It was not until 1975 that the GDR published her essay on the Russian Revolution in which she warned of the dangers of denying freedom of speech to the party's critics.) But she probably would have recognised the difficult path by which it came into being.

Until 1914 the debates on tactics took place within the ranks of the SPD. The outbreak of the First World War brought an open rift. On December 2 1914 Karl Liebknecht broke ranks and became the only SPD member to vote against the Kaiser's war credits in the Reichstag. In January 1916 Liebknecht, who had by then been joined by a few colleagues from the left wing of the SPD, formed the Spartacus League as a revolutionary faction inside the party. Two years later the Spartacists founded the KPD, but not before the centrist group in the SPD, which included Bernstein, had itself split off and formed the Independent Social Democratic Party. By then the so-called German Revolution had begun. The Kaiser abdicated at the end of the war, and Friedrich Ebert, leader of the SPD, was entrusted with the creation of a new Government. The Independent Social Democrats served under him for a time. When they resigned, the Government was left in the hands of the majority faction of the Social Democrats plus the army which had pledged itself to fight 'Bolshevism'. Although spontaneous councils of workers and soldiers sprang up in many German towns, they lacked central co-ordination. Backed by the SPD and unofficial vigilante units known as the Freikorps, the army gradually took the offensive. In a short and premature armed uprising in Berlin in January 1919 Liebknecht and Luxemburg were captured and killed. Four months later the Government and the army moved in to smash the newly proclaimed Bavarian Soviet Republic in Munich.

For the fledgling Communist party the Government's offensive against the workers' councils was new proof of the right-wing Social Democrats' 'treason', matching their support for the Kaiser during the war. Two men, who were later to be founders of the German Democratic Republic, were participants in some of these stormy events which must have affected their subsequent outlook. Walter Ulbricht, a 21-year-old SPD worker, broke with party discipline two months before Liebknecht's historic vote in the Reichstag against the war credits. Although often portrayed in the West as a dull conformist, Ulbricht was out on the streets distributing anti-war pamphlets in defiance of party policy and at some risk from the authorities. He was conscripted the following year but in 1918 he deserted twice and was caught twice. In the end he escaped from military prison and helped to organise the workers' and soldiers' councils as a member of the Spartacus League. Wilhelm Pieck was in the same building as Luxemburg and Liebknecht on the day they were caught and murdered. He managed to escape and hide with party comrades until the hunt subsided.[7]

Throughout the 1920s the tensions between Communists and Social Democrats increased. In 1923 Germany seemed to be poised once again on the brink of revolution. In a crisis brought on by the collapse of the currency and the French occupation of the Ruhr the middle class lost almost all its savings. There was a general strike in Berlin and spontaneous strikes in several parts of the Ruhr. Heinrich Brandler, leader of the KPD, hurried to Moscow for discussions with Trotsky, Radek and Zinoviev. They gave him confusing advice. In a series of badly co-ordinated moves the Communists succeeded only in launching a futile uprising in Hamburg which was rapidly crushed.

The episode caused deep disillusionment within the KPD. Thousands of potential supporters who had moved towards the party during the economic crisis drifted away again. Under a plan drawn up by the Allied Western Governments – the Dawes plan – Germany's reparations burden was eased. American loans and investment were pumped into the economy. The Communists watched as German society seemed to have been stabilised again. Brandler was removed from the leadership of the KPD and in Moscow Stalin argued that the period of capitalist instability in Europe from 1917 to 1924 had given way to a second period of consolidation. The KPD was encouraged to co-operate with the Social Democrats.

In 1927 Stalin suddenly changed his line. Having expelled Trotsky and the Left Opposition from the party the General Secretary was now turning on Bukharin and the right-wing Bolsheviks. In an apparent move to the Left he ended Communist co-operation with private traders and farmers and prepared for the total collectivisation of agriculture. By a kind of illogical extension Stalin ordered foreign Communists to abandon their alliances with other parties, particularly the Social Democrats. The KPD's failure to gain power in Germany, the Soviet party's moral and financial pre-eminence as the only ruling party in the international movement, and Stalin's ruthless use of power had transformed the Communist International from a meeting place of Communist ideas and experience to nothing but an instrument of Soviet policy. At its congress in 1928 the

Comintern announced that the period of capitalist consolidation was over.

A third period had started in which the contradictions in the capitalist economy would continue to develop rapidly. Out of the imminent general crisis, wars and revolution would 'inevitably' follow. Communist parties were told to prepare their final offensive against capitalism. An earlier quotation from Stalin that social democracy was 'objectively the moderate wing of Fascism' was revived to justify a policy in which Social Democratic parties were described as the most dangerous enemies of Communism. On the grounds that 'the more Left they are, the more dangerous they are', the leaders of the left-wing Social Democrats were considered the greatest threat to the revolution because of their ability to mislead the working class.

In Germany the policy was not followed without some qualms. During 1931 a group of the KPD's top men, including Pieck, and Franz Dahlem, who was to become one of the party's most respected leaders in the early years of the GDR, argued that the Communists' main blow should be against the growing strength of the Nazis.[8] But Ernst Thälmann, the party's first secretary, followed Stalin's line closely. As late as February 1932 he emphasised that the main priority was to fight social democracy. The line was reaffirmed by the Comintern the following September.

At times it produced a tactical alliance with the Nazis. In November 1932 the KPD in Berlin joined the Nazis in organising a strike against the Berlin transport company which was run by Social Democrats. That was an extreme case. In general the Communists did believe in a united front with Social Democrats as long as it was 'from below'. It was with the SPD leadership that the Communists would not co-operate. As had happened during the 1914–18 war the Communists hoped to wean left-wing rank-and-file members away from the SPD. They wanted to split the trade union movement which was largely under SPD control and create an independent Communist trade union movement. In some German cities in the early 1930s there were locally organised strikes and spontaneous action in which members of the SPD and the KPD joined forces.

24

But there was no move to get together with the SPD leadership. Equally the SPD leaders rejected any alliance with the Communists. After Hitler was already in power, the KPD finally tried to set up secret contacts with leaders of the SPD and the Social Democratic trade unions. Their approach was turned down. The SPD leaders rejected a Communist proposal for a general strike with the curt reply that Hitler had come to power legally and everyone should wait until he broke the law. If this seems naive, the KPD itself took time to realise the enormity of Hitler's plans, and what was happening in Germany. Long before he actually assumed constitutional power as Chancellor, the KPD considered Germany was already 'becoming Fascist' or, as some argued, 'was Fascist'. Even after January 1933 they saw him as 'a prisoner of finance capital'.[9] At least one Comintern official, Waldemar Knorin, felt Hitler's coming to power was Germany's 'February' which could lead the way to a victorious Communist revolution in 'October' on the pattern of events in Russia in 1917. The hope was that Germany's economic crisis would produce a split between the 'capitalist Nazi leadership' and its petty bourgeois and proletarian following.[10] It never happened, and the KPD paid dearly for its mistake. Although some preparations had been made for the possibility that the party might be banned, no one expected that the Nazi persecution would be so severe. Few serious precautions were taken. According to the party's own figures, by the end of 1933, 130,000 Communists had been put in concentration camps and 2,500 were murdered.[11]

At its party conference held in exile near Moscow in 1935 the KPD admitted that it had made 'tactical mistakes' during the Weimar Republic. But it put the blame on the SPD for rejecting a common policy against Hitler and splitting the working class. The SPD was charged with making one concession after another to the right wing and thus allowing it to gather strength. At public meetings in the early 1930s Communist orators thundered out the rhyme 'Wer hat uns verraten? Die Sozialdemokraten!' ('Who betrayed us? The Social Democrats.')

The SPD stood condemned of triple treason — over its attitude in 1914, in 1919, and in the last days of the Weimar Republic. Yet in spite of this hard public line against the Social Democrats, many Communists felt some doubts about their own party's role. They were also inhibited from too implacable an attitude by the fact that they still hoped to win the SPD rank and file over to their side. Numerous SPD members were also to suffer under Hitler. As the Nazi regime continued, the need for solidarity became obvious. In 1935 the KPD and the Comintern moved to an official policy of a united front with Social Democrats at all levels.

Later on, KPD members made a more sophisticated analysis of the end of the Weimar Republic. They accepted that they had been over-ambitious and had pressed the SPD leadership too hard for a deal while simultaneously criticising them too drastically. But these mistakes were still seen as side-effects of the bitter struggle for a common front. The main reason for the failure to achieve it was considered to have been the fact that the SPD and the centre parties had become Government parties after 1918. In 1928 their membership in all the various representative bodies from local government in the villages to the Reichstag was more than 60,000. Whereas the KPD had almost no access to the state apparatus, members of the SPD and the centre parties provided hundreds of thousands of people in the police, the trade union administrations, and the social insurance organisations. As one KPD member put it in 1943 'the leaders of this formidable social democratic and centrist machine were full of contradictory tendencies'. He listed them as: concern for their own safety, underestimation of the Nazis, over-estimation of their own strength, fear of the Communists and a 'holy terror of encroaching via the state on to the monopolistic financial and economic centres in order to overcome the economic crisis and create work for the unemployed – as Roosevelt did'.[12]

If German Communists have always had a mixed and at times ambiguous attitude towards Social Democrats, the same is true on the other flank about their attitude towards the Soviet Union. Uncertainty about Moscow's aims and tactics has been a constant concern for German Communists. It was as strong after the war when the GDR was founded as it had been before. In some ways the complex relationship between the German Left and the Soviet Union is the mirror image of the KPD/SPD split. While the norm in KPD/SPD relations has been public coolness and hostility, tempered by a certain grudging respect expressed in private, the norm in relations between the German Left and Moscow always was public warmth but private misgivings. Communists look on the Soviet Union with a mixture of pride, gratitude, guilt and mistrust.

Pride in the Soviet Union comes from its position as 'the first socialist state', and its effort in building itself into a powerful industrial nation against heavy foreign and internal odds. Admittedly even some of the most loyal party members sometimes experienced surprise and disappointment at what they saw in Russia. Karl Mewis, elected a member of the Politbüro in 1935, described his first impressions thus: 'On the one hand we had always said that socialism in the Soviet Union had won with the revolution; on the other hand labour productivity was still at a relatively low level. After all we came from an industrial country and expected that people would only talk of the victory of socialism once the scope and character of production had reached a higher level than under capitalism. But in the end we convinced ourselves that in fact an important stage in the Soviet Union's development had been achieved and that because of the international situation it was necessary to have a clear expression to describe the social level reached.'[13]

There was gratitude for the Soviet Union's enormous sacrifices in eventually helping to defeat Nazism and bring the Thousand Year Reich to an end. None of the Communists who returned to Germany after the war had any illusions but that the Russians had borne the main brunt of the struggle against Hitler. Those that had spent the war in the Soviet Union knew it at first hand. They had shared the anguish when the German war machine pushed towards Moscow itself. They knew the indescribable relief caused by the victory of Stalingrad. Those who had been in exile in the West or had spent the war in concentration camps reserved their main thanks for the Russians. After the war there was an extra reason for gratitude. Who but the Russians had installed Germany's Communists in power in the GDR?

But there was also mistrust and lingering resentment that Moscow had all too frequently used Germany's Communists for its own ends. Party loyalists were aware that in any clash between their interests and those of the Soviet party the Russian comrades invariably chose the latter. One of the earliest examples was the Comintern's policy of calling the SPD 'Fascists', which most KPD members accepted at the time but which left others unhappy. Then came the Moscow purges in 1936 to 1938 in which numerous German Communists died along with Soviet and other foreign Communists at the hands of the Soviet secret police, the NKVD. Some 70 per cent of the KPD's members in the Soviet Union at that time are thought to have perished.[14]

The Germans formed the largest community of foreign Communists and anti-Fascists, as the Soviet historian Roy Medvedev has written:

> They had fled to the Soviet Union – or on party orders had moved – to save themselves from Hitler's terror. But an even crueller terror was waiting for them in the USSR. The NKVD tried to give an 'ideological basis' to the mass arrests of German anti-Fascists. The *Journal de Moscou* declared 'It is no exaggeration to say that every Japanese living abroad is a spy or that every German citizen living abroad is an agent of the Gestapo'. Towards the end of April 1938 the arrest of 842 German anti-Fascists had been recorded by the German representative to the executive committee of the Comintern. The actual number was considerably greater. Many Germans were arrested right in the House of Political *Émigrés* in Moscow. Among those arrested were Hugo Eberlein, a participant in the First Comintern Congress, Werner Hirsch, the secretary of Ernst Thälmann, Leo Flieg, a central committee secretary, Hermann Remmele, a Politbüro member, Heinz Neumann and Hermann Schubert, both central committee members, and Heinrich Susskind, chief editor of *Rote Fahne*. Willi Münzenberg, one of the best Comintern officials, was expelled from the party for refusing to leave Paris for Moscow and certain death. The family of Karl Liebknecht which had received asylum in the Soviet Union was persecuted. His son was expelled from the party and his nephew Kurt was arrested.[15]

Perhaps the biggest psychological blow was the Soviet non-aggression pact with Hitler in 1939. According to Margarete Buber Neumann, Heinz Neumann's widow who later broke

28

with the party, some members of the KPD's underground inside Germany committed suicide on hearing the news.[16] Loyal Communists admit that many party members could not understand it. The pact came like a bolt from the blue. Even now it remains an awkward subject in the GDR, and history museums pass it over with barely a mention. The official explanation is that Stalin had to choose the lesser of two evils in order to forestall an agreement by Hitler with England and France. The Western powers, he was convinced, would have been happy to watch Hitler attack the Soviet Union.

A respectable case can be made out in defence of Stalin's decision. What was unnecessary, horrendous and incomprehensible (and a fact now totally suppressed in the GDR) was the pact's repercussions inside the USSR. Overnight the position of the German community changed. Wolfgang Leonhard, who came to Russia with his mother and was at a children's home for exiles, has recorded how the home was simply closed down from one day to the next without warning. In the Library of Foreign Literature in Moscow Nazi newspapers were substituted for the *émigré* press. Anti-Fascist books were removed from the library, and the word 'Fascism' virtually ceased to appear in the Soviet media.[17] In the Nazi prisons and concentration camps where German Communists were held there were brief hopes that for them at least the pact might have benefits. Prisoners thought that the Soviet Union might call for a mass amnesty for all anti-Fascists including Ernst Thälmann as its price for signing the pact. Nothing happened except that Stalin handed over to Hitler some 500 German and Austrian Communists who were living in the Soviet Union. They included several Jews.[18]

Some of them were described as suspected Gestapo agents, but in the context of the numerous false suspicions during Stalin's purges it is impossible to say how plausible those allegations were. After their hand-over to the Nazis, a few rushed to ingratiate themselves with their Gestapo guards. This could have been a sign of desperation as much as of guilt. In return Hitler released some Soviet agents, but no Germans. In Moscow there was a debate among some of the *émigrés* as to whether to approach Stalin to ask Hitler for Thälmann's release. The idea was rejected on the grounds that the party might look as though it was only interested in saving the leadership and not the rank and file. It is hard to gauge what psychological effect Stalin's purges and the non-aggression pact had on those who survived. Could a man like Alfred Kurella, later chairman of the Polit-büro's cultural committee after the war, who lost his brother in the purges, really ever trust Stalin again? Or Werner Eberlein, whose father was murdered? Those who were in Moscow rarely if ever spoke about their experiences later. Those who spent the war in exile in the West say they hardly dared to ask.

Yet at the same time as mistrust, many East German Communists feel an element of guilt towards the Soviet Union. The KPD failed to create a revolution in Germany in 1919 or 1923. It left the Soviet Union isolated, a fact which profoundly affected and distorted its internal development. The KPD failed to stop Hitler from coming to power. Most important of all, it failed to mount a significant internal resistance to Hitler right up until the last days of the war. During the war virtually the only Communist resistance was some minor sabotage and go-slows in munitions factories and the distribution of a few anti-Fascist leaflets in German cities. This was hardly dramatic.

In recent years GDR historians have been publishing more on the resistance. The party wants to give more prominence to the lesser-known martyrs in its midst. Public buildings are being decorated with plaques commemorating resistance fight-ers who lived or worked in them. Many individual German Communists, it is true, took enormous risks, particularly in intelligence work. Germans worked in the legendary Soviet spy network in Western Europe, known as the Red Orchestra. Scores of Germans helped the French Maquis. But the sum total of this activity inside Germany remains small, especially in comparison with the partisan activity of other nationalities in occupied Europe. In all the fanfare in 1975 over the thirtieth anniversary of Germany's 'liberation' one of the most embarrass-ing questions to ask any German Communist was 'Where were the German partisans?'

Objectively the defeat of Hitler was indeed Germany's liberation, but how many Germans felt that at the time? After the Nazi defeat at Stalingrad, the exiled German communities were full of talk about the chances of an uprising against Hitler.

It never came. Right up until the end of the war the vast majority of Germans remained loyal to the regime, or at best apathetic. Not one town liberated itself before the arrival of the Allied armies.

There were few partisans, even on the scale that there were Italian partisans in Italy. Elli Schmidt, who spent more than two years underground in Germany after 1933 and was in Moscow from 1940 onwards, gives *three* explanations. One was the ferocious Gestapo persecution of the slightest act of defiance, and the mass arrests and preventive detention in concentration camps of thousands of Communists, Social Democrats, and other potential rebels. Second, there was the virulently chauvinistic Nazi propaganda and the ideology of Fascism which not only persuaded Germans of the justice of their cause but also created an aura of Nazi invincibility. Finally, when the war started to go wrong and the German retreat began, Germans were moved by fear of their victims' revenge. Even if they disbelieved in the war, people knew that their side had started it. The enemy was expected to want to exact a fearful toll.

For the older generation of German Communists who survived the war these factors have left a deep and painful memory. Individually they themselves suffered under Nazism and bear no guilt. Collectively, the KPD's failure to stop Hitler's rise to power can be seen as a mistake of catastrophic proportions. But it was not a crime, and the Communists' role was not as great as that of most other political groups. Nevertheless, as Germans, sensitive party members could not help but feel at least a sense of shared responsibility, if not outright guilt. In public the current official line in the GDR makes no mention of this. But the feeling is there, and occasionally an oblique reference appears in print. In his recent memoirs, Karl Mewis wrote: 'Many comrades found it hard to understand how the Nazis took over power without any resistance, even though we had the best organised and biggest Communist party in any capitalist country.'[19]

After the war Walter Ulbricht and his colleagues wanted the great mass of Germans who had never opposed Nazism to recognise the guilt of the German people. It was guilt not so much for the millions of murdered Jews or Poles or for the numerous other peoples who suffered under Hitler's bestial rule.

Only a handful of Communists argued for compensation to the Jews. Paul Merker, a pre-war member of the Politbüro who became a leading figure in the German exile community in Mexico, wrote in October 1945 that restoration of Jewish property and other reparations were essential 'and should cause no difficulty'.[20] But the GDR authorities ended up by only giving special pensions and medical facilities to the survivors of Nazism who lived in the GDR. Compensation for loss of property was never paid, mainly on the grounds that no pre-war capitalist, whether Jew or Gentile, should be compensated for loss of property stolen or destroyed by the Nazis.

Ulbricht felt that German guilt should be shown primarily towards the Soviet Union. Anti-Communism and anti-Sovietism had been main factors not only in Nazi ideology but also among other parties, including the SPD. This was what had to be eradicated. The German people must recognise its guilt on this. 'Anti-Communism is the great folly of the twentieth century. Friendship with the Soviet Union is a duty of the heart for every German', as one KPD veteran wrote.[21] Some German Communists always doubted how seriously the Russians took them. Germany may have been the land of Marx and Engels, but where was the revolution? Lenin, according to a frequent but probably apocryphal quote, had said that there would never be a revolution in Germany because Germans did not like stepping on to the grass. Or, as Stalin is reported to have told the Polish politician, Mikolajczyk, 'Communism fits Germany as a saddle fits a cow'.[22] These were prejudices which Germany's Communists wanted to disprove. For ideological, emotional, and practical reasons they saw their role after the war as that of creating the closest possible links between Germany and the Soviet Union. Yet many of them also wanted to bring to power a specific form of German socialism at last. Somehow these two goals had to be made compatible and kept in harmony. But it soon became clear that an over-close identification of German Communism with the USSR could prove a handicap in the party's attempts to win popular support.

2

A German Road to Socialism

In February 1945 some 150 German *émigrés* gathered in the headquarters of the Moscow city committee of the Soviet Communist Party. Hitler's Germany was on the verge of collapse. At their conference in Yalta, Stalin, Roosevelt and Churchill had just agreed to divide Germany after the war into four zones and ensure its complete de-militarisation. For the exiles it was an exciting period. At last the nostalgic prospect of returning home was assuming the concrete outlines of reality. Many of the exiles had not been in Germany for a decade or more. They had left their homeland illegally on false passports and under the threat of persecution. Now the day when they could come back in triumph was fast approaching. They knew they would find a very different Germany – a country in ruins, its people demoralised, and all civic institutions destroyed other than those which the Nazis had turned to their own ruthless purposes. How would one build a new Germany on these shaky foundations?

Wilhelm Pieck and Walter Ulbricht, the two senior party leaders, lectured the assembled company on the tasks that awaited them. The message was simple and blunt. They told their audience to put any ideas of promoting a socialist development in Germany out of their minds. That was a dangerous tendency. Germany was about to embark on a transformation which would complete the bourgeois democratic revolution of 1848. To insist on socialism at once or to brandish socialist slogans would be demagogy.[1] Germany's anti-Fascists would have to support the actions of the occupying forces of the Soviet

33

Union, Britain, France and the United States. Their aim was to root out Nazism and militarism, re-educate the German people and carry through democratic reforms. These would include the trial of Nazi war criminals, measures against monopolies, and reforms in agriculture and education. Although the programme might lay the basis for a later transition to socialism it was a long way from socialism as such.

This muted policy was the outcome of Stalin's strategic considerations. He hoped for continued collaboration with his two major allies once peace had broken out. Above all, he wanted to destroy for ever Germany's ability to make war. At Yalta it was Stalin who had demanded for Russia the highest sum in reparations from Germany: ten thousand million dollars. It was Stalin who transferred the area east of the Oder and Neisse rivers to Poland. Most of these lands had been Polish centuries earlier but the Polish claim on them in 1945 was tenuous.

Had Stalin wanted to preserve the goodwill of the maximum number of Germans after the war in the hope of winning them to socialism, he might have drawn the country's Eastern frontiers differently. But he did not. He was quite happy to contribute to the mass deportations of thousands of Germans across the Oder–Neisse line. After all it was the Germans who had been directly responsible for the millions of acres of wasteland which the Red Army came across in its advance across Europe towards Berlin. As Isaac Deutscher put it, when the Russians finally hoisted the Red Flag over the ruins of the Reichstag, 'this was to symbolise the triumph of revolutionary Russia over Germany, not the triumph of the revolution in Germany'.[2] Or, in the words of Heinrich Mann, the brother of the great anti-Nazi writer Thomas Mann, Germany was 'free but conquered'.[3]

Stalin had shared the hopes of those German exiles who had waited in vain for a German uprising against the Nazis once Hitler's war machine had been forced into retreat. Long before then, on the day after the German attack on the Soviet Union in June 1941, Ulbricht had told the German exiles in Moscow that the first deserter had come over to the Soviet side.[4] At the end of 1941 the Russians organised a congress of German prisoners of war to send an appeal to the German front line for a popular struggle against Hitler. But with the storming Nazi advance through Western Russia German morale in the army improved. Deserters and prisoners became rarer. The exiles themselves went into retreat on an eastward evacuation from Moscow. It was not until after Stalingrad that Stalin began to hope again for some internal German resistance to Hitler. In July 1943 he launched the National Committee for a Free Germany. It started with an appeal to the Wehrmacht and the German people, calling for the overthrow of Hitler and the orderly withdrawal of German troops to the old Reich frontiers. The appeal put forward the mildest goals for a post-war Germany, including a strong democratic constitution, the re-establishment of broad political rights, and the restoration of economic and commercial freedom.

The National Committee for a Free Germany was given a flag. To the shock of some German communists, Stalin had recommended that its colours be black, white and red, those of Kaiser Wilhelm's Reich.[5] Its chairman was a Communist poet, Erich Weinert, but the two vice-chairmen were captured Wehrmacht officers, Major Karl Hetz and Lieutenant Graf von Einsiedel. Stalin hoped that the committee's composition and its offer of an honourable peace for Germany would be able to encourage a high-level mutiny against Hitler by the German army command. In January 1944 he changed the line. Now the aim was a popular uprising against Hitler. As the Red Army advanced, taking back more and more territory, the number of captured Wehrmacht officers rose. Field Marshal Paulus, the German commander at Stalingrad, fell into Soviet hands. With his brother officers, he issued a weighty and impressive radio appeal to his countrymen to overthrow Hitler.

It was all in vain. Germany went on fighting. There was neither a successful Generals' putsch against Hitler nor an uprising of the people. Even as the Russians entered Berlin, when there was nothing left to fight for, the Nazis sent schoolchildren into the front line to resist to the last. The tenacity and strength of German faith in Hitler and the absence of any uprising were bitterly disappointing to Stalin. While the war was still on he made one key statement which German Communists frequently quoted afterwards — 'Hitlers come and go, but the German people and the German state remain.'[6] The statement was meant to encourage the Germans to get rid of Hitler and not to be afraid of Russian revenge. Like the other appeals, it failed. The minimal extent of German resistance inevitably coloured Stalin's attitude to Germany after the war while the fearful destruction the Nazis had wrought in the Soviet Union left him in little mood for forgiveness. Like the other Allied leaders he saw himself in 1945 as the conqueror of a sullen nation.

He considered Germany mainly in strategic terms. But his position contained a fundamental ambiguity which was to remain in Soviet policy long after his death. On the one hand he wanted to ensure that Germany never again would start a war. He tried to keep open the possibility of a united Germany, as long as it was emasculated militarily. In his occupation zone he wanted a gradually recuperating and non-revolutionary economy from which he could draw reparations payments. All this meant playing down the role of the Communists in the zone and confining the changes to those that were agreed at Yalta and Potsdam. On the other hand Stalin wanted to guarantee that things in the Soviet zone remained under tight Soviet control, and the best instrument for that was a well-organised Communist party. There were massive contradictions in these two approaches, and as a result Stalin's tactics frequently wavered. When it came to supporting a Communist Government, there was a further dilemma. Should he try to put it in power and keep it there largely by force, or hope to let it win popular support by democratic means? This was another fundamental issue which neither he nor his successors ever resolved.

As the wartime alliance with the West collapsed, Soviet thinking moved towards strengthening the Eastern zone under Communist leadership. A similar psychological process was going on in the Western camp. George Kennan, the United States chargé d'affaires in Moscow, whose views carried considerable influence in Washington, cabled home on March 6 1946 with a recommendation for dividing Germany and consolidating the Western zones against the East.[7]

At Potsdam the previous summer the Allies had resolved to set up a central control council whose task would be to 'prepare for the eventual reconstruction of German political life on a democratic basis'. The German system of education and justice was to be reformed. The economy would be decentralised so as to 'eliminate the excessive concentration of economic power, exemplified by cartels, trusts, syndicates and other monopolistic arrangements'. 'Pending the final determination' the Allies gave East Prussia to the Soviet Union and the Oder–Neisse territories to Poland. Kennan argued in 1946 that the Potsdam decision to give up the German territories east of the Oder–Neisse provisionally was a serious mistake.

'This amputation of Germany's Eastern territories,' he cabled to Washington,[8] 'must surely have left a country seriously crippled and unbalanced economically, and psychologically excessively dependent in first instance on the great land power to the East which controls or holds great food-producing areas so necessary to German economy. It seems to me unlikely that such a country once unified under a single administration and left politically to itself and the Russians would ever adjust itself to its Western environment successfully enough to play a positive role in world society as we conceive it.' Denied the chance of fashioning a united Germany in a Western image, Kennan saw only two possibilities. One was to leave Germany nominally united but open to Soviet political influence. The other was to carry partition to its logical conclusion and 'endeavour to rescue Western zones of Germany by *walling them off* [author's italics] against Eastern penetration and integrating them into the international pattern of Europe rather than into a united Germany.'

For the exiles returning to Germany in the spring of 1945 all this was still in the future. Of the roughly 150 who had met in Moscow towards the end of the war to be assigned their tasks in the new Germany a score flew there in two secret planeloads shortly before the final surrender. On April 30 Walter Ulbricht and nine colleagues left their headquarters in the Hotel Lux in Gorky Street for the airport. From there they flew to an emergency military airfield in Germany several miles east of Berlin.

Ulbricht by then was fifty-one. In Stalin's eyes and among his colleagues he had won a reputation as a tireless organiser and activist, a practical man without much imagination but endowed with vast reserves of energy. Throughout the turbulent Weimar years he had shown persistent loyalty to Moscow in all the various changes of ideological course. After the Nazi–Soviet non-aggression pact when some comrades had wavered, Ulbricht had vigorously argued Moscow's case. Few people got on easily with Ulbricht. He was stiff and awkward in public. But he had a single-minded determination to bring German Communism to power. In the days of opposition and exile when the KPD had almost no bargaining position in Moscow he had followed Stalin's line faithfully. This did not mean that once in power Ulbricht might not find himself at variance with some aspects of Soviet policy and be bold enough to resist. His youthful experiences in the party showed that he was not without physical and moral courage in the service of a cause he believed in. He had worked with the KPD ever since its foundation. During the period of frequent rioting and strikes in 1919 and 1920 he was active in his native Saxony in Leipzig. In May 1919 he was put under surveillance by the Leipziger Freikorps and the following March during four days of rioting in the city he commanded a fighting sector at a barricade.

Ulbricht was also a shrewd tactician. He took a broadly centrist position in the numerous ideological struggles within the party, carefully never aligning himself too closely with either right or left. After the failure of the risings in the early 1920s Ulbricht's instincts seemed to become more cautious. He was suspicious of spontaneous mass action and concluded that a tight party organisation and careful preparations were essential before workers were to be called out on to the streets. At the age of 30 Ulbricht had been elected to the 21-member central committee of the KPD in 1923. He lost this position after the abortive Hamburg general strike when there was a considerable shake-up in the party leadership.

Over the next few years he visited Moscow several times, first as a delegate to the fourth world congress of the Comintern and later as a student at the Lenin School. From 1928 until 1933 he served as a deputy in the Reichstag and he was the top KPD man in Greater Berlin after 1929. When Hitler came to power Ulbricht escaped to France. He was active with the KPD in exile in Paris and Prague and spent some months in Spain during the civil war as political organiser (though not at the front line) before returning to France and Moscow. At one point Ulbricht was summoned for an investigation by the control commission of the Comintern after he had alienated several KPD colleagues in Paris because of his alleged arrogance and high-handedness towards the non-Communist exiles with whom

the party was in temporary alliance. Somehow Ulbricht satisfied his interrogators and became the KPD's representative on
the Comintern in 1938. In spite of this feat of survival there is
no hard evidence, as some of his detractors have claimed, that
Ulbricht ever denounced any of his colleagues to Stalin's
executioners. In her critical biography of Ulbricht, Carola
Stern does not believe he collaborated in the purges.[9] For most
of the time he was in Paris, and only made short trips to
Moscow.

As he led the first group of exiles back to Germany in April
1945 Ulbricht was acknowledged by the Russians as the party's
effective leader. Ernst Thälmann, the first secretary, had been
murdered by the Nazis in Buchenwald after twelve years of
detention. Wilhelm Pieck, the senior man in the party, was
already almost seventy. Although Pieck lived for another
fifteen years and became the GDR's first President, his age
prevented him from playing a full role after the war. For many
party members this was a matter for regret. Compared with
Ulbricht Pieck always had the image of a conciliator. Warmer
and more ready to display his emotions in public, Pieck never
forgot that he had grown up in the working class. He liked to
meet workers and preferred to play the role of a cheerful man
of the people rather than the efficient functionary.

Pieck had left Germany in July 1933 for Paris where he set
up the first headquarters of the party in exile. During the
various quarrels inside the party and with the other exile
parties over the policy of the Popular Front, Pieck worked with
Ulbricht. But his more sympathetic personality left him with
fewer opponents. He later moved to Moscow, and was in charge
of the *émigré* community there. On several occasions he took up
the cases of German Communists arrested in the purges. When
most of the community was evacuated from Moscow, Pieck
stayed behind to organise work among German prisoners of
war.

Besides Ulbricht and Pieck there were two other men who
stood out in the party, Anton Ackermann and Franz Dahlem.
Ackermann, leader of the second group of Moscow *émigrés* who
flew to Dresden shortly after Ulbricht returned to Germany,
was also a self-taught working-class Communist. A member of
the pre-war Politbüro he was a man of considerable intelligence

and charm, who wore his authority in the party lightly. He was known as the KPD's main ideologist. On the exiles' return to Germany he was put in charge of culture, education and the press, as well as the key job of training new party members.

Franz Dahlem's career was different from the others. He spent a long period with the International Brigade in Spain, and then moved to France. After the internal party row over the KPD's relationship with non-Communists when Ulbricht had to face a Comintern investigation, Dahlem replaced him as head of the Paris section of the party. That episode seems to have aroused a suspicion between the two men which neither of them ever got over. Dahlem stayed in France too long. When the Nazis came in, he was arrested and interned. In 1942 they transferred him to Mauthausen concentration camp. Three years later on the eve of the camp's liberation, when the SS was preparing to liquidate the inmates in revenge, they rose up and freed themselves. For two days they held the nearby bridge across the Danube as the Americans and Russians approached. Dahlem slipped behind the Russian lines and was flown to Moscow. On July 1, 1945 he went back with Pieck to Berlin.

For the returning exiles, whether they came from Moscow, from the West, or from the most fearful experience of all, the 'internal emigration' in the concentration camps, the home-coming to Germany was a shock. They found an appalling sight. Wolfgang Leonhard who was in the first group led by Ulbricht recalled it in his memoirs: 'The scene was like a picture of hell — flaming ruins and starving people shambling about in tattered clothing; dazed German soldiers who seemed to have lost all idea of what was going on; Red Army soldiers singing exultantly and often drunk; groups of women clearing the streets under the supervision of Red Army soldiers; long queues standing patiently waiting to get a bucketful of water from the pumps; and all of them terribly tired, hungry, tense and demoralised.'[10]

Anton Ackermann, the leader of the second group, wrote later:

Hundreds and thousands were moving westwards: every-where we came there were waves of refugees who had been launched westwards by the Wehrmacht and the SS

so as to depopulate the East. Now they were being overtaken by the advancing Soviet troops. We ran into them
at the edge of the road, deep in the woods, in village
meadows and school yards, in the squares of the larger
towns – homeless, starving, ill, desperate, aimless and
hopeless. Hundreds of thousands! ... Particularly shock-
ing was our encounter with the freed inmates of concentration camps and prisons. The reality exceeded our worst
expectations and fears ... We discovered a totally agonised
people. That is the truth. They were incapacitated by the
poison of despair, a mixture of shellshock from the nights
of bombing and war, of deeply ingrained fear of Bolshevism
and the gradual awareness of their own guilt at everything
that had befallen Germany.[11]

The first task for Ulbricht and his colleagues was to find in
this shifting sea of refugees a basic core of reliable people to
help with the administration. In line with the policy of enlisting
all anti-Fascists in the job of reconstruction, people of different
political persuasion were approached. Every district was to
have a Mayor and two deputies. Ulbricht laid down that at
least half the posts must go to members of the bourgeoisie or to
the Social Democrats. The Communists would appoint their
men mainly to the jobs of popular education, personnel and the
police. The first city government of Berlin, announced on May
17, consisted of seven members of the middle class, six Communists, two Social Democrats and two non-party members.
In numerous towns and villages spontaneous anti-Fascist groups
had sprung up to run basic services. They organised the clearing of rubble; found specialists to get the water, gas, and electricity going; and restarted schools and hospitals. But by June
Ulbricht and the Russians decided that these committees would
have to be wound up to make way for 'official' Government
services. Political parties were also to be restored.

On June 11 1945 the KPD published its new programme.
The main themes were those already outlined by Ulbricht in
Moscow. It was too early for socialism. It would be wrong to
impose the Soviet system on Germany. The common goal for
all Germans was the creation of a united peace-loving anti-
Fascist and democratic German republic. It was taken for

granted that Germany would remain a single unit. In a ten-point programme designed for all Germans the party called for:

1 The complete liquidation of the Hitler regime and the Nazi party; the purging of all Nazis from public office.
2 An all-out fight against hunger, homelessness, and unemployment. Complete, unhampered development of trade and private enterprise on the basis of private property.
3 The establishment of democratic rights and civil liberties. The restoration of free and legal trade unions for workers, white-collar employees and Government officials. Re-establishment of anti-Fascist democratic parties.
4 Restoration of democratic local government at all levels.
5 Protection of workers against any arbitrary treatment and exploitation by employers. Free democratic elections of representative bodies of workers in the factories, and of white-collar employees and Government officials.
6 The expropriation of all property belonging to Nazis and war criminals, and its transfer into public ownership via the local and provincial authorities.
7 The liquidation of the large estates of the Junkers, counts and princes, and the transfer of their entire land, livestock and equipment to the local authorities for distribution to peasants who were ruined by the war, and to people who have no possessions.
8 The transfer to public ownership of all public utilities (transport, gas, water, and electricity) and of all enterprises abandoned by their owners.
9 Peaceful and neighbourly co-existence with all other peoples. A decisive break with the foreign policy of aggression and threat, of conquest and plunder.
10 Recognition of the obligation to pay reparations for the damage caused to other peoples by Hitler's aggression. A just division of the burden on the principle that the wealthiest should bear the heaviest load.[12]

The Soviet administration moved rapidly to discover and replace former Nazis. Under Hitler the Nazi party had been dominant in the law, in education, and in the medical professions. According to East German figures,[13] an average of 80 per cent of all German judges had belonged to the Nazi party

or one of its subsidiary organisations. The authorities in the
Soviet zone made a clean sweep. In 1945 in Saxony 1,000
judges and 800 public prosecutors were removed. To stay in
office judges had to prove they had engaged in anti-Fascist
activities during the Hitler period. Out of 1,129 judges and
prosecutors employed in the Soviet zone in 1947 less than 10
were such exceptions. Many former Nazis fled to the West
before the arrival of the Russians on the assumption that they
might get more lenient treatment in the West. A number of
people suffered rough justice in the East at the hands of newly
released camp inmates and particularly from the foreign forced
labourers who had been dragged off to Germany from all over
central Europe and now understandably wanted revenge. Other
Nazis were either purged from their positions or in more serious
cases were tried. The Yalta conference laid down separate
categories. The major war criminals went before an International Tribunal. Others were tried in the countries where
their crimes were committed. According to an order from the
Allied Control Council in September 1946 Nazis who committed crimes against Germans were to be tried in German
courts. In capital cases the occupying power had to confirm the
death sentence.

In the period after 1945 the East Germans say they tried
16,572 people for Nazi and other war crimes. Of these 12,807
were convicted (118 were sentenced to death, 231 to life imprisonment and 5,088 to imprisonment of more than three
years, and the rest to shorter sentences).[14] East German sources
are proud of these figures which they contrast with West
Germany's record. In West Germany which has three times the
population and where many former Nazis fled there have only
been 13,000 trials. In more than half the cases the accused were
acquitted or the proceedings were dropped. In addition
British, French, and American military courts in the Western
zones tried and sentenced some 5,000 former Nazis.[15]

To make up for the vacancies in the judiciary the authorities
in the Soviet zone opened emergency training programmes.
Judges and lawyers who had retired before or immediately
after 1933 were brought back into service. New people, a third
of them from working-class backgrounds, took crash courses in
the law, lasting from six to nine months. It was a similar story

43

in education. At the end of the war there were 39,000 teachers in the Soviet zone, of whom 28,000 had been members of the Nazi party.[16] Special commissions consisting of members of the three political parties and the trade unions investigated each case. An entire new generation of teachers was trained, three-quarters of them under thirty years of age.

Apart from Nazis who were tried for war crimes, the authorities distinguished between people who had been active Nazis and mere party members. Most of the latter lost their jobs if they were in the professions. They had to report to the local labour exchange and take up a job in one of the permissible categories, mainly as manual workers. Active Nazis could be forced to work on reconstruction projects. The minimum period was thirteen weeks. More serious offenders had to do manual work for six months after which one of the de-Nazification commissions decided whether they should be freed or made to do another spell. In the beginning a large number of people were sent to the mines. But when the professional miners protested that the intake was excessive the ex-Nazis were parcelled out among all the main industries. These measures were rough. While they undoubtedly achieved a creditable purging of Nazi influences it would be foolish to pretend that they did not also serve the authorities' purpose of promoting a social revolution by removing ideological opponents. Other Communist countries in Eastern Europe adopted a similar purge of middle-class and conservative elements. In the Soviet zone of Germany it was easier to justify this as being simply the eradication of Fascists.

The Potsdam Agreement spoke of decentralising the German economy at the earliest possible date for the purpose of eliminating the excessive economic power of cartels and monopolies. The Russians partly anticipated this by closing all capitalist banks in July 1945. After Potsdam they used the Agreement's provisions to take over parts of industry. The drive against Nazi-owned business gave a further justification for introducing some socialist ownership. The moves were not unpopular. In Saxony (though not in the other provinces) a plebiscite was held on June 30 1946 to ask whether people approved of the transfer of Nazi enterprises to public ownership. A vote in favour was given by 77·6 per cent. Nationalisation mainly affected the commanding heights of the economy. A substantial group of private entrepreneurs was allowed to remain in charge of medium-sized and small-scale business. In 1948 39 per cent of the zone's gross industrial product was still contributed by factories in private hands.

In agriculture the authorities also moved relatively slowly. The KPD had declared that the 'historical omission' of the uncompleted bourgeois revolution of 1848 was that it did not give the peasants the land. The land reform of 1945 was designed to repair this by breaking the power of the large land-owners or Junkers who had been one of the mainstays of Prussian militarism. Estates of more than 100 hectares and all lands owned by former Nazis were taken over. A few of the large capital-intensive farms were turned into state enterprises. But the majority was divided between more than half a million peasants with a maximum farm size of five hectares for regions with good soil, and eight hectares for those with poor soil. In order to prevent new capitalist relations developing, the land handed over during the reform could not be sold, leased or mortgaged. This parcelling up of the large estates made sound political and economic sense. It was a way of settling some of the thousands of landless refugees from the East and winning the traditionally conservative peasantry to the regime. Even had the authorities wanted to set up large-scale collective farms from the start, there was no infrastructure for it. Most agricultural machinery and equipment had been destroyed in the war. The stock of animals was very low, and there was a shortage of seed and fertiliser. But the authorities maintained control over agriculture by demanding a certain part of the peasants' crop as a compulsory delivery to the state. The rest could be sold at higher prices either to the co-operative retail societies or on the free market. Incentives were needed to ensure a fast enough rise in output to feed the almost starving city population. Rationing was strict. Cards were allocated on the basis of work, with people in heavy industry getting the most and the unemployed (e.g. housewives and pensioners) getting least. Their share was known as 'the cemetery ration'. Workers in the major towns got higher rations than non-agricultural workers in villages who were assumed to be able to buy direct from peasants.

In spite of their generally flexible policy in the economy, the Soviet administration and the German Communists wanted to guarantee political control. A few months after the re-establishment of the KPD and the SPD they mounted a campaign for the merger of the two. The original post-war SPD programme was not very different from that of the KPD's moderate appeal in 1945. Perhaps precisely because of the similarity, the two parties were in tacit competition from the outset. But the KPD had the disadvantage of being closely identified with the Russians. When things went well, people tended to praise the Social Democrats. When they had complaints they blamed the Communists. Although in the Soviet zone the SPD had to be careful not to criticise the Russians publicly, the SPD in the Western zones and in the Western sectors of Berlin continually played on German fears of Russia and stressed the links between the KPD and their 'Soviet masters'.

Ulbricht and the KPD leadership decided to push for a unification of their party with the SPD. They had initially hoped that the KPD would emerge in open conditions as the stronger party. If anything, the opposite was happening, especially in the villages where the Communists had never been strong. It was clear too that the old split between right and left wings inside the SPD was reappearing, this time manifested in more or less anti- and pro-Russian factions. The KPD wanted to merge the two parties before the right wing of the SPD took control. The merger aroused some doubts among SPD members but it was by no means universally unpopular. In several factories local SPD and KPD trade union branches united spontaneously. One East German source who later defected to the West wrote that many SPD members had shown real enthusiasm 'with the hope that the unhappy division would at last be overcome and that the new party would unite the best traditions of both parties'.[17] He reports that there was some pressure against Social Democrats who opposed unification. As an official in the agitprop section of the KPD central committee he was in a position to know. But he heard of only one case where an opponent of unification was arrested by the Russians. It caused a considerable outcry among Berlin Communists.

Nor was there a free play of forces in the Western zones. The

Western allies were slower to permit political parties to reform. Trade union activity was forbidden for several months.
Soon after the merger of the KPD and SPD, Germans in the
West demonstrated publicly for a similar move in their zones.
The British military authorities forbade them and after July
1946 refused visas to leaders of the new united party in the East
who wanted to enter the British zone.[18] In the Soviet zone the
leader of the pro-unity faction in the SPD was Otto Grotewohl,
the head of its Berlin section. He had been a member of the
Reichstag in 1933. Now he carried the SPD central committee
with him in accepting unity. Opponents of the move in the
Western sectors of Berlin held a plebiscite of their members.
Altogether 32,547 SPD members were eligible. The results of
the poll on March 31 1946 were: 2,937 in favour of immediate
unification; 14,763 for an alliance between the KPD and SPD;
and 5,559 against any unification or alliance. Some 9,000 members did not vote at all, either out of apathy or in loyalty to
Grotewohl's appeal for a boycott of the plebiscite. The result
was therefore ambiguous. Both sides could claim victory.

The authorities' drive for unity went ahead. On April 21 the
two parties' delegates met in the Admiralspalast in Berlin.
Wilhelm Pieck, the chairman of the KPD and Otto Grotewohl
shook hands on a stage, and the new party, the Sozialistische
Einheitspartei Deutschlands (Socialist Unity Party), was
formed. Its symbol was clasped hands on a red flag against a
white background. The two leaders became joint chairman, a
Communist and a Social Democrat were joint vice-chairmen
and the executive and central secretariat were also divided
equally. The new party's most notable feature was its programme. It stressed that there would be a specific German road
to socialism, and appealed to the best traditions of German
nationalism. Both approaches had strong support in the SPD
and the KPD.

In December 1945 at the request of Ulbricht and the rest of
the leadership, Anton Ackermann had published an article
'Is there a separate German road to socialism?' It caused considerable enthusiasm among German Communists. It provided
an acceptable synthesis between the views of those who had
hoped for rapid moves towards socialism in Germany at the
end of the war and those who not only counselled a slower

transition but also seemed more inclined to take Soviet advice on most issues. Ackermann pointed out that Marx had thought the transition to socialism could be achieved by peaceful means only in England and America which already had bourgeois democratic Governments. On the European continent these conditions did not apply in Marx's day. Now, Ackermann argued, the possibility of a peaceful transition to socialism in Germany existed. Germany had a higher level of production than Russia had had in 1917, a bigger working class and a greater reserve of skilled labour.[19]

In his speech at the foundation of the SED Otto Grotewohl, the leader of the Social Democrats, spoke of the traditions of his old party. But he reached conclusions similar to Ackermann's. He said the SED rejected anti-Bolshevism, but this was far from being 'a surrender of our internal affairs to foreign influences'. He stressed the need for personal freedom inside the party and referred to Germany's special conditions: 'In no other party was there so warm and staunch a respect for human rights as there is in the Socialist Unity Party'. And he held out the prospect of a Socialist Germany that would not rely on the Red Army for backing. 'I do not think it presumptuous, and I do not think the Soviet occupation authorities will take it amiss,' he said, 'if I make it clear that at least in the Soviet zone of occupation the SED which we have created today represents, thanks to its immense political strength, a guarantee of our stability to an extent which makes us no longer dependent on Russian bayonets.'[20]

3

The Soviet Connection
causes Problems

It is easy to look back nowadays at the period from 1945 to the
creation of the German Democratic Republic in 1949 as a slow
and deliberate strangulation of all independent non-Communist political activity. The Cold War provides a constant dis-
torting lens. At the time events were more haphazard. German
Communists wanted control over the commanding heights of
the economy, over the banks and heavy industry, and over production and distribution. They considered these essential. But
they had hoped to guide the political process in the Soviet
occupation zone by consent as much as by coercion.

Just as the Russians and the German exiles during the war
had hoped for some form of popular upsurge against Hitler, so
now there were differences of view over how far people could
be trusted in peacetime. Was it an illusion to think that
Germans would willingly consent to socialism, and help to
build it up or would they have to be forced? Was the working
class really ready to take power or had it been totally corrupted
by the Nazi experience? There were bitter exchanges among
party members. Some argued that the working class was so
permeated by Nazi thinking that the only hope lay with the
next generation. This argument had already emerged towards
the end of the war. In a fierce letter to his brother who argued
that the German working class had betrayed its comrades in
other countries, Paul Merker wrote that it had been misled by
Nazi propaganda. It was up to Communists to trust German
workers again. The party had to find a policy which would
'show the masses the way to freedom'. The path would be hard

and stony, but the policy would have to ensure that Communists 'rid themselves of all tendencies towards school-masterliness, arrogance, superficiality, and heartlessness'.[1]

The formation of the Socialist Unity Party was the first major break in the process of relying mainly on trust in the working class. Control over the class was the top priority and by the end of 1945 the KPD felt that two working-class parties constituted an excessive risk. Nevertheless, for almost two years after that, political debate in the Soviet zone remained intense. Sections of the middle class, the church, and a number of alienated groups, including refugees and former Nazis, still contested official policy. The SED's close identification with Russian policy was a constant liability for the party. The Russians' every mistake and misdeed could be blamed on the Communists. As the tension between the Russians and their wartime Western allies grew over policy towards Germany as a whole, Stalin's fears for future Communist control in his zone sharpened. His imposition of a tight clamp on political activity was as much a casualty of inter-allied tension as it was its cause.

In June 1945 the Soviet military command had authorised the creation of two middle-class parties, the Christian Democratic Union (CDU) and the Liberal Democratic Party of Germany (LDPD). Both were members of the 'block of anti-Fascist democratic parties'. The CDU, as official East German historians describe it, represented 'religious circles of the bourgeoisie and petty-bourgeoisie as well as Christian workers'.[2] The party's first two leaders, Andreas Hermes and Walter Schreiber, had opposed Hitler and were in sympathy with the abortive 'Officers' Plot' to assassinate him on July 20 1944. The CDU called for private ownership of the means of production and wanted religious education to be part of the school curriculum. But the party supported nationalisation of natural resources and the mines. The LDPD appealed mainly to owners of small and medium-sized businesses, to craftsmen and intellectuals and the middle class. It too supported de-Nazification but wanted to retain private enterprise and restore the old-style German civil service.

From the beginning the role of both parties was limited. In December 1945, for example, the Soviet military administration used its rights as the occupying power to remove the CDU's first leaders, Hermes and Schreiber, because they opposed the expropriation of the large estates. On other occasions the two parties both opposed Communist policy with some success. In the parliament of Saxony, the zone's largest province, the LDPD and the CDU in 1946 defeated an SED proposal for the introduction of the death penalty for black market offences. In many towns and villages the CDU had a majority on the local committees of the newly formed youth organisation, the Free German Youth. The relative freedom of party activity in the first year after the war helped to attract a substantial number of qualified people into the Administration, regardless of their attitudes to Communism. One technique used by the Russians to speed up reconstruction was to encourage one town to compete against another in restoring normal life. This instant approach to rebuilding was effective. One Western source has written that the 'Russians obtained the services of some of the most capable men in the Zone while in the West there was a tendency on the part of many such Germans to stay away from work under the occupation authorities. Those who blame the Russians for the large-scale desertion of German civil servants in the years 1947 and 1948 never stop to enquire how the Russians came to obtain the services of these men in the first place.'[3]

But the Russians also incurred a substantial amount of popular ill-will. By the end of the war German fear of the Soviet Union was at its highest. The Nazis had always directed their special hatred against Bolshevism. Even before Hitler came to power the links between his party and the army were based on the creed of anti-Communism. The Freikorps officers who murdered Karl Liebknecht and Rosa Luxemburg in 1919 were in contact with the Nazis by 1927. Hitler labelled Communism a Jewish ideology. In his propaganda against the Soviet Union he managed to mix hatred for the Jews with contempt for Slavs and fear of Communism. Except for the two-year period between 1939 and 1941 after the non-aggression pact with Stalin, the Germans had been subjected to continual anti-Russian stories for a decade and a half. Hitler deliberately exaggerated these fears by meeting any suggestion of a slackening-off of the German military effort against Russia in 1944 and 1945 with the threat that the Russians would raze Germany to the ground if they won the war.

The Red Army broke into German territory for the first time in East Prussia in January 1945. Germans fled westwards with stories of looting, rape, and murder. Wild rumours swept through Germany of Russians on the rampage. All the old prejudices about the Russians were revived and redoubled. The Nazis hardly needed to exaggerate. Spontaneously, people let their imaginations run riot, and they believed the worst. The Russians came in as conquerors. After sweeping across miles and miles of devastated Russian and Polish territory, the feelings of revenge among sex-starved and exhausted troops must have run high. Discipline broke down in several units. But the excesses which many of them committed were a shock to Soviet officers. The diary of a young Lieutenant, Yuri Uspenski, who died in East Prussia, was captured by the Germans. It shows how at first he felt the Germans deserved anything they got. A few days later his mood had changed, and he was condemning the appalling things he saw. His attitude was shared at the highest levels of the Red Army.[4] According to other documents captured by the Nazis and which later fell into American hands, on January 29 1945 Marshal Zhukov sent out an order to all battalions of the 1st Byelorussian Army forbidding any actions of revenge, from rough measures against the German population to looting and the burning of houses.[5] Marshals Rokossowski and Konev issued similar orders. Severe punishments, including the death penalty, were carried out on troops who disobeyed. By the time the Russians approached Berlin in April, discipline was considerably improved.

It was impossible to expect all incidents of rape and looting to be stamped out. The German population responded with gross exaggeration. Heinz Brandt who later defected to the West recalls that when he first arrived in Berlin from Buchenwald he lived in the Christian Hospital in Wedding 'where terrified nurses announced from one day to the other "Tomorrow the Mongols will be here". For them this meant the end of the world. In point of fact the Mongols never came to Berlin, and later we heard that these same troops had been among the most disciplined of the Soviet occupation forces.'[6] Gordon Schaffer, who toured the area for ten weeks at the end of 1946 and wrote up his impressions in *Russian Zone*, reports a trivial but typical conversation with a woman employed in a Government department in Saxony. She complained bitterly that a Russian took her bicycle during the Red Army advance through the town. The very next day the discussion turned to wireless sets. She volunteered brightly that she had a beautiful set. Her husband had sent it to her while he was stationed in France. Schaffer goes on to record that 'the Germans in the Russian Zone as in all other zones are much more ready to pity themselves than to recognise their guilt and join in an effort to make amends to the nations they wronged'.[7]

German feelings of bitterness in the Soviet zone were directed mainly against the Russians. Although it was British and American planes that had wrought most destruction in Germany's cities, it was the Russians who felt the brunt of German resentment. Russia was the occupying power. It was responsible for redrawing Germany's Eastern boundaries, for the loss of resources in the Eastern territories, and the aggravation of the refugee problem. Russia was in charge of reparations in the Soviet zone. The Potsdam Agreement of August 1945 gave each occupying power the right to exact reparations from its zone. (In addition the Russians were to settle Poland's claims from their share.)

Estimates of the effect of Russian reparations on the East German economy vary. One Western source suggests that the dismantling was equivalent to a reduction of between 37 and 45 per cent of the economy's capacity in 1936.[8] This source also says that the programme was carried out in such a way as to magnify its damage. No plan was announced, so that no one knew which plants would go. The Germans were deterred by this uncertainty from repairing and reconstructing factories. Sometimes a factory lost its main equipment, leaving the rest worthless. Another Western source identifies six waves of dismantling, in the first of which some 460 plants were removed in the Berlin area alone. The Russians took 32 per cent of the Soviet zone's railway track as well as mine installations, railway repair shops and power plants. In the mechanical engineering sector Russian reparations took more than twice the toll of the war itself. Dismantling amounted to 53 per cent of the industry's 1936 capacity, compared to 24 per cent which was destroyed or damaged in the war.[9]

Besides the dismantled equipment the Russians also took a

share of current production. To administer many of the zone's main firms they set up Soviet state joint stock companies. Most of their production was exported free of charge to the Soviet Union. In 1948 these companies included such key works as the Leuna chemical works, the Max metallurgical plant, and the Neptun shipyard in Rostock, and accounted for 22 per cent of the zone's gross industrial production.

The severe scale and crudity of the dismantling caused considerable resentment against the Russians even among Communists and other anti-Fascists. Trade union leaders found it hard to explain to workers why whole factories which had just been rebuilt had to be sent off to Russia. There were cases where the material removed was allowed to rot in railway sidings. Railway track was ripped up but not delivered to Russia for months. The reparations were run by a special department in Moscow rather than by the local Soviet administrator in Germany. Sometimes the local commanders tried to have decisions reversed. They usually failed.[10] As for Ulbricht and his colleagues, they did not tolerate any party discussion of the issue. For them it was taboo. They were prepared to make certain concessions to the population on internal matters – the postponement of agricultural collectivisation, the slow pace of nationalisation in industry and a limited role for parties other than the SED. These were features which formed part of the model of a 'people's democracy' and were approved by Moscow. But Ulbricht was not willing to make any moves which could conceivably antagonise the Russians at this stage. Where there was a clash between German and Russian sensibilities, it was always the Russian ones which came first.

Reparations were one such issue. The SED gave people the correct official explanation for reparations. Germany must repay the appalling damage it had caused in the Soviet Union. The Russians had suffered much more than the Western powers and could not afford to be as lenient. The SED would not concede that the policy could nevertheless have been handled more efficiently and smoothly. A similar issue was that of the refugees from the East. In the last months of the war and during the summer of 1945 some ten million Germans had left the former Eastern territories in East Prussia, Pomerania, Silesia and the Sudetenland. Some fled in terror. Others were forced out by the Nazis so that the towns they left behind could be devastated before the Russian arrival. Others were deported by the incoming Russians, Poles and Czechs. In all, the great trek westwards was probably the biggest movement of a national population in the entire war. There was historical justice in that fact, no doubt. It was not to be expected that anyone outside Germany would feel much sympathy for the displaced Germans who were paying the price for the Nazis' bestiality in the war. In Germany itself things looked different. The displaced people felt themselves no more guilty than other Germans, yet they suffered most. They came from the East with virtually nothing. They were homeless and starving and did not even have valuables, furniture or carpets that could be bartered or sold for food on the black market.

Most of the refugees moved immediately to one of the Western zones. Some three and a half million refugees stayed in the Soviet zone. Although some of these later left too, in the beginning they formed a sizeable addition to the population of the zone. As late as 1960 according to the Mayor of Frankfurt on the Oder, which suddenly found itself a frontier town, they represented between 15 and 20 per cent of the town's population.[11] This did not include people from the old Eastern and now Polish part of Frankfurt just across the river. For the authorities the refugees created massive extra problems in housing, food supply and welfare services. Some were given newly expropriated land. The majority were billeted on local people in the towns, frequently causing friction. The budget for the refugees was almost limitless. The story is told of an old pre-war Communist, a veteran of the Spanish civil war, who was put in charge of the refugee problem. On one occasion he was called in by the Soviet administrator and informed that his accounts showed an overdraft of four hundred million marks. What was he going to do about it? 'Lop it off my salary,' he replied. The Soviet officer laughed, and the matter was ended.

The refugees wanted more than shelter and security. They would have liked some psychological compensation for the homes they had lost. But officially no one sympathised with the relative injustice of their position vis-à-vis other Germans. In the Western zones the authorities came close to over-compensation. The issue of the 'Heimatsvertriebene' or 'people expelled from their homelands' was kept artificially alive as a political irritant and a stick with which to beat the Russians. In the Soviet zone the refugees were called 'Umsiedler' – 'resettlers'. Out of unwillingness to offend the Russians or the Poles Ulbricht refused to allow any public reference to the difficulties the refugees had had to face in leaving their homes. The new frontiers of Germany were fixed. Germany had to accept them, and any suggestion of sympathy with the resettlers could have looked like 'revanchism' or at least an unwillingness to face the new realities.

The third issue where Ulbricht forbade any emotional concessions to nationalism was that of the German prisoners of war still detained in the East. At the end of the war Stalin held on to an unknown number of Germans. Although many German POWs captured and held in the West had to wait up to two years before returning home, there were clear statistics on who was held where. The Russians by contrast released no figures. Some prisoners were allowed home. Others were not. The West used the issue for propaganda but Ulbricht had no convincing reply. Had it been merely propaganda, it might not have mattered so much. But for every man missing in the East there was an anxious German family in the Soviet zone, waiting desperately for news and indignant with the SED for doing nothing. Ulbricht was accused of being 'anti-German'. Just as right-wing nationalists in the West later accused Willy Brandt of having been a traitor and anti-German for wearing a Norwegian uniform in exile during the war, some reactionaries made the same charge about Ulbricht. At the Berlin Foreign Ministers' conference in 1954 the US Secretary of State, John Foster Dulles, referred to 'the Soviet citizen, Ulbricht'. The remark was untrue. Although the Nazis stripped Ulbricht of his citizenship because of his opposition activities, he never became a Soviet citizen. The remark was also psychologically inaccurate. Ulbricht was very conscious of his German-ness, even if like other exiles he had lost some of his feeling for the country during the ten years spent abroad. He too was torn between disillusionment with a nation that had so willingly remained Fascist to the very end and hope that it could be brought over to socialism one day.

Ulbricht made a strict, long-range calculation. By far and

away the first priority, he felt, was to guarantee the security of Communist control in the zone. That meant retaining the confidence and backing of Moscow. The Russians were the final arbiter of what happened to the zone. Ulbricht feared any move by the SED that could conceivably bring its loyalty to Moscow into question. Grumbling over reparations, the resettlers or the POWs were luxuries that the SED could not afford. Instead, it must emphasise its assets to the Russians. One of these was the uranium deposit in Aue. It was vital to the success of the Russian drive to break the United States' monopoly on the atomic bomb. Ulbricht sent in some 300,000 workers, most of them former Nazis but including other political detainees. They worked under grim conditions. To Germans who complained, Ulbricht replied that it was results that mattered. The zone was helping to strengthen the anti-Fascist and anti-imperialist camp. Otto Gotsche, Ulbricht's private secretary, put it bluntly: 'We bought our security.'[12] Only a handful of party officials protested against what they saw as the party's insensitive line on these 'national' issues. One of them, Walter Janka, a member of the exile community in Mexico during the war, resigned from the central committee secretariat in 1947.

One counter-move which the SED took to stress its Germanness to people in the zone was a mild relaxation of the de-Nazification measures. This did not affect the Russians directly, and was therefore 'safe'. Shortly before the local elections in the autumn of 1946 the party announced a new policy towards 'nominal Nazis'. People who had been 'nothing more than simple members or fellow-travellers of the Nazi party' should be 'incorporated into the democratic structure'. One reason for the change in policy was the enormous drain on efficiency caused by the purge of technical people. But the Communists were also afraid of losing too much popular support. The Austrian Communist party had performed disastrously in the Austrian elections in 1945. It was thought that a key factor had been their campaign against all former Nazis. The SED was afraid of a similar backlash in the zone. The slight softening in de-Nazification caused some Communists distress and anger. The authorities were later to relax it further. In February 1947 the three political parties sent a resolution to the Soviet administration calling for a clear statement offering former Nazis a chance to return to normal life. On February 13 the Soviet-run paper, the *Tägliche Rundschau*, wrote 'It is in the interest of the speedy reconstruction of the peacetime economy and of peacetime living conditions in Germany to draw former Nazis into the rebuilding process, particularly those who came from the working class. These nominal Nazis must be assured that they will find support in their efforts to return to the right path and to free themselves of their former errors and mistakes. There must be no obscurity or extremism in this matter ... '[13]

It would be easy to be cynical about this move, but the SED decided that former Nazis were reformable in practice. Those who had committed crimes had been punished through the courts. Others had lost their jobs. There was a large category of people with Nazi party membership numbers above the 8,000,000 mark who were virtually 'automatic' members. Towards the end of the war almost every school-leaver was enrolled into the party. If after the war they could show they no longer believed in Nazi ideology they were cleared. Former Nazis who had changed sides in POW camps and joined the National Committee for a Free Germany were considered to have reformed. (Hitler took the same view. Most of these men were tried *in absentia* and their families often faced severe reprisals.)

Against this background the first post-war elections in the zone were held on October 21 1946. They proved to be a watershed. Although the SED was the largest party it did not win as much as 51 per cent of the vote in any single province. In Berlin, where the SPD ran as a separate entity in the Western sectors of the city, the results were highly embarrassing to the SED. It came third behind the SPD and the CDU. The official East German history books describe the 1946 results as 'a great victory'.[14] The SED obtained 249 seats in the provincial parliaments, the CDU 133 and the LDPD 121. In fact the results gave the Communists something of a shock. The other parties had done better than expected. In Berlin the results showed too big a majority for the SPD for this to be written off as a consequence of the intense anti-Communist and anti-Russian campaign in the Western media. It was apparent that the SED was genuinely losing support, partly because of its close identification with the Russians, and partly because of its own policies.

In defence the Communists in the SED began to reduce the influence of former SPD members. Some ex-Social Democrats left the party voluntarily, and moved to the Western zones. Others were arrested as 'agitators'.

The SED also undermined the other parties' work. They denied them adequate newsprint for their papers. Workers were not given time off to attend party meetings, although for SED meetings all work ceased. Some CDU and LDPD members increased their defiance. At the CDU's conference in September 1947 the two leaders, Jacob Kaiser and Ernst Lemmer, rejected the Oder–Neisse line as Germany's Eastern frontier and called for the Soviet zone to accept Marshall Plan aid from the United States. The Soviet authorities were anxious not to close the parties down. They wanted to keep the semblance of official representation for different interest groups. They therefore brought about a second change in the CDU leadership in 1948. The 'block of anti-Fascist parties' increasingly became an out-and-out instrument of SED policies. The new climate also produced a split in the LDPD. At its 1947 conference the party's chairman, Wilhelm Kuelz, was bitterly attacked by several members of a pro-SED faction who later brought it round to accepting the nationalisation of the larger enterprises and of the zone's natural resources.

By the middle of 1947 tension between the Russians and the Western Governments was acute. It was the logical outcome of their different approaches to post-war Germany from the moment a Nazi surrender began to seem likely. Stalin's main aim at the Yalta and Potsdam conferences had been to use German resources to pay for Soviet reconstruction and to end for ever any chance of Germany's revival as a military power. Both objectives assumed some form of central control over Germany. In 1944 the Russians became the first of the Allies to provide a specific plan. Germany's main industrial areas lay in the West, and were concentrated in the Ruhr. Stalin favoured central control over Germany partly in order to get his share of the Ruhr's resources. Within the framework of a central administration Stalin readily agreed with the Western Allies on a zonal division of Germany between himself, the Americans, and the British (and later the French). But he was more interested in a vertical division of Germany, that is, by democratising the sources of power within Germany as a whole – by expropriating Nazi-owned and controlled industry, breaking the hold of monopoly capital and eliminating the springs of Nazi ideology.

The American view tended in the opposite direction. Washington was afraid of strengthening the economy of post-war Russia. In January 1945 Stalin asked the Americans for a six thousand million dollar loan at low interest. The request was turned down, and the official American 'Lend Lease' programme was even cut off. (In May it was resumed, at a much lower level.) Washington was also reluctant to concede Stalin's desire for heavy German reparations. The Americans felt that a weakened Germany and in consequence a weakened Europe would be in the interests of the European Left, and would help it to gain strength in Western as well as Eastern Europe. They also wanted to prevent the Russians from having any control over the Ruhr.

The British position before the end of the war was slightly different. Their projected zone of Germany had always had a food deficit. If excessive reparations weakened Germany and prevented its recovery, they would have to pay for their zone's food imports out of British reserves of hard currency. This gave London a greater interest in ensuring that the agrarian areas of Eastern Germany be reintegrated into a centrally controlled economy. Churchill told Stalin on July 25 1945 that the Ruhr's industrial output should be traded for food.[15]

At Potsdam a compromise was reached. Each Ally would take its reparations from its own zone. In addition the Russians could also have 10 per cent of the industrial output of the Western zones for nothing plus another 15 per cent in exchange for supplying food and raw materials. The Ruhr was not internationalised. Four-power control was to operate in finance, foreign trade, and transport but basic economic partition had been largely conceded. Moreover, shortly before the Potsdam conference the Russians had said that the economic disintegration in their zone was too great for them to supply food and coal to the Western sectors of Berlin. Reluctantly the West agreed to supply them themselves. Small though the issue was in comparison with the other matters affecting Germany, it showed that by sacrificing a potential tool for blockading Berlin economically Stalin had as yet not thought of such pressures.

Things began to go sour in March 1946 after the detailed reparations programme had been settled. Faced with the enormous needs of their zone and the Russian economy itself, the Russians claimed they could not supply the Western zones as planned. But they added (correctly, in terms of the Potsdam Agreement) that the extra 10 per cent of reparations due to them from the Western zones was a separate matter to which they were entitled whether or not they continued their supplies to the West. Britain and the United States disagreed. They argued that a common export–import programme for all Germany had to be established promptly.

Certainly the Russians had broken the Potsdam Agreement by hindering free trade between their zone and those of their Allies. The Americans decided to force the issue. On May 3 1946 they halted the dismantling of machines in the American zone which were due to be delivered as reparations to the Soviet Union. In September 1946 after two Allied foreign ministers' conferences in which little progress was made, the US Secretary of State, James Byrnes, threatened unilaterally to create an economic entity with any other zonal powers that were interested. By then each of the Allies had gone a long way in putting its own stamp on its zone. In the East the major industries were nationalised, and a land reform had been carried through. In their zone the Americans were anxious to restore a free enterprise economy. In the British zone the Labour Government wanted to nationalise the mines in the Ruhr (but were discouraged and ultimately prevented by Washington).

In the autumn of 1946 the Americans and British decided to fuse their zones into a single economic unit on January 1 1947. By March when the British, French, Soviet and United States foreign ministers met in Moscow, mutual suspicions between the Russians and the three others had increased. The Americans had a new Secretary of State, George Marshall, who was a passionate anti-Communist. He saw Russian insistence on 10,000 million dollars' worth of reparations and their determination to fix the Oder–Neisse frontier as parts of a master-plan for communising Germany as a whole. Even though the French were also being highly obstructive to US policy in Germany, Marshall chose to ignore that. Only the Russian obstruction mattered to him. He close to see it as sinister.

Marshall's fear of Communism was matched only by President Truman's. Two days after the Moscow conference began, Truman launched his 'Doctrine' of an all-out crusade against Communism wherever it held sway. Every nation, said Truman, must 'choose' which side it was on. The occasion for the speech was a plea to Congress for aid for the Royalist side in the Greek civil war. Although it was clear that Stalin was honouring his commitment not to intervene in Greece, Truman felt the need to escalate his Congressional appeal into a worldwide clarion call against Communism and to brand Stalin as an exporter of revolution.

The Moscow conference broke up in disarray. On June 5 the United States announced the Marshall Plan which was meant to ensure that the Western Zones should take part fully in Washington's general programme for economic recovery in Europe. Under the plan the United States, which had emerged from the war relatively unscathed and clearly the world's richest power, was offering aid ostensibly to all of Europe, East and West. In fact Marshall never intended or expected that Stalin would accept it. For one thing Soviet acceptance would probably kill the plan in Congress. He also calculated that the Russians would not be able to keep their hold over Eastern Europe if those countries joined the co-operative venture. But a Soviet refusal would have good propaganda value for the West, Marshall thought, 'particularly in countries with large Communist parties'.[16]

For a time Stalin showed interest as did many other Communists in Eastern Europe. He sent his Foreign Minister, Molotov, to Paris in June to discuss the details of the plan. But Molotov soon discovered that the aid was contingent on the integration of Europe's national economies. This, the Russians felt, would mean abandoning their plan to industrialise Eastern Europe in favour of keeping it as a subservient granary for the West. The Russians would also be required to submit a balance sheet of their economic resources, a demand which wounded their national pride. The war-torn Soviet Union was not going to go cap in hand to the affluent United States, especially when it also became clear that the Marshall Plan was based on the restoration of free enterprise and an end to nationalisation schemes. Finally the Americans had shown that they were going to ignore for ever Russia's claims for reparations. Two days after the start of the Paris meeting, as the Americans had calculated, Molotov brusquely walked out. Although Stalin had a justifiable case in being suspicious of the motives behind the Marshall Plan and its likely effect, his curt public rejection of it shocked many people, Communists included.

Inside the Russian zone it severely sharpened the authorities' already mounting problems. Private traders distrusted the Administration and what they saw as its exclusively working-class bias. Many felt the zone's economy was in hopeless chaos. They longed for the injections of capital that were being offered through the Marshall Plan. Strong anti-Russian feelings among many sectors of the population were heightened further by the contrast between the apparent generosity of the Americans to their zone and Stalin's continuing reparations in the East. Even the SED's historians admitted later that the position in the zone was serious. Party policy was facing 'countless obstacles in an extremely complicated position. The consequences of the war had not yet been overcome. People's needs could only be satisfied in a modest way. In spite of the efforts of anti-Fascists and the self-sacrificing labours of many work-people, hunger and cold could not be banished completely. The continuing scarcity of nearly all essential commodities led many people to see their salvation in the chance for American goods provided by the Marshall Plan.'[17]

In fact the British historian J. P. Nettl has calculated that in 1946 the standard of food consumption in the Soviet zone was higher than in the West. In 1947 it was still as good as that of the American zone and considerably better than the British zone. The Soviet zone consisted primarily of agricultural land. Nettl writes: 'Both in 1946 and 1947 serious distribution breakdowns occurred which directly affected the consumer's ration while the same on an even more catastrophic scale repeatedly occurred in the West. But in any comparison of production and consumption between East and West, the Russian zone – mostly in spite of, but partly because of, land reform – must come out more favourably.'[18] Even in industrial production the Soviet zone did comparatively well until the end of 1946. 'On the whole its [the American zone's] recovery would seem to have been slightly less than that of the Russian Zone and rather greater than that of its northern neighbour [the British zone].'[19]

The Marshall Plan's attraction to many Germans was that it offered a hope of rapid improvement. It was a psychological master-stroke. To counter it Walter Ulbricht and his colleagues decided to play their own nationalist card. In their propaganda they increasingly stressed the argument that it was the Western side that was to blame for splitting Germany. The SED central committee condemned the Marshall Plan on July 23. The SED invoked 'the bitter experiences which the German people had gathered after the First World War from American economic aid which had strengthened the power of the monopolies. Dollars had smoothed the way to crisis, Fascism, and war.'[20] The inclusion of the Western zones of Germany in the Marshall Plan, the SED went on, was a further step on the road to Germany's economic and political division. At its second congress in September 1947 the SED resolved to work out a 'real' plan of reconstruction for all Germany and to 'answer the Marshall Plan with a German plan for an economic revival based on Germany's own strength'.

In June 1947 the Russians had already started to centralise economic policy in the zone by setting up the German Economic Commission above the provincial governments, which had earlier taken the key economic decisions. In February 1948 the Russians gave the Commission full powers and in July Ulbricht announced a two-year plan for 1949–50 to supersede the earlier yearly plan. Increasingly too, the SED sought to weaken the two middle-class parties where national feelings were still strong. Ulbricht wanted to capitalise on the nationalist feeling among the population and divert it into manageable channels. On March 22 1948 the authorities opened a newspaper, the *Nationalzeitung*, to provide a psychological outlet and a controlled safety valve for people who felt this way. On September 7 the National-Demokratische Partei Deutschlands (NDPD) was founded to provide a 'political homeland' for former Nazis and other members of the petty bourgeoisie whose loyalty to the new system in the zone was in some doubt. The NDPD never had even the qualified independence which the LDPD and CDU once had.

Soon afterwards former Nazis were given back the right to vote. The last formal step in the process was taken on November

11 1949 when a law was passed 'On the Cancellation of Atonement Measures and the Granting of Civil Rights to former members and supporters of the Nazi Party and to Officers of the Fascist Wehrmacht.' The law was based on the argument that all the levers of power were now firmly in the hands of anti-Fascist forces. There was no danger of former Nazis gaining influence over the administration. At the same time a category of disgruntled second-class citizens might be created if former Nazis were to be penalised for ever. The law restored their civic rights and their right to work in their former professions (except in the police and the administration of justice). It did not give them any right to reclaim the jobs they had had before, or any confiscated property. Nor did the amnesty apply to former Nazis who had served a year or more in prison or who were still at large. The law was described later in the East German press as a 'triumph of reason over emotion'.[21] And so it was. It was a clear example of the pragmatic and careful policy followed by East Germany's Communists in most spheres at that time.

The emerging split between the Russians and the West developed rapidly throughout 1948. On March 20 the Soviet delegate, Marshal Sokolovsky, had walked out of the Allied Control Council in protest at the conference held by the Western powers in London the previous month whose results, he complained, had not been transmitted to the Russians. On June 18 the Western zones' Administrations announced a currency reform for all three zones. In protest the Russians retaliated by ordering a ban on all land traffic between the Western zones and Berlin. Four days later the Western powers extended the currency reform to Berlin. For the Russians and the East Germans this was seen as a particular threat. They feared the change in values would allow West Berliners to raid East Berlin's supplies of goods at artificially low prices. The following day the Russians announced their own currency reform, and refused to lift the blockade of Berlin.

As well as marking the decisive division of Germany, the two currency reforms showed the different economic tendencies in the two parts of Germany. In the West the reform was designed to alter the price ratio between labour and capital and give an incentive to the revival of a capitalist economy. In the East the reform amounted to a transfer of resources to the state. Citizens had to change their old notes at the ratio of from 3:1 to 10:1 while state institutions, political parties and the trade unions changed at par. The result was that 'while the entrepreneurial class turned the currency reform in the West to its own profit at the expense of the wage-earner, the Eastern reform was planned to benefit the State and all organisations under its control, as well as the various State authorities and organisations. It made little difference to the majority of wage-earners and "liquidated" a number of individuals and groups.'[22]

Though Stalin's decision to blockade Berlin was prompted by the Western currency reform, its aim was much more than a defence against Western economic penetration. Stalin hoped to take over control of the city's Western sectors and eliminate their potential nuisance value to him once and for all. With the division of Germany by then a reality, Stalin saw no reason to tolerate what was an enemy enclave within his territory. Russia had liberated Berlin unaided and at a cost of 305,000 men killed or wounded, half as many again as the Americans and British had lost in the whole of 1945. Admittedly the Western powers had obtained their sectors of Berlin by wartime agreement and had since withdrawn their troops from those parts of Germany which were designated as the Soviet zone. But Stalin knew that the Western leaders had at one time seriously considered violating the agreement and not retreating. Now that the alliance had broken down, Stalin felt no further justification for a Western presence in the city. He apparently did not count on the ability of the Western airlift to continue throughout the winter of 1948–9. It is sometimes argued that Stalin also wanted to use the Berlin crisis to prevent the formation of a West German Government. Whether this was his intention or not, the result was the reverse. On April 8 1949 the American, British and French Foreign Ministers agreed on an 'Occupation Statute' which gave the three zones legislative autonomy as a federal state. A fortnight afterwards – by now too late – Stalin lifted the blockade of Berlin. The Federal Republic of Germany was officially proclaimed by Dr Konrad Adenauer who became its first Chancellor on May 23.

The Russians moved rapidly to match the new state with one of their own. A number of local and national 'People's Congresses' had already been held in the Soviet zone, but on May

15 and 16 elections for a new People's Congress took place with a single list of candidates. Two weeks later it met to approve a Constitution for the whole of Germany. It called for a peace treaty based on the Yalta and Potsdam Agreements, the re-establishment of German unity through a Provisional German Government, participation by the Government in negotiations for a peace treaty and the end of zonal barriers to trade, currency, and transport. On October 7 1949 the German People's Council, elected by the Congress, proclaimed the foundation of the German Democratic Republic.

While the two sides of Germany were drawing apart, the SED was growing closer to the Soviet Communist Party. The decisive event was President Tito's break with Moscow in June 1948 which unleashed a wave of hysteria in Moscow and demands for conformity. Even before that the SED had begun to follow the Soviet line more faithfully. While Walter Ulbricht and his colleagues were playing the nationalist card more openly in their propaganda towards the population, the party itself was going in the opposite direction. At its second congress in September 1947 the three leading speakers, Walter Ulbricht, Wilhelm Pieck and Otto Grotewohl, repeatedly stressed the pre-eminence of the Soviet Union. By January 1948 the SED had taken over more and more of the various provincial Government posts. They held the Prime Ministership in every province, except Saxony-Anhalt, and exclusive control of all Ministries of the Interior and Education. Several more ex-SPD members left the party or were expelled. At the end of 1947 a control commission was set up in the SED to investigate cases of 'personal dishonesty' within the party's ranks.

In July the SED declared its support for the Cominform resolution which condemned Tito and Yugoslavia. Tito was accused of a variety of heresies, but his main sin was determination to go his own national way towards Communism. To affirm its loyalty and appease Stalin, in September 1948 the SED's executive committee rejected the thesis of a 'German road to socialism' and resolved to turn the SED into a party of a 'new type'. The leadership stated that the party either had to become 'a vanguard party of the working class in the spirit of Lenin' or it would not be able to master the complex conditions of the class struggle. The first task was to 'help all party members to find a class attitude towards the Soviet Union and recognise its leading role in the international workers' movement'.[23] The concept of a special German road to socialism was condemned as a device for denying the fundamental experiences of the Soviet party. It was a shield for anti-Communism and anti-Sovietism and a cover for people who were working in secret for the Social Democrats in the Western zones. Anton Ackermann, the chief exponent of the German road to socialism, was pressed by the leadership to retract. He made a public self-criticism. In an article called 'On the only possible road to socialism' he recanted his former theory which he said 'contains the seeds of a split from the working class and the Bolshevik party of the Soviet Union'. Throughout the party at all levels meetings were held to confirm the new line. In January 1949 the SED's first party conference took place. The central secretariat of the SED was replaced by a nine-man Politbüro, six of whom were former KPD and three former SPD functionaries. Walter Ulbricht took charge of a small secretariat for day-to-day work. Potential new party members had to go through a probationary period as 'candidates'. Above all, the status of parity between former Communists and former Social Democrats was abolished.

So by 1949 the division of Germany was complete. In the GDR the authorities sought to satisfy nationalist feelings by pinning all the blame for the split on the Western side. Inside the party Soviet-style discipline and orthodoxy were enshrined. According to the official East German history, the zone already exhibited various features in 1948 which created the 'elements of future socialism'.[24] The working class, it says, was strengthening its leading role at the head of the alliance of classes. In the economy there was a substantial state sector which limited capitalist profit making and restricted the laws of capitalism. The working-class alliance with the peasantry was getting stronger. With the beginning of long-term planning it was becoming an alliance for production.

The official history also points out some of the differences which the SED faced in contrast to other Communist parties in Eastern Europe, except in Czechoslovakia. It had to bring about a democratic transformation in an industrially developed country – in one of the countries where the revolution according to Lenin 'would be harder to begin but easier to continue'. It had to bring democracy to a country where Fascism had appeared in its most barbaric form and had had a particularly deep impact on the population. It had to operate in complicated conditions arising from the occupation of large parts of Germany by armies of imperialist states and the continuing division of the country. 'The SED's battle was a constant effort to preserve the unity of the national and social struggles.'[25] What the official history does not discuss is the effect on the party of excessive Soviet control. In spite of Germany's specific conditions the SED was still developing primarily according to Stalin's interests. As he told a delegation of visiting Bulgarian and Yugoslav Communists in early 1948, 'The West will make West Germany their own state, and we shall turn East Germany into our own.'[26]

4

Birthpangs of a Divided Nation

From Stalin's point of view the founding of the German Democratic Republic on October 7 1949 was only the second best solution to the German problem. He was realistic enough to see that the creation of two separate German states had become virtually inevitable, but he did not welcome it. Throughout 1948 and 1949 as the Western powers pushed on with their plans for building a Westward-leaning state in the American, British, and French zones, Stalin repeatedly tried to forestall it. He would have preferred a united but neutral Germany. He felt confident it would either be left-leaning or else sufficiently open to Soviet influence not to swing to the right. The effect of a united and neutral Germany in strategic terms would be to give Russia another large buffer zone beyond its Western borders. The front line of Western Europe, armed and potentially hostile to Russia, would then be the Rhine and the industrial power-house of the Ruhr would be denied to the Western Allies. On the other hand a West German state that was pro-American and eventually re-militarised would bring the Western camp's front line several hundred miles further forward to the Elbe. And it might not stop there. Article 23 of the Basic Law, or Constitution of the Federal Republic of Germany claimed to extend the provisions of the new state, at some future date, to East Germany and the entire region of Germany's prewar territories, parts of which had been incorporated into the Soviet Union itself.

Stalin's proposals at the Paris conference of Foreign Ministers in May 1949 were an attempt to reverse all that. He suggested

70

a peace treaty for Germany and the withdrawal of all occupation troops. The Western powers countered with a demand that on the road to a future united Germany there should be an Allied High Commission where decisions should be taken by majority vote. This clearly deprived the Russians of a right of veto. Nevertheless, the American military governor, General Lucius D. Clay admitted later that he had been concerned that Stalin might accept it. 'It would have been the end of our efforts to form a West German government,' he wrote in his memoirs. He was glad when the Russians finally turned it down.

At every step of the way towards the division of Germany, the Russians followed rather than led. They reacted hastily to Western initiatives. Their currency reform in the East came after the Western reform and was badly prepared. The East German draft constitution was announced after West Germany's Basic Law had been passed by the West German parliament. The founding of the GDR came five months after the Federal Republic was proclaimed in Bonn. Even with the creation of the GDR the Russians did not give up their hopes of achieving a neutral united Germany. It was not until five years later in March 1954, a year after Stalin's death, that the Soviet Union recognised the GDR's formal sovereignty in a treaty. After 1949 Stalin made two more attempts to negotiate the neutralisation of Germany, first in 1950 and then again in 1952. Even the founding of the GDR was justified not as a step away from German unity but as a move towards it. In his inaugural speech the GDR's first president, Wilhelm Pieck, stated 'We can now recognise with satisfaction the fact that the struggle of the national front of all Germans for German unity and a just peace treaty has entered a new phase with the formation of the German Democratic Republic. More than ever before we can now carry on our fight for our just aims with a good prospect of success.'[2]

Official East German histories stress two aspects of the GDR's foundation. One was that it 'dealt German imperialism and militarism its biggest blow since the surrender of the Hitler regime in 1945. The possibilities for the imperialistic high bourgeoisie to prepare and unleash a new war were limited. The monopolists' and militarists' plans to expand their rule over all Germany were broken through. German imperialism

71

and militarism found the way to the East was blocked.'[3] The GDR's other feature was that it gave the 'working class and its allies the basis for Germany's national rebirth as a united peace-loving, democratic state and for the entire German people to move peacefully towards the construction of socialism.'[4]

Details of the East German leadership's relationship with the Soviet Union are still shrouded in considerable secrecy. But it is safe to assume that Stalin was more interested in the first consideration, that is, the security implications for the Soviet Union of the founding of the German Democratic Republic. For Walter Ulbricht it was equally important to build up German socialism. He wanted to create a state that the Russians could not afford to sacrifice, and he wanted to do it fast. For one thing he feared that in a united Germany he would be hard pressed to keep his own power. Some time soon after the founding of the GDR the first really major differences of opinion emerged between Ulbricht and the Soviet Administration. At the same time the tensions between Ulbricht and the less dogmatic and more idealistic groups in the SED began to grow more acute. In the immediate aftermath of the Nazi defeat, Ulbricht had been the faithful servant of Moscow's cautious line. With Ulbricht's complete agreement, Stalin wanted to soft-pedal any rapid moves towards socialism – to the disappointment of men like Ackermann. But by 1949 the position had changed. Apparently dubious of Soviet intentions, Ulbricht was in a hurry to socialise and to create a strong state power. While sharing his doubts about Moscow, other groups within the party favoured a more flexible strategy. For some the idea of a German road to socialism still lingered on. Some simply felt the party should rely less on coercion and should make its first priority the retention of support among the working class. This could best be done, they argued, by improving living conditions.

After 1949 the Russians rejected both the idea of any easing of the German Communists' tasks or of a speeding-up of Germany's socialisation. Again they turned down pleas for an end to reparations payments. They delayed the incorporation of the GDR into the rest of the Soviet bloc. And they continued to keep open the option of a neutralisation of Germany regardless of its social system. Ulbricht later gave a rare admission of his doubts over Soviet policy when he commented on Stalin's offer to the West of free elections for an all-German Government in 1952. 'Had the Western powers accepted the Soviet Note of March 1952, the position of the party and the state in the GDR would have been greatly endangered.'[5] The SED leadership probably felt similar doubts about the Soviet Union's earlier proposals. But at least the foundation of the GDR gave Ulbricht a certain security. For the first time in history Germany's Communists were in charge of a state. Thirty years after the KPD was formed, its successor the SED had control of a piece of German soil. Admittedly it was only a tiny rump of land compared with the Germany of 1919. Nor had it come into existence by virtue of an armed popular uprising or on the wave of a massive working-class strike movement. It was born on the ruins of a destroyed and divided Germany, and the midwife was the Red Army.

Circumstances were hardly propitious. Official sources made no bones of the problem. Unlike the other peoples' democracies in the rest of Eastern Europe which had had successful anti-Fascist and national liberation movements during the war, Germany's anti-Fascists had achieved very little. Many of Germany's people still felt resentment, bitterness, and a desire for revenge after Hitler's defeat. The GDR was also faced with the need to compete with another powerful German state whose Chancellor, Konrad Adenauer, had declared his government's goal to be 'the absorption of all Germany into a European order'.[6] The Federal Republic was incomparably the stronger state. In the Ruhr and along the Rhine it had most of pre-war Germany's raw materials. In 1939 the area occupied by the GDR had only produced 1·3 per cent of Germany's pig-iron, 7 per cent of its steel, less than 1 per cent of its coke and 3 per cent of its hard coal.[7] The only indigenous fuel supply was poor quality lignite. Its transport system was totally disrupted by the division of Germany. It had no river or canal flowing exclusively through its territory, and its road and rail network were geared to trade with the West.

The division of Germany was followed by a politically inspired boycott of the GDR by traders not only in West Germany but throughout Western Europe. In February 1950 at the Allies' suggestion the Federal Republic broke off the steel deliveries originally stipulated in the inter-zonal trade agreement. With other goods also being blocked, the volume of inter-zonal exchanges dropped by 75 per cent between December 1949 and February 1950.[8] The GDR was cut off from its natural hinterland, and had to forge completely new links with the East. Because of its lack of raw materials before the war, Eastern Germany had concentrated on light industry, textiles, precision tools and optics. This left it after the war with serious disproportions between its low raw material base and its processing industry. To fill the gap with its own heavy industry needed massive investments which left little room for private consumption. The final difficulty for the GDR which its East European neighbours were spared was the open frontier with the West. In 1949, 130,000 refugees went to the Federal Republic, mostly for economic reasons. In addition under its de-Nazification programme, in spite of the slight easing up in 1948–49, more than half a million people were forced out of the Administration. Many of them were experienced technocrats and skilled people.

Against this background Ulbricht decided after the foundation of the GDR to tighten its control over the other parties and move to a clear-cut dictatorship of the proletariat. The democratic bloc of anti-Fascists was now a Government coalition. Some groups within the two middle-class parties, the CDU and the LDPD, still hoped to be able to oppose SED measures. The CDU's vice-president, Hugo Hickmann, had gone on record against the creation of the GDR. Other MPs hoped that they could revise some of the nationalisation laws. On January 10 1950 Ulbricht declared that the 'central task for the defence of freedom and the security of the nation's future, was to create a strong National Front, in which all parties would agree on a common programme.' Over the next few weeks local committees of the National Front were formed throughout the country. The People's Councils which had been elected the previous year became a National Council. After struggle inside the ranks of the CDU and the LDPD, Hugo Hickmann and his sympathisers were pushed aside. And in May it was decided that the National Front would put up a single list of candidates for the elections in October 1950. The proportion of seats would be decided as follows: SED 25 per cent, CDU and LDPD 15 per cent each, NDPD and the DBD, the peasants

74

party, 7·5 per cent each and the remaining 30 per cent would go to the trade unions, the FDJ, the women's organisation, and other social groups.

From then on the original post-war distinction of anti-Fascist versus pro-Fascist shifted to pro-Soviet versus pro-American. As Wilhelm Pieck put it in July 1950: 'It is quite simple. Germany will either become a united peace-loving and democratic country developing independently of the American, British, and French imperialists or it will be a tool of the war kindlers and so be destroyed as an independent, national state.'[9] This crude differentiation led to the purging from any active social role of countless people who were accused of being pro-Western.

The SED held its third party congress in July 1950. The congress decided that the SED should also purge its ranks of all 'bourgeois influence'. The new ideological stiffening which had already led to tighter controls over the CDU and the LDPD was turned inwards on the SED itself. The leadership was particularly worried by the fact that social democratic influences still survived, particularly among the working class. Since the beginning of 1949 the SED had been trying to create as many party cells as possible in the factories. By the time of the congress the proportion of the party's 1,316,700 members who were enrolled in factory cells had jumped to 43·6 per cent compared with 28 per cent in 1947. After the congress every member had to hand in his party card. He was only issued with a new one after careful screening to determine his suitability. About 69,000 members were expelled from the party or struck from the rolls. Most of them were workers.[10] In some nationalised enterprises entire cells refused to hand in their cards. Many workers were accused of being agents of the West German SPD's so-called Eastern bureau, which had been set up originally to keep contact with East German Social Democrats but was infiltrated by Western intelligence. The SED later admitted that unfair decisions were taken during the purge.[11] This particularly affected old Communists who had been members of splinter-groups before 1933 or who had emigrated to the West while Hitler was in power. Many of them were Jews. In the climate of hysteria which Stalin generated after the break with Tito, and with the Cold War developing, the SED was terrified of 'revisionists' and potential imperialist agents. In the summer of 1950 a number of senior party officials were purged on the grounds that they were connected with Noel Field, an alleged American spy. They included Paul Merker, Leo Bauer, Lex Ende, Willi Kreikemeyer and Bruno Goldhammer. Over the next two years several other senior people were removed from the party or excluded from their jobs. Almost none of the Moscow *émigrés* who were close to Stalin and accepted by Stalin were affected. But many of those who had spent the war in America suffered – Albert Norden and Alexander Abusch, to name but two. Of the English *émigrés* there were the economists Josef Winternitz and Grete Wittkowski, and the philosopher Klaus Zwerling. In addition, almost everyone who before 1933 or during the emigration had not been in the mainstream of the KPD but had indulged in some form of factional activity now paid the price and was removed.

Officially, the party was still not calling for socialism. At the third party congress the country's first five-year plan was adopted with the aim of proving that the new system was superior to capitalism because of its economic results. At the time the GDR was founded the leading sectors of industry were nationalised but almost half the country's gross national product was still produced by private enterprise. The congress said there would be no more expropriations for the moment. But with the creation of a state wholesale system in 1950 the SED was able to influence developments in the private field through taking charge of bulk buying and selling. The five-year plan foresaw substantial investment in heavy industry in order to overcome the problems caused by the splitting of Germany. The output of the metal-working industry was to rise two and a half times and that of machine-tools was to double. Mining, the chemical industry, and energy production were all to be stressed while the working class, it was officially admitted, would have to make 'considerable sacrifices and enormous efforts'.

Over the next three years the main testing-ground for Ulbricht and his colleagues was indeed on the factory floor. Two months after the party congress the Federation of Free German Trade Unions (FDGB) held its own congress. One of its stated aims was to convince all union members of the need

76

to recognise the party's leading role. Hundreds of workers still felt that trade unions should remain outside politics and be independent of the state apparatus, if necessary representing workers' interests against the state. Their views were strengthened by the new 'collective agreements' brought in to the nationalised enterprises in 1951. The party's plans for the economy rested on a rapid increase in productivity. During the two-year plan which began in 1948 the authorities had relied mainly on Stakhanovite methods of raising productivity by finding a local hero whose example could be held up to everyone else. A coalminer, Adolf Hennecke, achieved a phenomenal output of coal on October 13 1948, fulfilling his norm by 387 per cent. He was turned into a national symbol overnight.

By 1950 something more comprehensive was needed. The SED took over from the Russians the notion of collective agreements. Under Lenin the first such agreements in the Soviet Union in 1922 were similar to those of the capitalist world in that unions and management agreed on safety measures, rates of pay, and fixed hours of work. Later towards the end of the 1920s the agreements became simple instruments of the state. Collective agreements were abandoned in 1934 but Stalin reintroduced them in 1947 as nothing more than contracts in which workers bound themselves to fulfil and over-fulfil the annual and five-year plans. The SED wanted to bring in this model of the collective agreement. By a Government decree in February 1951 every nationalised enterprise had to draw up an agreement as soon as possible. This was easier said than done. The workers as a whole had to endorse the agreements. German workers had a long industrial history and the traditions of trade union independence had not been entirely lost during the period of totalitarian government under Hitler. Under the new collective agreements workers had to contract to fulfil the norms laid down but management fixed the wages and how much was to be spent on social measures. The work norms were increasingly calculated by new technical bureaux. Although these bureaux included some workers' and trade union representatives they were frequently met with suspicion. Many workers saw the norm bureaux and the collective agreements as a device for getting more work out of them for less pay.

The introduction of the agreements went more slowly than

77

the authorities had hoped. At the important Carl Zeiss optical works at Jena numerous discussions were needed to persuade a workers' delegate conference to accept the new agreement. Only after a stormy meeting lasting all day did delegates approve it by a majority of 265 to 56. There was protracted resistance at the 'Walter Ulbricht' chemical works at Leuna. This was one of the GDR's largest and most prestigious enterprises, situated in the 'Red' district of Halle, a pre-war Communist stronghold. Workers at Leuna had a tradition of good organisation and solidarity, what SED historians later referred to as a 'company ideology'.[12] Talks over the collective agreement dragged on for months and progress only began to be made once the party cell in the plant had been brought round to accept it. (Even then some truculence remained among party members at Leuna. In December 1952 the SED journal *Neuer Weg* criticised party members for not buying more party journals. Only 11·8 per cent were regular subscribers to *Neuer Weg*.)[13]

The difficulties in implementing the collective agreements were a warning to the party. The year 1952 turned out to be full of crises. There were clear signs of uncertainty and indecision in the party leadership. Harsh measures were followed by concessions which were then themselves rescinded. Ulbricht was impatient to move the country on to a new institutional basis. In July at the SED's second party conference he announced that it was time to start 'the building of socialism' and that 'state power' was to be the main instrument in building it. The decision had several practical effects.

The GDR formed its first official armed fighting units with the ostensible aim of counterbalancing West Germany's signature of the European Defence Community treaty two months earlier. Before this the GDR had already had armed men, formed into so-called Kasernierte Volkspolizei, people's police in barracks. These had been set up in July 1948 when the GDR was still the Soviet zone. For many years the question of which German state was the first to arm was a major East–West dispute. Both sides had paramilitary units of uncertain capabilities from an early period. By the end of 1945 the Americans were employing armed Germans in uniform for guard duty. Some were in mobile units. Other Germans wearing American uniforms were formed into 'labour units' and the 'industrial police'. A year later on December 1 1946 the East German Grenzpolizei or frontier police were unified into a single administration, which had 18,000 men under arms by the time the GDR was founded. SED spokesmen recognised that the creation of the fighting units in 1952 produced some propaganda problems. At the party conference Pieck said that if the GDR were weak and unprotected it would be a temptation for aggressors. The official history claims that it would have been easy to reverse the decision to set up the armed units if the West had stopped rearming. It also says that as the war had created a pacifist attitude 'in petty bourgeois circles as well as for many workers' the party found it difficult to convince people of the need for defence.

Ulbricht saw the creation of the new fighting units as another step towards the legitimisation and strengthening of the state. He followed Stalin's view that state power was the essential weapon for building socialism. The idea of a strong state was of course a traditional German concept.

Another consequence of the 1952 party conference was a new impulse for the collectivisation of agriculture. By the end of 1952 some 37,000 peasants had formed almost 2,000 co-operatives thanks to a mixture of incentives and pressure from the authorities. At a conference in December 1952 the presidents of the first co-operatives laid down three models for other cooperatives to follow. In the first type peasants continued to own and have the use of all their animals, tractors, and other agricultural machines. They had to lend them out in return for rent to help with the joint cultivation of the entire co-operative's fields. They also pooled all their arable land. In type two, horses, tractors, and other machines which the peasant did not need for his own household were handed to the co-operative and repaid in instalments until they became its full property. Meadows and pasture land were given over to the co-operative. In the third type members pooled their farm buildings and all their land except for a small garden plot. The only property a member kept was his house, one cow, a pair of pigs, and some poultry.

In the beginning the main recruits to the new co-operatives were landless refugees and farm labourers. They formed the cadres for running the co-operatives. The so-called middle peasants, who were the mainstay of most villages, held back. The 'big farmers' who owned more than eight acres and employed labourers were not allowed to join at first, even if they wanted to. But both groups had to make compulsory deliveries of their produce at fixed prices to the state. It was bad luck for the party that the stiffening of its agricultural policy coincided with exceptionally bad weather. A wet autumn followed spring frosts. The tough new measures for collectivisation and the high compulsory deliveries led to a sharp exodus of farmers. In 1951 4,343 farmers fled to the West. In 1952 the number had more than trebled to 14,141. By the end of the year abandoned land accounted for 13 per cent of the GDR's entire agricultural area. The result was a poor harvest and a shortage of food. The authorities did not publish any statistics on agricultural output.

The Government compounded the shortage by stockpiling food. The enlarged police force also needed extra rations.[14] In November the authorities prohibited sales of food to West Berliners as a way of conserving supplies. Earlier sales to West Berliners had been allowed as a way of showing that socialism was superior because it could produce cheaper food than the West. The move was a further step towards the division of Berlin. A campaign was also launched against food speculators, some real, but many imaginary. 'Class justice' became more severe. The Minister of Trade and Food plus his two secretaries of state were arrested.

The food crisis was caused partly by Ulbricht's impatience. The GDR was already 'behind' its neighbours Hungary and Czechoslovakia which had already almost completed collectivisation. Although Poland still kept private peasants, Ulbricht felt this was an aberration. He was anxious to stress the differences between the GDR and the Federal Republic. As for the sharpening of tensions in society which collectivisation caused, Ulbricht was prepared to live with them. Stalin had written that the class struggle would sharpen during the transition to socialism. Ulbricht agreed. The attack on 'speculators' was matched by new moves against the church. Numerous parsons and church officials were arrested. Members of the evangelical Junge Gemeinde were expelled from universities. Stalinist control over science and the arts was tightened.

Only on the industrial front was Ulbricht more conciliatory for a time, or at least more flexible. After the problem with the collective agreements in 1951 he made some concessions. The issue of pay and conditions was taken out of the agreements and laid down by statute. The FDGB was officially criticised for having 'bullied workers'. The use of technically based norms diminished, and in the union elections in the autumn of 1952 about 70 per cent of the candidates were not SED members.[15] Although this result showed some tolerance on Ulbricht's part, it also suggested – ominously – that the SED's stock among the working class was not very high.

5

A New Course after Stalin's Death?

The SED designated 1953 the year of Karl Marx, 'the greatest son of the German people'.[1] It turned out to be one of deep crisis for the party and for Ulbricht. The simmering disappointment of a section of the leadership which had hoped to see a more sensitive application of socialist principles coincided with the anger and bitterness of a large element of the working class. Eight years after the end of the war there was a widespread feeling that the first blueprint for socialism had failed and now needed substantial modification. Symbolically Eastern Europe's first major post-war revolt took place in Germany where the working class had always been more militant.

As 1953 opened it was still official policy to try to deal with the economic crisis by putting the main burden on to the middle class. It was blamed for causing the food shortages by resisting collectivisation and by indulging in black market speculation. Under a decree which came into force at the beginning of April about two million people lost their ration cards. In future small retailers, craftsmen and people in freelance professions had to buy their food in state co-operative stores at high prices. Workers retained their ration cards and also had access to special shops which were opened on factory premises. Although these moves affected the way the country's economic burden was shared, they did little to find a way out of the crisis. In the first quarter of 1953 the output of several branches of industry fell a long way short of the plan. Since December 1952 the number of people leaving the GDR for the West had become a flood. It was to reach its peak in March when as many as 58,605 refugees were registered in West German transit camps compared with 7,227 in January 1952.[2]

Otto Grotewohl, the Prime Minister, revealed that by February a majority of the Politbüro already realised that drastic steps were needed to increase production.[3] Ulbricht was suspicious of their views and motives. At the end of 1952 he had abolished the Politbüro's information office, directed by Gerhard Eisler, on the grounds that too many of the staff had spent the war in emigration in the West. In February 1953 he dissolved the Association of Victims of the Nazi regime to prevent it becoming a focal point for veterans of the Spanish civil war who opposed him. He overruled an attempt by the trade union movement to set up its own youth organisation for fear that it would escape the control of the centralised Free German Youth (FDJ) and encourage clashes with official SED policy.

In the midst of these competing tensions a political earthquake suddenly occurred. On March 5 Stalin died. For Ulbricht and the rest of the leadership the news raised a host of questions. Who would emerge on top in Moscow? What would his commitment be to the GDR? Would he want a unified Germany? Some senior SED members, though not Ulbricht, hoped that Stalin's death would at last produce a relaxation of the political climate throughout Eastern Europe and ease the pressure for trumped-up trials. These had reached their nadir with the false confession extracted under torture from Rudolf Slansky, once the first secretary of the Czechoslovak Communist Party. He and several other distinguished Communists were executed. In the last months of Stalin's rule the anti-Semitic 'doctors' plot' led to fears among the Jews in the GDR's leadership that they too would be made scapegoats. In earlier and less severe purges several Jews had lost power in the SED. Some thought that the reason may have been that they were Jews rather than the fact that they had spent the war in the West. Some of those who had survived in power began now to prepare to escape from the GDR on the S-Bahn, the suburban railway which thousands of lesser refugees had used to go from one side of Berlin to the other.

To test the new mood in the Kremlin the SED approached Moscow for special economic help to overcome the country's crisis. Stalin's successors replied with a polite but firm 'No'. They urged the Germans to abandon their hard line on internal dissidence and slow down their programme of socialisation. The Kremlin's message was a strong rebuke for Ulbricht. He chose to defy it. In a speech published in the next day's *Neues Deutschland*, Ulbricht invoked the ghost of the dead dictator. He praised his 'wise leadership', and appealed for greater vigilance, and the 'exposure of agents and disrupters'.[4] He blamed the country's problems on 'sabotage, arson, and the theft of documents' and said that the most pressing task for the state was to overcome low work norms. He provoked a new clash with church authorities by announcing plans for a new 'socialist' city to be called Stalinstadt which would have no churches. Ulbricht's defiance of the new Soviet leaders was probably not based on loyalty to Stalin nor on traditional conservatism. He shrewdly calculated that the Kremlin itself was divided between those like Molotov who wanted to retain Stalin's hard line and others like Malenkov who favoured change. There was also the question of the survival of the GDR itself. At the end of April President Eisenhower and the new Soviet Prime Minister, Georgi Malenkov, made conciliatory speeches on the need for *détente*. Churchill called a summit conference on Germany. The idea was unwelcome to Adenauer who feared the neutralisation of Germany. He wrote to Eisenhower on May 29 stressing that any peace treaty for Germany must allow a reunited country to enter into any alliance it chose.[5] He clearly had in mind the European Defence Community.

Ulbricht was equally suspicious of the Allies' intentions. The old spectre of the Russians one day giving up the GDR raised itself again in his mind. He framed his tactics accordingly. It would be hard for him to oppose Soviet foreign policy outright. Instead he decided to play up to the Soviet conservatives by resisting any softer line on domestic affairs. He also wanted to move against the moderates in his own Politbüro. The device he and his two closest allies chose was to remove Franz Dahlem, one of the party's most respected members. A veteran of the Spanish civil war and the symbolic leader of the 'Western *émigrés*' Dahlem seemed to many of the old Communists the only possible alternative party leader. He had been a rival of Ulbricht's since the days of the Weimar Republic. After the war

he served as party secretary in charge of cadres and head of the
SED's department dealing with the West.

On May Day the crowds that paraded through the streets of
Berlin were thinner than usual in spite of measures to compel
attendance. Those who were there noticed that Dahlem's
picture was not being carried in the parade of Politbüro
members. A fortnight later the rumours which this strange
omission had aroused were confirmed. The central committee
met and Ulbricht pushed through an astonishing three-point
resolution. The first part dealt with the Slansky trial in Czechoslovakia and its 'lessons' for the SED. One might have thought
that Stalin, the instigator of the purges of the 1950s, was still
alive. The resolution condemned the destructive activities 'of
bourgeois elements and the whole iniquitous rabble of Trotsky-
ites, Zionists, freemasons, traitors, and morally depraved
individuals'. It said that enemies of the state were bringing up
the 'so-called theory of the weakening class struggle', which was
said to go with the establishment of socialism. It declared war
on 'saboteurs, parasites, and traitors'. Dahlem was excluded
from the Politbüro and central committee after Ulbricht and
Matern accused him of having shown 'total blindness towards
the attempt by imperialist agents to infiltrate the party'. It was
announced that the investigation into Dahlem's case and all its
ramifications was continuing. The second part of the resolution
called for the work norms to be raised by at least 10 per cent.
This ended the policy of shifting most of the economic burden on
to the middle class. From now on workers were being asked to
work 10 per cent harder for the same pay, all at a time of
growing shortages. The third part of the resolution added insult
to injury. It called for Ulbricht's sixtieth birthday to be turned
into a 'political climax'. While criticism of the personality cult
had already begun in Moscow, June 30 in the GDR was to be
the occasion for every worker and official to make 'self-commit-
ments in honour of the sixtieth birthday of our belovey Walter
Ulbricht'.

The central committee's defiant tone roused the Russians
into giving the SED a new warning. On June 3 the Soviet
Politbüro, though itself divided, made it clear that it was
watching events in the GDR with concern. In the SED leadership Wilhelm Zaisser, the Minister for State Security, and

Rudolf Herrnstadt, the chief editor of *Neues Deutschland*, were organising against Ulbricht. They argued that the party's existing policies were wrong and divisive, and that a new leadership and a new party policy were essential. Heinz Brandt, the secretary for agitation and propaganda on the SED staff in Berlin, wrote later that the aim was 'a peaceful democratic change-over in the GDR' and thereafter the reunification of Germany. He foresaw that 'the present regime would slide, as it were, towards disintegration in stages and finally be fully replaced after free parliamentary elections had been held. SED rule would be dismantled, not blasted sky-high; the terror abolished; the secret police dissolved. In this way an explosion with unforeseeable potential conclusions would be avoided.'[6]

Zaisser and Herrnstadt were apparently backed by Malenkov and Beria in Moscow. On June 5 Vladimir Semyonov who had been political adviser to the Soviet Control Commission returned to Berlin as High Commissioner. He came with a sheaf of written resolutions which the SED Politbüro and central committee were to adopt. For a start he told the Politbüro: 'We recommend that Comrade Ulbricht celebrate his sixtieth birthday in the same way that Lenin celebrated his fiftieth.' When someone obligingly asked how that was, Semyonov replied, 'He invited a few friends to drop in for dinner.'[7] Semyonov then outlined the 'new course' which Moscow wanted to see in the GDR. The programme was published without comment in *Neues Deutschland* on June 11. Investment in heavy industry was to be cut and production of consumer goods stepped up. A series of taxes on farmers, craftsmen, shopkeepers, and private firms was lifted. Private businesses that had been closed down by the authorities could start up again. Refugees who had gone to the West were invited to return and offered help. Farmers were promised back their land. They could borrow money, machines, and seeds. Intellectuals received permission to attend conferences in West Germany, and West Germans could get passes more easily to visit relatives in the GDR. Students expelled from university because of their religious beliefs could come back. All those arrested on religious grounds were to be released, and the campaign against the church was to end. The idea of 'class justice' was to go. The middle class would get ration cards back, and some recent price increases were revoked. The SED Politbüro admitted to 'errors in the past'.

The whole package was said to be aimed at the great goal of 'reunifying the German people into a national German state', and the Politbüro called for measures on both sides that would 'materially facilitate a rapprochement between the two parts of Germany'. What this last phrase meant is unclear. Were the Russians prepared to see the SED and the West German KPD go into opposition in a united German Parliament? Or were they just hoping to restore the Four-Power dialogue, and thought that a conciliatory offer on Germany would get them to the negotiating table? Ulbricht himself was probably in doubt. At all events he was unwilling to take the risk that Beria and Malenkov, the Soviet initiators of the 'new course', might be serious. It was an amazing reversal of most of the measures taken since the Second Party Conference in July 1952 which had been proclaimed as 'building socialism'.

Ulbricht looked for ways of undermining it. In subsequent speeches he emphasised the 'all-German' aspects of the Politbüro resolution less than the rest of it. On two points he successfully resisted Semyonov. He did not let the Politbüro rescind the 10 per cent increase in the work norms, and he did not call a central committee meeting although under the party constitution only this body could ratify the proposed changes. Ulbricht was afraid that supporters of Dahlem might reopen his case and call for a change of leadership. There might be an embarrassing post mortem on the whole Stalinist nature of Ulbricht's domestic policies. Ulbricht was also concerned that there might be demands for a return to the old work norms. He may genuinely have thought that the 'new course' could not be paid for economically without an increase in production which would have to mean maintaining the new norms due to go into force on June 30. Or he may have deliberately tried to sabotage the 'new course', and hoped that the imposition of the new norms would do the trick.

At all events on the same day that the Politbüro decision was published, *Neues Deutschland* printed a virulently hostile analysis of the Federal Republic. It predicted an imminent popular uprising in West Germany where, it said, 'the isolation in which the traitorous Adenauer clique finds itself is growing from day to day ... the patriots' will to struggle is constantly kindled anew'.[8] It is impossible to say whether this article's language was personally approved by Ulbricht. It certainly sounds more like his voice than that of the editor Herrnstadt who supported the conciliatory line towards West Germany. But *Neues Deutschland* was full of contradictory pieces in those days. Certainly the bitter attack on Adenauer went against the Malenkov and Beria policy of *détente*, and reflected Ulbricht's main tenacious concern not to see the GDR liquidated.

Unexpected and unexplained, the 'new course' hit party members like a bombshell. Some of them were so used by then to the suggestion that imperialist agents were active under every bed that they thought the Politbüro announcement must be a Western forgery, planted in *Neues Deutschland* to confuse the party. Confusion was indeed the outcome. The progressives in the SED felt it was the last chance for the liberalisation which they had long been hoping and waiting for. Admittedly the lack of any announcement about a central committee meeting was strange, and went against the democratic spirit of the new measures. The conservatives, meanwhile, feared the worst but took comfort from the retention of the higher work norms. In the West the Federal Government played into Ulbricht's hands by denouncing the changes as proof of the 'bankruptcy of the SED'. The Social Democrats welcomed the changes and called for Four Power negotiations on Germany. They were drowned out by Adenauer and his inflexible colleagues. Adenauer wanted unification, of course, but he also wanted to discredit and destroy Communist rule in the GDR. The second goal was by far the more important in his eyes.

Through his mouthpiece in the GDR, the Soviet-run *Tägliche Rundschau*, Beria appealed in vain for Western understanding. 'Our enemies are working overtime to present the new resolutions as symptomatic of a mood of panic ... A segment of the West German press has shown an understanding of the importance of these resolutions to the GDR and has taken an attitude of good will towards them ... '[9] Events were now overtaken by the working class. For workers the 'new course's significance was its silence on the issue of the work norms. In contrast to the middle class who were being given all kinds of concessions, there was no hint of the work norms being lifted. A mood of anger, bitterness and incipient revolt set in.

The events of June 16 and 17 have since become a casualty of Cold War propaganda. Two rival myths have appeared. In the West the conventional wisdom is that a country-wide popular uprising for reunification on the Western model was suppressed by Soviet tanks. June 17 has become a national day in the Federal Republic, an occasion for anti-Communist speeches and sanctimonious passing thoughts by politicians for 'our oppressed brothers and sisters on the other side'. (The Social Democrats stopped their June 17 speech-making after Willy Brandt became Chancellor). In the East the SED's brief moment of self-criticism on the morrow of the events gave way within days to an attempt to write them all off as an operation by Fascist bandits and imperialist agents in the West to incite East Germany's workers. According to the official SED history, the imperialists had long prepared a 'Day X for a counter-revolutionary putsch'.[10]

The truth was more complex. On June 14, a Sunday, *Neues Deutschland* published an article which only added to the confusion already caused by the Politbüro decrees. Called 'Time to put aside the sledgehammer', the article criticised the way the work norms had been introduced. It said they should only be made legally binding once workers had been convinced of their necessity. The next morning the article was passed from hand to hand among building workers on the site of a new hospital at Friedrichshain in Berlin. They decided to send a delegation to the Government the next morning to find out once and for all what was happening about the work norms. They sent a letter to Grotewohl demanding a meeting and threatening to strike if he refused to rescind the increase in the norms. At first Grotewohl hesitated about whether to meet the delegation. But he was persuaded by his staff to adopt well-worn elitist tactics. Bruno Baum, a member of the SED secretariat in Berlin, who had been criticised in the 'sledgehammer' article suggested that once they entered the Council of Ministers building the workers would be so over-awed by the chance to speak to the Prime Minister himself and hear a few soothing assurances from him that their militancy would evaporate.[11]

The next morning, June 16, the building workers found an

article in the trade union newspaper *Die Tribüne* confirming the higher work norms. It was written at Ulbricht's request. Traditionally, building workers are militant in most countries. The seasonal nature of the job, ramshackle working conditions, the absence of the discipline of an industrial site, and the tough requirements of hard, outdoor, physical work tend to create an attitude of dare-devil militancy. In East Berlin building workers were paid piece rates, but their comparatively good earnings had already been threatened by the introduction of technically based norms. The idea of yet higher norms was anathema. On reading the article in *Die Tribüne* building workers at the Stalinallee, which was intended to be East Berlin's most prestigious street, decided to march immediately to the Council of Ministers. On the way they were joined by the workers from Friedrichshain. The move was entirely spontaneous, as was admitted on the day by Fritz Selbmann, the Minister for Heavy Industry, and by Max Fechner, the Minister of Justice, in an interview in *Neues Deutschland* on June 30. The workers went to the Council of Ministers *en masse*, partly because feeling was running high and partly for fear that a small handful of representatives might simply be arrested.

Their move was patently not counter-revolutionary in intention. Their banner read 'We demand lower quotas'. They had not even elected a strike committee. As the march went on, it gathered new recruits, including many young people not in working clothes. Now, in addition to the demand for lower norms, there were chants of 'Free Elections' and 'We are not slaves'. In the square in front of the House of Ministries in the Leipzigerstrasse the crowd stopped and demanded to talk to the Government. 'Pieck and Grotewohl, Pieck and Grotewohl,' they shouted. At the SED headquarters some way off, the Politbüro had been in session for some time anxiously discussing the crisis. Heinz Brandt was called in and told to go out to the workers and tell them that the new work norms were cancelled. Climbing on to the seat of a bicycle Brandt stood up and gave the crowd the news. The response was a 'remarkable roar of triumph, mingled with joy, anger and laughter', according to an eye-witness.[12] He was Robert Havemann, another old Communist, a professor of chemistry at the Humboldt University who was later to break from the establishment himself and become one of its most celebrated critics. He wrote later that after the first reaction to the news that the work norms had been revoked there came calls 'Down with the Government' and 'We want free elections'.

He climbed up himself to try to address the crowd, and control its mood. 'Yes, we want free and secret elections for a Government in the whole of Germany – free, equal, and secret elections. But you know our Government has proposed this to the West German Government ... We must go to the West. That is where we must demand free elections ... ' The crowd shouted him down. Fritz Selbmann, a member of the Politbüro, was the next to speak. His voice too was drowned. No one else even tried to speak to the crowd, which gradually dispersed of its own accord after an hour. Later, on their way back from the Leipzigerstrasse, some of the demonstrators hijacked a loud-speaker van. One man broadcast an announcement of a general strike for the following day and a mass meeting at the Straussbergerplatz on the Stalinallee. The Politbüro issued a statement that it had been wrong to want to raise the work quotas by 10 per cent by administrative order. This should only be done 'on the basis of persuasion and voluntary co-operation'. But this still left an area of ambiguity. Was the Politbüro only trying to buy time? Did it still hope to bring in the increase, but by other means? The statement was a disaster. Throughout the night, in the absence of any relevant news on the East German radio, Western stations broadcast accounts of the day's events, and plans for strikes in several large factories the following day.

On June 16 the upheaval had been largely confined to Berlin. The next day there were disturbances in several parts of the country. Eastern and Western sources agree on the extent. Western estimates list 274 towns and 372,000 strikers.[13] Otto Grotewohl said, a month later, that 300,000 strikers had been involved in 272 towns. In either case the figure is around 6 per cent of the total work force. Several aspects of the day were remarkable. The vast majority of strikers and demonstrators were workers. Peasants and farmers were more isolated, and took no part. In the cities the middle class and the intelligentsia were hardly involved. Partly they were demoralised by the experiences of the past few years. And partly they felt unaffected by the strikers' main issue, the demand for a reduction in work norms. Many probably felt too little solidarity with workers on any issue to throw off their inhibitions about joining a workers' demonstration.

In most towns the protests had a broadly similar pattern. Besides Berlin, the main centres were Bittersfeld, Halle, Leipzig, Magdeburg and Merseburg, and to a lesser extent, Brandenburg, Görlitz and Jena. In all these districts the strikes began in large industrial installations. Workers in heavy industry in general took a more active part than those in the state trading concerns or the food, hotel and textile industries. Although they were better paid, workers in heavy industry had been the main target for the Government's propaganda about the need for higher work norms. They were more aware of the contradictions involved in the party's call for socialism to be built on the basis of more work for less pay. As workers in vital industries, they knew their bargaining power was greater than that of other workers. The only big works that did not strike was the new iron foundry being built at Stalinstadt, now Eisenhüttenstadt. Later the authorities made much of its failure to join the strike. The main reason appears to have been that workers at Stalinstadt were new arrivals who had little time to form a cohesive unit. In other towns where there was a long working-class tradition of organisation, strikes took place. The largest were in Halle and Merseburg, where the Communists had been the biggest party before 1933. Leipzig and Magdeburg, the two other main strike centres, had been SPD towns.

Although working-class traditions die hard, it would not be accurate to claim that the work force was the same in 1953 as in 1933. Arnulf Baring, who has undertaken the fullest Western investigation of the June 17 events, points out that few men on the locally elected strike committees were over forty. A surprising proportion, around 10 per cent, were former professional soldiers. Among this group were many who were 'violently opposed to Communism in general, and the SED regime in particular'. They held right-wing political views, for which they had suffered a loss of status, and they resented the official propaganda of anti-militarism. It is also true that many of the most left-wing workers had been promoted into Government and civic jobs. The strikers' four commonest demands were a revocation of the new work norms, an immediate lowering of the cost of living, free and secret elections, and no victimisation for the strikers. The day began with industrial workers marching in orderly fashion to the city centres. In most towns they tore down posters of the party leaders and other official slogans and banners. They occupied the town hall and various public party buildings, and tried to release political prisoners. There was little rioting and looting. Later on the mood and emphasis changed, as other people – especially women and teenagers – joined the protests. In several areas members of the local police (though not the paramilitary units) also took part. The demands became more political. Discipline collapsed, and there was looting and arson. In a number of morning incidents crowds beat up some party and Government officials who had unpopular personal records. Officials thought to be decent were spared. 'In the afternoon,' Baring writes, 'no such distinctions were made, and anyone wearing a party badge on his lapel was immediately seized and beaten up.' Rioters stormed the prisons, and released criminal and political detainees alike.

But – and this is one of the most important aspects of the day's events – Soviet tanks were only brought in after the demonstrations had assumed a direct political character. Although the Soviet military commander declared a state of emergency during the day, he did not send in troops against the demonstrators until very late on. The Red Army was originally confined to holding strategic positions, such as the docks along the Baltic, railway stations and post offices in the larger towns, as well as the border with West Berlin. On June 16 Waldemar Schmidt, the head of the Berlin police, was forbidden by the Russians from using force to disperse the first march.[14] The demonstrators themselves did not direct their anger against the Russians, except in some instances in Berlin. The target was the SED. Events in Berlin were different from those elsewhere in the GDR, mainly because of the open border with West Berlin and the extra tension caused by the risk of an armed East–West clash.

Official Western reaction to the disturbances was generally cautious. The American 'Radio in the American Sector' (RIAS) broadcast regular news items about the events, and this undoubtedly played a large part in helping workers in different cities to co-ordinate their activities. But Western politicians kept to a very restrained line. Jacob Kaiser, the former CDU leader in the GDR and then Federal Minister for all-German Affairs, broadcast an appeal to East Germans on the evening of June 16 not to be persuaded to take rash or dangerous action. During June 17 the Allied Control Commission, as well as West German and West Berlin politicians, tried to avoid any statement that could look like interference in the GDR's internal affairs. All public transport in West Berlin was blocked in the areas near the border, while police and troops were used to prevent crowds gathering there. These measures were only partly successful. Heinz Brandt reported that innumerable West Berliners, mostly young people, joined the strikers and acted as couriers. 'Many hoodlums and political adventurers with shady designs of their own' came over from West Berlin and found a favourable field for activity. Many 'had been hired by obscure agencies in West Berlin to fish in troubled waters.' There is no direct evidence that the United States Central Intelligence Agency was involved, but now that the extent of its 'dirty tricks' has begun to be documented in various parts of the world, it would be surprising if it had not taken some part in Berlin. The West German Intelligence Service, the Bundesnachrichtendienst, run by the former Nazi, General Gehlen, certainly did. The SPD's Eastern bureau, the 'Ostbüro', was also involved. As the centre of Cold War confrontation, Berlin was a hot bed of rival espionage and disinformation agencies. The West German magazine *Der Spiegel* reported later on a typical organisation, the 'Kampfgruppe gegen Unmenschlichkeit' ('Fighting group against inhumanity') which for a time received American funds.[15] Staffed partly by former SS men, it made food unusable, gave out fake ration cards, created food shortages, sabotaged industrial enterprises, tried to destroy bridges and intimidated the families of SED officials.

In spite of this external interference in the June 17 events the current official line in the East is false when it denies that there was a genuine and spontaneous workers' revolt. All the evidence is that the events were an unplanned popular outburst of indignation at the SED's economic policies. On the other hand the Western myth that it was cut down by Russian tanks is also wide of the mark. On the basis of meticulous study Baring concludes that with the exception of Berlin 'the Soviet intervention was not a turning point. It merely served to mark the end of the day's events: the demonstrators had run out of steam. Their rising came to a standstill before it really got off the ground.'[16] This largely accounts for the fact that in the whole country the number of dead was only twenty-one. Contemporary newspaper reports of the events in Berlin generally agree with this interpretation. 'The Red Army troops evidently were given the strictest instructions to behave with restraint. There are few cases reported of their having opened fire on demonstrators even though they were stoned and insulted, and their tanks and armoured cars were physically attacked by the demonstrators', wrote the *Manchester Guardian*.[17] Precisely because of their spontaneity, people just drifted home after the meetings were over in all the larger towns. There were no contingency plans to continue or expand the rising, and no attempt, except in Dresden, to take over any communications centres. Workers had achieved their main demand, the reduction of the work norms, the day before. Eye witnesses recorded that after the meetings people felt 'that nothing else would happen' and that the movement had 'faded away'.[18] The subsequent looting and rioting showed how unplanned the events had been. Robert Havemann wrote later after his expulsion from the SED, 'The uprising lacked political leadership at the decisive moment. It lost sight of its original aim and in effect assumed counter-revolutionary aspects. Thus it was fated to collapse.'[19]

The events had a profound effect within the GDR and particularly within the party. The struggle inside the Politbüro which had been apparent since the beginning of the year had grown since Stalin's death and the introduction of the 'new course', and was now intense. Each side privately blamed the other for what had happened on June 16 and 17 although the immediate result was a public façade of unity and calm. Both wings in the Politbüro were stunned by the events, but wanted to convince the Russians that the SED was in full control. Behind the scenes the in-fighting went on. A temporary compromise was arrived at under which the 'new course' was reaffirmed but all the blame for the upheaval was put on American and West German 'war-mongers'.

At its fourteenth plenum on June 21, the central committee approved a Politbüro declaration calling the events 'a Fascist provocation'. But it also announced that the old work norms would be maintained, pensions would go up, the housing programme would be intensified, and the social services would have more money. Domestic power cuts were to be reduced by cutting the amount of electricity going to heavy industry. The central committee even had the grace to make a remarkable self-criticism. It declared that if the masses no longer understood the party, it was the party's fault and not the masses'. For two weeks party leaders toured the factories, explaining the decision and trying to restore workers' confidence. From the different tone of their speeches, it was clear that the leaders were split. Anton Ackermann, the original spokesman for a German road to socialism back in 1945, and Otto Grotewohl, the Prime Minister and a former Social Democrat, admitted that the Government was responsible for the miserable state of the economy. Neither man mentioned 'Western provocation'.

One issue was whether to punish the strikers or at least their leaders where these could be identified. On June 30 in his interview in *Neues Deutschland*, Max Fechner, the Minister of Justice, and another former Social Democrat, said that the right to strike was written into the Constitution and that no one had been guilty of an offence merely by striking. The events in the GDR also affected the power struggle in Moscow. Ulbricht did his best to play on the fears of the conservatives there by arguing that the 'new course' had been brought in too abruptly and that he had always had doubts about it. The argument carried some weight. The Russians were concerned about the upheaval, but in Moscow too the Politbüro reached a compromise on what to do next. In contrast to their earlier refusal of aid, they now authorised a massive grant of economic help to allow the SED to make concessions to the population, which in effect bought off the working class. They also shelved all plans for revising the status of Germany. It was obvious that any chance that in a unified and neutral Germany the Communists could be a major political force was in present circumstances an illusion. The Soviet Politbüro found a scapegoat in Lavrenti Beria, the notorious Minister of the Interior, whom a majority already wanted to eliminate. On June 26 he was ousted from power under the accusation, among other things, of having wanted to turn the GDR into a bourgeois state.

How serious Beria had ever been in wanting to give up the GDR in return for Germany's neutralisation will probably never be known. At all events, Ulbricht took the cue from Beria's downfall to launch his own purge of the SED. On July 16 Max Fechner was dismissed from his job and arrested. His 'soft' line towards the strikers was presented as an incitement to anarchy. By extension Herrnstadt, the editor of *Neues Deutschland*, was guilty of a serious error in publishing Fechner's interview. The SED central committee was called back into session from July 24 to 26. Ulbricht managed to have Herrnstadt and Wilhelm Zaisser, the Minister for State Security, removed from the Politbüro. They had had good contacts with Beria, and were accused like him of advocating defeatist policies. Later Ulbricht claimed that if their policies had been carried out they would have restored capitalism in the GDR. Hermann Matern argued that they had wanted the SED to become 'a party of the people' which 'would represent the just interests of other classes and groups'.[20]

The exact content of the programme which Herrnstadt and Zaisser proposed remains a mystery. To judge from Herrnstadt's last article in *Neues Deutschland*, it seems he advocated some form of humanistic socialism. 'Isn't it the soulless bureaucratic attitudes behind which we have so often evaded workers' demands that is really reactionary and the worst form of opportunism?', he asked.[21] Herrnstadt had the reputation of being arrogant and ambitious. But as a man who had lost all his family in the Nazi gas-chambers, he opposed Ulbricht's strong-arm methods. Zaisser was an unlikely security chief, a secret policeman with a mild manner who believed in a united and neutral Germany. Besides Zaisser and Herrnstadt, several of their supporters lost their jobs – Anton Ackermann, Elli Schmidt, his former wife who was President of the Democratic Union of Women, and Hans Jendretzky, an old Communist who spent the war years in concentration camps and who for a time headed the trade union organisation before becoming first secretary in Berlin. The secretariat was reduced to six members. Sensing that even he must make some self-criticism, Ulbricht told the central committee: 'I bear the greatest responsibility for the errors that have been committed.' His only penance was that his title was changed from general secretary of the central committee to first secretary.

The central committee's decision had two significant aspects. It endorsed Ulbricht's general line for building socialism and said it was as correct as ever. The 'new course' was implicitly abandoned. More importantly, Ulbricht had defeated his political opponents. He had gambled on 'his' side winning the power struggle in Moscow. Beria's fall helped to save him. But probably the main factor was the upheaval on June 16 and 17 itself. Faced with such instability, and with Franz Dahlem, the only credible alternative to Ulbricht, so recently sent into disgrace, the Russians were unwilling to change helmsmen in the GDR. It might have looked too much like a victory for the strikers. And so, ironically, the workers' demonstrations ended by preserving Ulbricht in power. There is one theory that Ulbricht deliberately provoked the revolt by his original obstinacy over the norms in the hope that this would bring the Russians in on his side — as indeed happened. But the notion is too Machiavellian and not in tune with Ulbricht's usual caution. No one could have foreseen how such a revolt would turn out. Ulbricht survived partly through luck, and partly through his canny strategy of removing Dahlem on the morrow of Stalin's death.

In the immediate aftermath of the revolt Ulbricht was strong, but the GDR had rarely seemed weaker. Yet it soon became apparent that the country had emerged from the unexpected upheaval in a more durable form. Although there was no real prospect of the Western powers' intervening during the crisis — and it would have been madness if they had tried — their restraint had the effect of stabilising the SED's authority in the country. All Mr Dulles's talk of 'rolling back Communism' was seen to be nothing but sabre-rattling. When it came to the crunch, the West accepted that the GDR was a Soviet sphere of influence. The Western commitment to reunification was exposed as mainly rhetorical. Those who suspected that the United States, Britain, and France were not really interested in the revival of a strong Germany, even if it were capitalist and Westward-leaning, felt justified.

East Germans who had looked on the GDR as a temporary phenomenon or a nightmare which one morning would have disappeared realised that they had to face the facts. After June the country gained a new dimension of permanence. In order to discredit Communism in general, the Americans tried to capitalise on the continuing unrest by stepping up the propaganda war. President Eisenhower offered food aid to the GDR and set up distribution stations in West Berlin, where East Germans were invited to come and help themselves. Of course thousands did. But the cynicism of the American move was obvious to all since the elderly and poor of West Berlin were offered nothing. Those with false hopes of more forceful Western intervention in the GDR's crisis now had to live with reality. Indeed after that NATO had a contingency plan based on the assumption that there might be a sustained revolt later on in the GDR and the Federal Republic would not effectively prevent intervention by 'private' West German groups crossing the border to 'help'. This could have led to a full East-West confrontation, which NATO wanted to avoid.

The Soviet leadership showed by its actions that it too accepted the existence of the GDR, and would stand firmly behind it. Over the next few months the Russians repeated their diplomatic approaches to the West for a solution to the German question. For a time there was still enough uncertainty among some SED leaders for the Soviet overtures to cause them panic. In a Note to the Western powers on August 15 1953, the Russians proposed the creation of a provisional all-German Government. According to Heinz Lippmann, who was Erich Honecker's deputy at the head of the FDJ, the proposal 'hit Berlin like a bombshell. The self-confident façade vanished'.[22] People could not imagine why the Russians should make what looked like such a defeatist proposal so soon after June 17. Lippman maintains that an emergency staff within the central committee began work on plans for the SED to go underground in case the West accepted the Soviet proposals. Their fears were unfounded. With their accusations against Beria of wanting to give the GDR up, the Soviet leadership had made it clear that they wanted to keep their own German state. Their proposals to the West had only tactical significance. Unlike Stalin's Note of March 1952 which suggested free elections for an all-German Government, the new Russian note proposed that the Parliaments of the GDR and the FRG form a joint provisional Government. This was a device for achieving some form of Western recognition for the Government of the GDR which would have helped to stabilise the situation there. In the GDR's moment of weakness it was a repetition of the old attempt to appeal to nationalism by showing the Western powers up as the country's real dividers. It was also hoped that the proposal might influence the forthcoming elections in West Germany and prevent the FRG's military integration into the projected European Defence Community.

In the very same month the Russians pledged their support for the GDR by concrete actions. Ulbricht and Grotewohl were invited to Moscow and given the massive economic help which the Russians had denied them only four months earlier. After the workers' revolt the Russians accepted that the GDR could only make economic concessions if it had the funds to pay for them. The Russians renounced all further reparations payments, which amounted to US $2,537 millions. They promised that as from January 1 1954 the last Soviet companies in the country would be turned over to the GDR. They offered extra supplies of consumer goods, coal, cotton, and other materials plus a multi-million dollar line of credit to enable the GDR to buy goods in the West. In March the Soviet Union announced that the GDR had the right to take all its own decisions on foreign policy. In August it declared that the GDR was a fully sovereign state.

Ulbricht felt more secure than he had ever done before. He had survived his most serious leadership crisis, and the GDR was firmly backed by Moscow. By its grudging inactivity in June the West had implicitly given the GDR *de facto* recognition. The division of Germany had been dug a little deeper. Ulbricht was emboldened to start publicly promoting the idea that there were now two German states. Since the war the notion of a single Germany had remained in official SED statements. The GDR's Constitution of 1949 said in Article One that 'Germany is an indivisible democratic republic; its constituent parts are the German states. The Republic decides on all matters essential for the continued existence and development of the German people as a whole.' There was no indication of the geographical area for which the Constitution was valid. It said there was only one German citizenship. In other statements the GDR was said to represent the true national interests of the German people because it alone had overcome the causes and effects of Fascism and was building a new democratic Germany. The Federal

Government in Bonn was regarded as a usurper, a continuation of monopoly capitalist rule in a different guise.

From 1953 onwards Ulbricht developed the more pragmatic concept of two German states. The first mention came in his speech at the sixteenth plenum of the central committee in September 1953. 'In present conditions,' he said, 'where two states in fact exist in Germany, the unity of Germany can only be achieved by negotiations between the two.'[23] Over the next few months the two-state theory was developed more frequently in the party. The first public mention of it in a Government statement came from Grotewohl in a speech to the People's Chamber in November 1954. The West still refused to accept the GDR's existence in any formal or diplomatic sense. It maintained a tight economic boycott and political and diplomatic pressure against the Soviet zone, as it continued to call it. The Western powers, and the West German Chancellor, Konrad Adenauer, in particular, argued that the West must deal with the East from a position of strength. The rhetoric of reunification was kept up although there was little hope of achieving it. The West's main aim was to win the psychological allegiance of the East German population in the global crusade against Communism.

For their part the Russians had also become more pessimistic about the chances of achieving a united and neutralised Germany. The kind of neutral solution which was in the process of being reached for Austria was practical mainly because there was a single Austrian Government which was prepared to agree to it. And Austria's strategic significance was less. Germany was another story. Adenauer had no intention of presiding over a neutral Germany, even if unified. Every time the Russians suggested this, he replied stiffly that a united Germany must be free to choose its own foreign policy. His whole aim was to create an integrated, rearmed, and anti-Communist Western Europe. He even wanted the Allies to concede that the GDR had a 'right' to opt for membership of NATO. The British Government in particular saw this as excessive and unreasonable. They were embarrassed by Adenauer's zeal in promoting German nationalism, and frequent tensions arose between London and Bonn, even though Britain backed the Federal Republic's integration into the Western alliance.

Throughout 1954 and 1955 the process of integration went on. In March 1954 the FRG ratified the European Defence Community treaty. In October it signed a treaty of friendship with the USA, and in February 1955 it joined NATO. On the eve of the Bundestag vote on whether to enter NATO, the Russians made one last effort to dissuade Adenauer. They promised to normalise relations provided the Paris agreements were left in abeyance. The West Germans rejected the proposal and joined NATO. So anxious were the Russians to achieve better relations with Bonn in the vague hope of holding back its rearmament plans that in June they invited Adenauer to visit Moscow. In a surprise move they offered to open diplomatic, trade, and cultural relations with West Germany.

Adenauer and his state secretary, Walter Hallstein, flew to Moscow in September. They returned not only with an agreement to exchange ambassadors but also a Russian promise to release almost 10,000 Germans still held in the Soviet Union since the war — 'war criminals', according to the Russians, 'prisoners of war' according to Bonn. For Adenauer the visit was a triumph. He made no major concessions. Even while in Moscow he argued that the Federal Government spoke for all Germans, and not just the population of the Federal Republic. He explicitly stated that new relations with the USSR did not mean that Bonn was accepting the Oder–Neisse line as Germany's Eastern frontier.

In the GDR Ulbricht and the Stalinists were unhappy with the Russians. They saw the Soviet leadership shake hands with the man they considered Hitler's heir. It must have been a blow to Ulbricht's pride to watch Moscow open diplomatic relations without obtaining any *quid pro quo* for East Germany from the West. The nearest that the Russians came was when Marshal Bulganin said that if Adenauer wanted to talk about the Germans held in Russia, then the GDR should be represented equally in the discussions. By the end of the visit the Russians dropped this point. They agreed to release the Germans unconditionally as a gesture of goodwill. To add insult to injury from the GDR's point of view, three months after the Moscow talks Bonn launched the 'Hallstein doctrine' by which it threatened to cut off relations with any country that recognised East Germany. The doctrine was juridically inconsistent,

since Bonn itself had breached it by opening relations with the
Soviet Union which already recognised the GDR. But it was a
powerful political weapon against weaker nations which wanted
links with the Federal Republic.

In spite of the wound to his ego Ulbricht could welcome the
Adenauer visit to Moscow for one reason. It pushed off any
notion of reunification on more or less Western terms. By opening diplomatic relations with Bonn the Russians were accepting
the *status quo* of a divided Germany and the two-state theory.
As a reward for the GDR immediately after Adenauer had left
Moscow, Ulbricht was invited to lead a large delegation there
to sign a treaty between his country and the Soviet Union.
This gave the GDR full responsibility for military security on
its territory (except for the access routes for Allied troops and
goods between West Germany and West Berlin). The Russians
also decided that the GDR should join the Warsaw Pact, which
had been set up that May. The official history of the GDR
proudly states that the treaty confirmed that 'Germany could
only be reunited through a gradual rapprochement of the two
German states and if the Paris treaties were lifted'.[24] 'All imperialist speculations that the Soviet Union would agree to
negotiate with the Adenauer regime about the dismantling of
the GDR were shown to be groundless,' it went on, adding that
'it was clear that workers' and peasants' power in Germany
could no longer be set aside.'

While the Adenauer visit to Moscow was at first a shock to
the Stalinists,[25] it was welcomed by another group in the SED.
The reform Communists who still looked for a German road to
socialism that might be less dogmatic than Ulbricht's rejoiced
at the news. They interpreted Moscow's invitation as a sign of
a liberalisation of attitudes among the Soviet leadership. The
entire period from June 1953 to 1958 was one in which such
hopes of reform were rife. It was the time of de-Stalinisation par
excellence. If in those years the GDR's existence as a state was
more firmly established than ever before, it was still unclear
what kind of internal regime it was to have. The workers' revolt
had sparked off a widespread move towards de-Stalinisation in
the lower levels of the party, in the trade unions, and among the
intellectuals. In an article in *Neue Deutsche Literatur* immediately
after the June events, Günther Cwojdrak wrote that literature

must be the voice of the people, and that if a writer noticed that the people's and the Government's voices did not agree, he should point it out.[26] The German Academy of Art published a bold statement calling for an end to every form of state intervention in art, drama and publishing.[27] Berthold Brecht criticised the vulgar Marxism of the cultural authorities, and wrote his poem (not published in the GDR) on the June events:

> After the rising of June 17
> The secretary of the Writer's Union
> Had leaflets distributed on the Stalinallee
> In which one read that the people
> Had lost the Government's trust,
> And that it could be restored
> Only by redoubled work.
> Would it not have been simpler
> If the Government had dissolved the people,
> And elected another?[28]

At the top levels of the party among the 'Old Communists' the advocates of a softer and less dogmatic line had lost out at the fifteenth plenum, but hopes were still bright among intellectuals. Most of them were younger people in their thirties who had no experience of the pre-war splits, and were optimistic that the GDR could now open a new chapter. All the compromises, the distortions and the bureaucratic crudities of the Stalinist period could be put aside. For a time the SED tolerated this explosion of critical discussion and even made some concessions. It fostered a relaxation of relations between the church and the state, between the SED and the other parties, and towards the middle class. Ulbricht was preoccupied with bringing the working class and party officials back into line. The fifteenth plenum had called for a purge of the party. In the general climate of the 'new course', and the Soviet Union's economic support for the GDR, recalcitrant individuals were increasingly isolated and punished. An unknown number of strikers and demonstrators, more than 1,300 according to Western records, were sentenced for their roles on June 16 and 17. Six were condemned to death. Others got long prison terms.

Inside the party the purges were wholesale. In most industrial towns the local party secretaries and about half the other officials were replaced. A similar shake-out affected the trade unions. Ulbricht criticised the view that 'the Government is no real workers' and peasants' Government, but is some kind of indefinable Government to which the trade unions stand opposed'.[29] 'Social Democratism' was attacked as the main deviation in the party. It was said to have many forms; the rejection of democratic centralism; the damaging theory of spontaneity; the tendency to look for a 'third way' on the issue of German reunification, typified by the demand for the resignation of particular SED leaders said to be too closely identified with hard-line policies in the past; an artificial confrontation of Lenin with Marx, based on different emphases in their works; and insufficient trust in the Soviet Union.[30]

By the beginning of 1954 Ulbricht was ready to start undermining the 'new course'. Collectivisation of agriculture began again. At the SED's Fourth Congress in early April the leader of the Soviet delegation, Anastas Mikoyan, said it was the party's first duty. The party congress revived the idea of rapid development of heavy industry, and said that it was a mistake to believe that it had been wrong to give it priority in the past. A change in the statutes gave party organisations in industry the right to control management.

In the Soviet Union the 'new course' introduced by Malenkov was also coming under stronger pressure. Part of the leadership argued that the need to keep defence spending on a level with Western rearmament required more emphasis on heavy industry and less on consumer goods. This was also Ulbricht's own argument. He was still more concerned with the GDR's security and the build-up of its military prestige vis-à-vis a rearmed West Germany than with satisfying popular economic demands at home. In February 1955 Ulbricht's hopes were fulfilled. Malenkov was dismissed as Soviet Prime Minister. Four months later Ulbricht buried the 'new course' at the twenty-fourth plenum of the central committee. 'Some of you will wonder why I have not used the phrase "New course",' he told them. 'The New Course has given a lot of people strange ideas – that it is possible to consume more than is produced, that wages can rise faster than productivity, that it is all right to slack on the job. What is remarkable about this course is not that it is new, but that it is wrong. I must warn people with these ideas that we never meant to embark on this kind of mistaken course, and we never shall.' In spite of the clampdown on the 'new course' the ferment among the intellectuals was still unchecked. The removal of Malenkov mainly affected the official line on economic issues. In foreign policy and on ideological matters the Soviet leadership was still acting in a very different way from Stalin.

In the spring of 1955 Khrushchev visited Belgrade and apologised to Tito for Stalin's attacks on him. In September there was the Soviet invitation to Adenauer to visit Moscow. But the worst event for Ulbricht came at the Twentieth Congress of the Soviet party in February 1956. Khrushchev's attack on the dead dictator gave the decisive impetus for reform and liberalisation throughout Eastern Europe. Ulbricht seems to have partly anticipated it. At all events it was shortly before it that he began a cautious and subtle policy of enlisting China on his side in the struggle against de-Stalinisation. In December 1955 he sent a strong Government delegation to Peking, and some months later himself led the SED team to the Chinese party's Eighth Congress. Ulbricht could not oppose de-Stalinisation outright. After Khrushchev's speech Ulbricht expressed a number of severe criticisms of Stalin. At the Berlin delegate conference in March he said that Stalin had made significant errors in agriculture, had not prepared the Soviet Union adequately for Hitler's invasion, and had given way to a personality cult towards the end of his life.

These criticisms apart, Ulbricht's tactics seemed to be to play down the idea that the GDR had any special lessons to learn from what Khrushchev had said. At the SED's third party conference in March Ulbricht concentrated on economic policy and managed to avoid mentioning Stalin's name even once. He turned the thesis of different roads to socialism to his advantage by arguing that Stalin's excesses had not been repeated in the GDR. If Stalinism had never existed in the GDR, there was no need for de-Stalinisation. There was a limited amount of truth in this. The GDR was the only country in Eastern Europe where widespread trials of party officials, let alone executions, had not taken place. The GDR had not forced through a wholesale collectivisation of agriculture. In 1956 the co-operatives still only accounted for 23 per cent of the country's arable land. Nevertheless, Ulbricht's attempt to play down de-Stalinisation provoked wide disagreement within the party. For a time it seemed that he was in a minority in the Politbüro and secretariat. Angry at the distortions of previous years, many of his colleagues wanted to draw out the full consequences of what had gone wrong under Stalinism. They were buoyed along by the workers' strikes in Poznan in nearby Poland in June.

But in Moscow the Poznan events shocked the leadership into instinctive retreat. *Pravda* wrote soon afterwards that Stalin's terror had been basically necessary.[31] In the GDR however the Politbüro met a few days afterwards and produced a resolution that went further in its support of liberalisation than anything since the Politbüro decision on the 'new course' in 1953. It called for self-criticism in the party, exposure of all the party's mistakes and failures, and a search for new solutions. It said that every Communist party was currently re-examining Marxism-Leninism to see how best to adapt it to national conditions, and the SED should do likewise. It called for more open discussions on culture and science. The resolution had the hallmarks of the reformist wing in the Politbüro which probably commanded a majority against Ulbricht. It certainly included Karl Schirdewan, the cadre chief, and Fred Oelssner, a former secretary for propaganda. Otto Grotewohl, the Prime Minister and a former Social Democrat, and possibly Heinrich Rau also seem to have supported the new line while Ulbricht was only left with Hermann Matern and Willi Stoph.[32]

Matern was always one of Ulbricht's closest associates. His career had been remarkably similar. As a young man he broke with the Social Democrats; in the 1920s he was a KPD official in Magdeburg and East Prussia; arrested in 1933, he later escaped to Prague and Paris, and then spent the last four years of the war in Moscow. Stoph was twenty years younger and had a different background. During the pre-war Nazi period he had done underground Communist work, but in the war he served in the Wehrmacht. After 1945 he was in the industrial ministries, and in the 1950s he took charge of the GDR's armaments programme. A competent but rather wooden official, Stoph later became Ulbricht's Prime Minister.

Shortly after the Politbüro meeting the full central committee approved its declaration but added some ambiguities. An appeal was made for 'a bold exchange of opinions'. At the same time the central committee opposed 'the slanders put about by the enemies of peace and socialism'. The party's old propaganda was said to have been crude and exaggerated and to have 'offended Christian workers'. The central committee rehabilitated Dahlem, Ackermann, Jendretzky, Merker and Elli Schmidt, but not Zaisser and Herrnstadt. The resolution clearly reflected the desire for change that was surfacing throughout the party. In general terms the current was described as 'revisionism', but it had several different strands. In the economic field revisionism covered those who wanted to modify the system of central planning and introduce some 'market' elements. Among the philosophers, political scientists, and intellectuals it meant those who were looking for ways of giving a voice to society's different interest groups. They wanted some form of political pluralism within a one-party system and a socialist economy.

The economists had been conducting a muted debate in the theoretical journals for more than a year. Professor Fritz Behrens, supported in part by Oelssner and Selbmann, the Minister for Heavy Industry, wanted to bring in a more flexible price system, a greater role for profitability, and much more use of economic indicators in supervising the plan. They advocated more autonomy for individual enterprises. Oelssner hoped to apply these criteria to agriculture too. Basing himself on the arguments of Professor Kurt Vieweg, a leading agronomist, he criticised what he felt was the excessive pressure for more collectivisation. In one of his essays Behrens wrote:

> The idea that the state can do everything and that every little concern, even the most private one, must be controlled and directed by the state is not socialist, but Prussian. It is 'Junker-monopolistic'. What is socialist, that is Marxist-Leninist, is the idea of the withering away of the state, as socialist relations of production are strengthened and the capitalist threat becomes unreal.[33]

This directly contradicted the Stalinist theory that the class struggle sharpens as socialism develops. One of Behrens's close colleagues, Dr Arne Benary, favoured a form of workers' self-management as in Yugoslavia, whereby workers' wages would depend on a factory's profitability as well as workers' performance. Other 'revisionist' tendencies appeared among historians, like Juergen Kuczynski and Joachim Streisand, and philosophers like Ernst Bloch. Bloch and the great Hungarian revisionist Gyorgy Lukacs, who contributed to several German journals, wanted to replace Stalinism by a 'genuine, humanistic socialism'. The dictatorship of the proletariat could not be reconciled with democracy, freedom or respect for the law. In a series of packed lectures at Leipzig University Bloch argued that Marxism, if correctly understood, was a method of analysis that had to be perpetually renewed. He attacked the dogmatism and petrification of Marxist studies in the GDR.

Among journalists and writers, and particularly the 'Kulturbund' with its 180,000 members, the revisionist wave was also strong. At several universities, among them the Humboldt University in East Berlin, Jena, Halle, Leipzig and Rostock (if one judges by the number of subsequent student arrests), there were lively discussion circles. They were all emboldened by de-Stalinisation in Hungary and by the events of the 'Polish October' when Gomulka returned to power and publicly recognised (in contrast to Ulbricht's reaction in 1953) that the workers' strike in Poznan was not the doing of counter-revolutionaries or hooligans.

The man who played one of the central roles in the revisionist movement in the GDR was Wolfgang Harich, a young philosophy lecturer at the Humboldt University. He had contacts with reform-minded newspaper editors, revisionist academics in the universities, and numerous writers, including Berthold Brecht. He had also made links with dissident intellectuals in the rest of Eastern Europe and with the SPD in West Berlin. The programme of Harich's group, published first in November 1956, pulled together many of the strands of the internal political opposition. It said the opposition wanted to function completely legally, but it would not shrink from factional activity and conspiracy if it were forced to by the Stalinist party apparatus. The opposition would forge close links with the population, criticise the existing leadership, but 'prevent a popular uprising'. Like a number of other party members, Harich believed in a 'third way' between East and West. Only a radically de-Stalinised system could ever have a significant influence on the West.[34] Vice versa, Western concepts of freedom and democracy could influence the East and gradually minimise its totalitarian features. 'After 1945', Harich wrote, 'the USSR played a progressive role vis-à-vis the people's democracies in destroying capitalism and the large landed estates. But the Soviet Union also transferred other political features which had already become obstacles even in the Soviet Union. This was its reactionary role.'

Harich's demands were for the abolition of the bureaucratic apparatus's primacy over the party's rank and file, a purge of the Stalinists, profit-sharing in the factories, raising of the standard of living, an immediate end to forced collectivisation and help for medium and small peasants. The programme called for the disbandment of the security police, a reform of government on the Polish model which would give parliament full sovereignty while keeping the block system of parties with a single list of candidates. On reunification Harich laid down a list of preconditions for the Federal Republic, designed to make a 'capitalist restoration' in the GDR impossible. The SPD would have to come to power, withdraw West Germany from NATO, nationalise the main industries, remove all former Nazis from jobs in the administration, and carry out a land reform.

Harich's ideas were probably already too late. In West Germany the SPD had moved a substantial distance to the right and towards NATO. Adenauer had that summer introduced conscription and banned the Communist party. In the East the carpet was pulled out from under the party opposition with the uprising in Hungary. The Soviet Politbüro decided on a massive use of troops and tanks against what they claimed was 'counter-revolution'. All over the Eastern world from Albania to China, from Czechoslovakia to the GDR, the Stalinists were heartened by the Soviet show of force. Ulbricht told the People's Chamber in November: 'History teaches that whoever gives even his little finger to reaction will end by losing his life.' He took the chance to blow up the issue of Harich's ideas as a warning to his political opponents. Most of Harich's activity could hardly be described as conspiratorial. He and his friends used to meet regularly every Thursday in the Kulturbund to discuss their programme. Harich had a reputation as a voluble and naive talker and on November 7 was even invited in to see Ulbricht. At a long meeting Harich argued for greater debate within the party.

But Harich had extensive contacts in West Germany and in West Berlin with the SPD. This was enough for Ulbricht to claim – and even some of Harich's colleagues later believed the allegations – that he had been in touch with intelligence agencies. On his return from a visit to Hamburg at the end of November Harich was arrested. In March 1957 he was tried and sentenced to ten years' imprisonment. Two colleagues got four years and two years respectively. The trial marked the symbolic end of de-Stalinisation in the GDR, at least in its most dramatic form.

It took Ulbricht several more months to gain the upper hand over his opponents in the central committee and the Politbüro itself. At the thirtieth plenum at the beginning of 1957 Ulbricht had the thesis adopted that the Federal Republic was the SED's main danger. This effectively crushed the hopes of those who wanted a reconciliation with West Germany. But it was not until the October plenum that Ulbricht engineered attacks on Kurt Hager, the secretary in charge of science and higher education, and Paul Wandel, the secretary for culture. Hager was accused of being too soft on Ernst Bloch. He made a grovelling self-criticism, apologising among other things for having supported 'the openness with which the party in Poland had talked about its economic difficulties'.[35] Wandel's apology was apparently insufficient. He lost his job in the secretariat.

In his speech at the plenum Ulbricht made it clear once again that the physical security of the GDR remained his first priority. 'Some people saw things one-sidedly,' he said. 'They only looked at the development of democracy in our system of people's democracies. They did not see that a class struggle exists, and that the fight to safeguard workers' and peasants' power can not only be waged by means of persuasion but also needs the state to show its power ... '[36] Shortly afterwards at the Moscow conference of world Communist parties Ulbricht and Mao set the tone with a call for a sharpening of policy against the West, and a radical confrontation with all tendencies towards revisionism and national Communism. On his return Ulbricht sacked Ernst Wollweber, the security chief.

Gerhart Ziller, another central committee secretary, committed suicide. The way was now open to remove his most senior opponents, Karl Schirdewan and Fred Oelssner, from the Politbüro in February 1958. Finally, in July 1958 at the fifth congress of the SED, Selbmann and 20 of the remaining 89 central committee members were not re-elected.

It was a quiet and delayed end to an upsurge of revisionism which was matched in no other country except Poland. The debate and dissension were more varied and deeply rooted than in Hungary. And yet the repercussions were less than in either Poland or Hungary. The main reason was that in the GDR the crisis over reform was confined to the intellectuals in 1956. Whereas in Poland and Hungary massive industrial unrest coincided with, and helped to accelerate, the intellectuals' revolt, the GDR was spared this explosive mixture. Workers had had their say in 1953. Three years later they kept quiet. A combination of repression against the ringleaders and some economic concessions for the rest was enough to silence people. Others, possibly including many of the most militant workers, left the GDR for the West. In each of the years 1955 and 1956 the number of emigrants exceeded a quarter of a million. Many of them seem to have shared the aims of the intellectual reformers. In 1956 the Munich-based Infratest Institute studied the attitudes of workers who had recently left the GDR. It found that 35 per cent had 'completely or predominantly Marxist-Leninist views'. Another 26 per cent had 'partly, though not predominantly, Marxist views'.[37]

The open border to the West also explains why revisionism in the GDR in 1956 was less nationalistic than its counterparts in Poland and Hungary. The vociferous anti-Russian sentiments that surfaced in those two countries were conspicuous by their absence in East Germany. Most of those who objected most strongly to tight Russian control had already voted with their feet and left. Ulbricht's point that the excesses of Soviet-imposed Stalinism had been avoided in the GDR also played a role. Perhaps the very existence of two German states helped to dampen nationalism down. Polish or Hungarian nationalists who tried to combat Russia's power may have had an idealised and over-romantic notion of national independence. East Germans could see the reality of the alternative state in West

Germany and had to face the sober and practical question of what reunification would mean.

The GDR's revisionists were in the main socialists. They were interested in a fundamental reform of the system – along socialist lines. Nationalism was not a dominant feeling for them. Some of them had come to East Germany from the West because they saw in the GDR the only chance for a socialist Germany. Ernst Bloch spent the war in the United States and moved demonstratively to the GDR in 1949. Stefan Heym, the writer, left the United States during the McCarthy era to settle in the GDR. Others, like Selbmann, Schirdewan, and Ziller, had been in Nazi concentration camps. This separated them from Ulbricht and the Moscow *émigrés*, but left them equally suspicious of German nationalism.

Above all, the East German revisionists were a loyal opposition. Their defeat in the period from 1956 to 1958 ended the last attempt in the GDR's history to change the country's course decisively at a stroke. From then on no faction was able to organise widespread support for a sustained critique of the system. The West's indifference in 1953 and during the Hungarian uprising showed the population that it had nothing to hope for from that quarter. People concentrated on their private lives and on improving their economic positions. The Federal Republic's increasing integration into the Western political and military system disappointed German socialists' hopes for early reunification. The meagre extent of actual de-Stalinisation in Russia and elsewhere disillusioned the revisionists. There was to be no new chance for reforming the system until the Prague spring in 1968, and that, too, ended in disappointment and despair. After 1958 differences within the SED were confined to smaller groups and narrow issues – economic reform, how to improve industrial democracy, changes in the school system, decentralisation of the economic ministries, professional training for factory managers and so on. What form of socialism the GDR should have was no longer an open issue within the party. The philosophers had failed to change the world. It was now up to the technocrats.

6

Shaping an Economic Miracle

After 1958 the German Democratic Republic entered a new stage in its development. The internal party opposition to Ulbricht was defeated. The SED's control over society had been stabilised. Five more years of consolidation were spent reinforcing the party's authority, until in 1963 the Sixth party congress launched a period of controlled experimentation. The party itself was changing. An elite of younger, better-trained professionals was moving into senior positions. Performance ('Leistung') became as important a principle in judging cadres as their loyalty to Marxism-Leninism. The emphasis on party traditions and the pre-war clashes with the Social Democrats receded into the background. Symbolically, the references to Karl Liebknecht, Rosa Luxemburg, Ernst Thälmann and the Spartakusbund were dropped from the party statutes in 1963.

It is appropriate then that the focus of this study should shift gradually from the GDR's birth and growth to an analysis of the kind of society it has now become. But first the final outcome of the Ulbricht years has to be told. Even with the defeat of his last major opponents in 1958, Ulbricht's problems were by no means over. In July of that year the Fifth Congress ordered the final collectivisation of agriculture and a sharp rise in industrial output as part of a seven-year economic plan to bring *per capita* consumption in the GDR up to the level of West Germany. One major loophole in Ulbricht's scheme of things remained – the open border to West Berlin through which hundreds of East Germans daily left the country. Nearly all of them went by underground or S-Bahn, undetected among the thousands of commuters who worked or shopped in the West. Regular spot-checks by the police on anyone carrying a suitcase had little impact. Most people easily evaded them by making repeated journeys with a few belongings at a time.

For years Ulbricht had hoped to end the exodus. His first preference was to convince the Russians to take over West Berlin once and for all by repudiating its Four-Power status and proclaiming it part of the GDR. But until 1958 Khrushchev wanted peaceful co-existence with the West above all else. Ulbricht's pleas went unheeded. Then in November 1958 Khrushchev for the first time publicly endorsed Ulbricht's line that 'all of Berlin lies in the territory of the GDR. The Western powers no longer have any legal, moral, or political basis for their continued occupation of West Berlin.' The Soviet leader demanded that West Berlin be turned into a demilitar-ised 'free city' within six months. The Western powers ignored the ultimatum. Khrushchev's bluff was called. When the six months were up, he did nothing.

For Ulbricht it was a fiasco, and the situation was worse even than before. The continued tension during the six-month period had only increased the flow of refugees who feared that time was running short. When the ultimatum ran out there was a brief respite but as the effects of the seven-year plan began to be felt the flow of refugees rose again. Forced collectivisation raised the amount of land in co-operative hands from 45 per cent to 85 per cent in the first five months of 1960. It also led to a new exodus of disgruntled farmers to the West. At the same time the pressure for increased industrial output was alienating factory workers. From a total of 144,000 in 1959, its lowest annual figure since the GDR's foundation the number of refugees rose to 199,000 in 1960. In the first seven months of 1961 the flow almost doubled to 207,000. The exodus included hundreds of professional people, a brain drain which few countries could have afforded. In 1960 688 doctors, 296 dentists and 2,648 engineers went West. The only comparable phenomenon in recent times has been the departure of panic-stricken settlers on the eve of independence in Algeria, Kenya and Angola.

In the summer of 1961 Ulbricht persuaded the Russians that force was the only way to stop it. On August 13 1961 the Berlin Wall went up. It was a humiliating admission of failure which to this day remains one of the ugliest sights in Europe. Ulbricht later admitted to visitors that it was his greatest propaganda defeat and that every bullet which the GDR fired at an escaper was a self-inflicted wound. But he claimed he had no alternative. Certainly the official GDR line that the Wall is a 'frontier of peace' is half-true in the sense that the Wall is no different from any other part of the heavily guarded frontier between Eastern Europe and the West which runs all along the GDR, Czechoslovakia, and Hungary. It seems worse because it is so visible, and bisects a city with all the obscenity of division which that entails.

After the initial shock most people adjusted to the fact of the Wall. If 1958 had shown the party opposition that it had no chance of changing the situation, the Wall did the same for the population at large. People now knew that no one could easily opt out. Gradually there developed a new 'shared consciousness' in the GDR which laid the basis for the reforms of subsequent years. Although the Wall was a propaganda defeat for Ulbricht vis-à-vis the West, it was a victory vis-à-vis the Russians. It was the culmination of more than five years' pressure by Ulbricht for some action on West Berlin. Originally he had proposed two options: either a separate peace treaty between the Soviet Union and the GDR and the recognition of GDR sovereignty over the access routes to West Berlin, if not over the city itself, or else a Wall. Khrushchev's decision to build the Wall was meant to end Ulbricht's demands. But even after the Wall was built Ulbricht continued the pressure in public declarations for a peace treaty as well. This was too much for Khrushchev. He was unwilling to give the GDR sovereignty over West Berlin's access routes and thereby the power to provoke war with the West. The GDR already had *de facto* control over the autobahns and was able to manipulate tension by impeding traffic. Instead of a peace treaty Khrushchev signed a twenty-year friendship treaty with the GDR in 1964, which went less far than Ulbricht liked. Although qualified, it was a triumph since it set the seal formally on the guarantees which the Soviet Union had given Ulbricht in 1961 when it authorised the building of the Berlin Wall.

Ulbricht had achieved what even his enemies fifteen years earlier had hardly thought possible. A man without personal charm, admired and trusted by few, he had created a state out of a rump territory, a quarter the size of pre-war Germany. He had ensured its continuity. He had pushed aside all domestic opposition. He had endowed the country with a sense of permanence which its people could feel themselves. And he had given it an industrial potential which its allies envied. Nikolai Fadeyev, the secretary-general of Comecon, the Council for Mutual Economic Assistance, put it like this in 1964: 'At present the GDR is one of the strongest industrial states in Europe and the world. It has a highly developed modern industry, particularly in machine building, chemicals and energy. With its industrial production the GDR occupies fifth place in Europe and eighth in the world. With its *per capita* production of electricity it is third in Europe, and of chemical products second in the world (after the United States)'.[1] Any suggestion that the Russians would be willing to give up an economic powerhouse of this kind must have been finally laid to rest by those comments.

Of course the GDR of the early 1960s was worlds away from the dreams and illusions of German Communists in the early 1920s. No one could claim that the GDR had a highly politicised working class. Or that it had married the traditions of bourgeois civil liberties to the advantages of a socialist economy. Or indeed, as the early proletarian Marxists in a combination of puritanism and Utopia had hoped, that physical labour would give way to the creative enjoyment of education, culture, and new spiritual values – in other words that people would be free to become consumers not only of goods but of leisure, learning and the higher things of life. That was not to be. The GDR's identity was already conditioned by the constant sense of competition with the West. Economic results and 'consumer' values were seen as the criterion for judging the society's success or failure. From 1963 onwards 'management' concepts began to be introduced increasingly in the running of the economy through the principles of cost accountability, the use of new technologies, and more rational investment procedures. In an obvious attempt to overcome the attractions of the West by imitating them, the GDR became a career-oriented society. At a youth rally in 1963 Ulbricht called for clear performance criteria to be set up in industry so that young graduates would know for sure what they would be doing and earning.

The new central committee elected in 1963 showed several changes. It was larger – with 121 members and 60 candidate members compared with 111 members and 44 candidates in 1958 and only 51 and 30 respectively in 1950, even though the country's population had declined. More importantly, the 1963 central committee was younger. The average age was 46, unusually low by comparison with the political leadership of other countries, including West Germany. (Wolfgang Zapf has calculated that the average age of political leaders in the Weimar Republic in 1925 was 53·9; in 1940 under Hitler it was 50·3 and in West Germany in 1955 it was 56·2.)[2] The central committee was also more professional, and had more graduates of universities and technical colleges and a larger number of people normally engaged in economic, technical and administrative positions.

For the first time the central committee reflected the style that has since become the norm. The Old Communists still had a monopoly of power in the Politbüro. Of the 14 members elected in 1963 11 were pre-1933 members of the KPD and the rest were former Social Democrats. But in the central party body their numbers were receding. The central committee had increasing influence. It was less a rubberstamp for decisions taken at the top by the Politbüro and more of a consultative co-ordinating body. From 1960 onwards its competence had begun to expand to cover a wide range of technical issues. It organised conferences addressed by scientists, technical experts and factory managers, and heard from its own professionally qualified members at plenary sessions. Ideological issues were increasingly balanced by concrete assessments of how to solve complex economic and social problems. The key decision which reflected all the other 'modernising' changes was taken at the party congress in 1963. Ulbricht launched the 'New Economic System of Planning and Directing the National Economy'. In spite of his earlier criticisms of the revisionist economists, Oelssner, Selbmann and Behrens, Ulbricht took over some of their ideas. His seven-year plan had failed. Ulbricht and his colleagues accepted that there were weaknesses in the planning system. Quantitative output targets were no longer appropriate for a sophisticated industrial economy and led to misplaced investments. Excessive subsidies on prices encouraged wasting of raw materials. The over-centralisation of decision-making stifled initiative and a sense of responsibility among workers and factory-managers. Modelling himself on the revisionists and on the reforms already proposed for the Soviet Union by the Russian economist, Yevsei Liberman, Ulbricht decided to apply a series of economic rather than administrative levers to the plan. Enterprise managers and workers were to get financial incentives to look for higher productivity. Indirect taxes and monetary incentives would supplement the long-term goals of the plan. Industrial prices would be gradually changed so that they could better reflect the scarcity value of the raw materials used. A new system of enterprise funds, based on a firm's profits, would be the source for workers' bonuses and social spending for crèches, holiday homes, and outings to the theatre or tourist spots.

These features were common to the reforms introduced in the Soviet Union and several other East European countries at about the same time. The GDR's changes had one major difference. This was the role of the so-called VVBs (Verein-igungen Volkseigener Betriebe) or 'associations of nationalised enterprises'. These had been formed in 1958 as groupings of enterprises making similar products, a kind of cartel. Originally they were simply links in the chain of command from the Council of Ministers to the enterprise, and were financed by the state. Under the new economic system they became semi-independent decision-making units. They guide the investment programme of their entire industry and of each participating enterprise. They realise their own profits, out of which further investment and wages are partially financed. They also have to organise marketing and consumer research, and maintain close links between industrial research institutes and all branches of scientific research. They themselves select and negotiate with their suppliers of raw materials, and semi-finished products.

In effect the VVBs function as large near-monopoly trusts. Although some other East European economies, particularly in Poland, Romania, and Bulgaria as well as the Soviet Union, have started to form similar combines in parts of industry, the GDR is the only country which has set them up throughout the economy. The history of economic reform in Eastern Europe has generally been one of alternate moves away from central planning towards more autonomy for the enterprises and then back to recentralisation a few years later. The GDR was able to find a more stable balance from the start by combining enterprises into VVBs and giving them autonomy.

This partly explains the GDR's recent economic success. The country has also made a virtue out of necessity in dealing with the chronic labour shortage, caused partly by the flight of people to the West and the loss of manpower in the war. For the drive to establish and expand new industries the country had few reserves to call on. In 1960 only 61 per cent of the population was of working age (compared with 70·5 per cent in 1939). Higher productivity had to be achieved by more investment, more efficient methods of organisation and better use of technology. Although the Eastern part of Germany was never as industrialised as the Ruhr, it had a longer industrial tradition than its Eastern neighbours. This too helped it to outgrow them. In the decade since the NES began, the GDR's overall growth rate averaged 5 per cent a year. The industrial growth rate averaged an annual 6·4 per cent. Taking 1960 as the base year (= 100), metallurgy and electronics had raised their output to 260 by 1973; the chemical industry was up to 265, light industry and textiles were up to 180, and food industries up to 175. These results were all the more remarkable because they occurred in a period when the GDR brought in a five-day working week (ahead of most of the rest of Comecon), extended the minimum holiday leave by three days and allowed more part-time working.

Before the war the area of the GDR had produced little iron and steel. Massive investments during the 1950s laid the groundwork for the expansion of the 1960s. Using its one indigenous source of energy, brown coal, the GDR built up a steel foundry in the early 1950s at Calbe. Some twenty miles south of Frankfurt on the Oder, on a green-field site near the Polish frontier, a new iron foundry was created at Stalinstadt, later renamed Eisenhüttenstadt. It used imported Polish coke and Soviet iron ore. At Merseburg near Halle the pre-war Leuna works which produced oil from coal and lignite was greatly expanded. Nearby, a new plant known as Leuna II became the basis for the GDR's chemical industry, which by the mid-1960s was the country's biggest single industry. At the Schwarze Pumpe complex near Cottbus the GDR has the world's largest lignite-processing plant, which feeds three power stations. The remarks made by Nikolai Fadeyev about the GDR's potential in 1964 have been amply reinforced since then. It has become the Soviet Union's biggest trading partner, accounting for 16 per cent of its total trade in 1973. It was the biggest source of capital goods for the Soviet Union in 1973, on the eve of the major Soviet decision to look for industrial co-operation with the West. A quarter of all the Soviet Union's imports of machinery and equipment came from the GDR. The proportions are higher still for individual items – 40 per cent of Soviet imports of ships and marine equipment and of agricultural machinery were East German. In return the GDR was intimately linked to the USSR through its imports; more than 50 per cent of its hard coal, between 35 and 50 per cent of its coke, between 60 and 95 per cent of its wheat, 75 per cent of its oil, and almost all its natural gas.

For ordinary workers and other citizens in the GDR the NES has produced impressive results (which are discussed more fully in Ch. 9). Here it is enough to say that average wages in the GDR have outstripped the rest of Comecon. According to Comecon's Statistical Yearbook, the average GDR citizen in 1972 earned 815 Marks a month compared with 693 in Czechoslovakia, 578 in Poland and Romania, 568 in Hungary, 537 in Bulgaria, and only 415 in the Soviet Union. East Germans ate more meat than any other people except the Czechs, more butter and margarine than all the others.

The NES's greater realism and rationality did not eliminate all the mistakes of earlier years. In 1968 the leadership laid down a new set of economic tasks under which leading sectors of industry were to be specially boosted. These key 'structure-determining' branches included chemicals, machine- and vehicle-building, electronics and electricity. They received special investments. But after two years it became apparent that this deliberate forcing of certain branches was producing a general imbalance in the economy. The building industry, in particular, could not meet the demands made on it. The capacity of the transport system and the country's energy supply were insufficient. At a central committee plenum in December 1970 the party restored some of the central control which the economic planners had given up in 1963. The amount of net profit which enterprises could retain was henceforth written into the firm's annual plan as a target. The way this profit was divided was also regulated in the plan. The central planners laid down new investment targets in order to even out the disproportions that had arisen in the previous six years. Recentralisation may also have been a partial political reaction to the 1968 events in Czechoslovakia. The Politbüro feared that excessive economic decentralisation could lead to pressures for something similar on the political front.

Later on in 1975, as a result of the effect of inflation imported from the Western world and the increase in the price of Soviet oil, the leadership launched a scheme to change industrial prices. Both sets of charges reversed some aspects of the NES. The blame for inflation was not of the GDR's own making. But Ulbricht was made the scapegoat for the problems facing the country. In the early 1970s visitors to the GDR were told that his well-known penchant for grandiose solutions, his impatience, and his tendency to demand results without knowing enough about the consequences were the reason for the faulty targets of the 1960s. Ulbricht by then was in the closing years of his rule. Like other elderly leaders he was unwilling to retire. His younger colleagues found more and more issues with which to charge him. But it would not be fair to blame Ulbricht alone for the economic mistakes which led to the disproportionate results of the late 1960s. They were the responsibility of the entire political leadership.

Since 1963 a complex relationship had grown up between the economic managers and the party bureaucracy. The party retained its political primacy but gradually extended the role of economic experts. In 1963 for the first time three young economists became candidate members of the Politbüro. The most outstanding representative of the new breed was Günther Mittag. Born in 1926 to a worker's family he joined the party in 1945 and worked himself up through the apparatus until he got a job in the central committee secretariat in 1951. He studied economics by correspondence and won his doctorate in 1958, the year he became secretary of the Politbüro's economic commission. Mittag was a combination of party loyalist and trained economist. His boss at the commission, Erich Apel, was never even a member of the party. He was a mathematician who rarely used ideological slogans. The third new candidate member of the Politbüro was Werner Jarowinsky. The same age as Mittag, he too was a worker's son and another brilliant student. In 1956 he won his doctorate from the Humboldt University in Berlin and then joined the party apparatus where he soon became state secretary for trade and consumer supply. There he distinguished himself for the unselfconscious way in which he advocated decisions, and for the precision of his economic speeches. He was the first expert to have the authority and self-confidence to use the first person pronoun in giving his views in a complex article in the main party paper, *Neues Deutschland*.[3]

The party's increasing use of men like Mittag, Apel, and Jarowinsky helped to win it extra legitimacy. In the early post-war days the SED had relied for moral authority on its claim to be heir to German revolutionary traditions and on its sacrifices under Hitler. But for large sections of the population, who were still infected with nationalism, the SED's attempts at self-legitimation were irrelevant or even counter-productive. In a mild way the SED had tried to appeal to nationalism with its argument that the West was responsible for splitting Germany. This did not convince many people. With the NES and the appointment of economic experts the SED could claim the legitimacy which comes from successful government performance especially in the economy. The use of experts symbolised the shift in the SED's ideology and propaganda towards modernisation and rationalisation. It was also a way of integrating the new professional elites into government. It has been said that the SED has had 'to address its legitimacy appeals to at least four often incompatible audiences: the Soviet Union, the party itself, the GDR's new professional elites, and the public. In the first ten years of Communist rule in East Germany only the first two audiences were successfully addressed, and then only intermittently.'[4]

Some analysts of the GDR and Eastern Europe have argued that there is an inherent conflict between the technical experts and party politicians. All depends on the word 'conflict'. It is one thing to identify different groups in the GDR's ruling stratum. It does not follow that changes in emphasis or approach constitute a situation of potential, let alone actual, conflict. Professor Peter Ludz, one of West Germany's leading students of the GDR, identifies a 'strategic clique' consisting of the political decision-makers, and a 'counter-elite' comprising the younger experts and revisionist party theoreticians, and including scientists, academics, and functionaries in culture, the economy, and agriculture. They execute but do not determine policy. He is careful to call them 'an institutionalised counter-elite'. By this he means that they too are part of the GDR's social elite and have a powerful vested interest in its values and stability. Even this distinction between an institutionalised counter-elite and a strategic clique may be less valid than when it was first pronounced in the late 1960s.[5] The interchangeability of party and state functions has increased, and the entire party leadership is becoming better educated. In the mid-1970s almost a fifth of the party's members and candidate members were university graduates. At the Eighth party congress in 1971 the central committee reported that 95·3 per cent of the members of the secretariat had a university degree or other vocational qualification.[6] Alongside the new technical intelligentsia another group has been identified – the so-called representatives of the 'new morality'. These are intellectuals such as the writers Christa Wolf or Stefan Heym, who accept the prevailing system and do not challenge its basic principles, but frequently take a critical stance vis-à-vis the party, particularly on the felt need for a wider public debate on the GDR's goals and performance. This group consists of writers, film directors, some of the staff of cabarets like 'Die Distel', and numerous journalists. Though many of them were active in the upsurge of revisionism and reform in 1956, they later took a generally friendlier and more optimistic view of the system's potential for change, at least until the sudden rift with the regime at the end of 1976.

Ludz calls the system which has developed since 1963 'consultative authoritarianism'. He identifies an earlier phase of totalitarian rule, which had been superseded by the early 1960s. Under 'consultative authoritarianism' the party remains determined to maintain political primacy but also shows 'openness towards new experience and the beginnings of non-coercive methods of co-operation and co-ordination and a willingness to consult technical experts'.[7] Interestingly, this concept is not totally different from that of some of the GDR's own social theorists. Professor Georg Klaus, a leading exponent of cybernetics at the Humboldt University and a veteran of Dachau concentration camp, sees the party's aim as 'finding a synthesis of a socialist consciousness and a socialist order with modern techniques and organisation'.[8] A system has to be created in which accurate information can flow from controller to controlled and back again so that ultimately society becomes dynamic and self-regulating. In the end 'the controlled' will be entirely machines and man will be released from the direct work process. Although this is a long-term Utopian vision, its immediate importance is that Klaus recognised that the Marxist concept of alienation can and does exist in socialist societies. He differentiates between a 'technical alienation' which exists under socialism and a social alienation which exists alongside it only under capitalism. 'The social alienation of man and his work is caused by the need for man to sell his labour and abandon its products to whoever may buy it. Without being identical technical alienation is closely connected to social alienation. Man's technical alienation is the need, inherent at a specific stage in the development of the forces of production, to perform monotonous physical or manual labour and subject himself to the pace of the assembly line.' Under conditions of technical progress, Klaus argues, this technical alienation can be abolished. Gradually only two types of labour will remain: work in an automated plant with its control personnel and maintenance brigades, and the creative labour performed by the designers of this machine environment and those who guide and direct the system, the planners. The importance of these theories is that they marry the philosophy of the 'scientific and technical revolution' to the traditional forms of SED ideology, the dictatorship of the proletariat, and the leading role of the party. They provide a dynamic philosophy of a society reacting to technical progress. And to go back to Professor Ludz's terminology, they assume a society in which the consultative mechanisms develop to the point where authoritarianism can fall away in favour of a self-regulating process. Other theorists see the problem in a similar light but focus more on the issue of linking group and individual interests during the development of socialism. Günther Mittag proposed the formula that the central authorities should formulate the general social interest while taking account of the legitimate separate interests of factories, local communities, social groups and individuals. There has to be some body always open to correction and improvement but which can formulate the common good in a modern efficient way. At the same time it must integrate and co-ordinate all legitimate interests.[9]

These theories are at least more up to date than those which were common at the top levels of the party in the 1940s. They are much discussed in the party as people look for the best kinds of organisation in practice. Sceptics may say that during the 1968 crisis in Czechoslovakia when Czech Communists were trying to find them the GDR took an extremely unsympathetic view. In part that was a throwback to the GDR leadership's old ideological caution at times of crisis. The veneer of modernity falls away. In part it was also a highly personal reaction by Ulbricht who always worried most about security-related issues. In 1968 the GDR was still unrecognised in the West. Willy Brandt's Ostpolitik had not yet begun. Ulbricht reacted to the Czech events in traditional Cold War style. Partly perhaps too, the GDR's ideologists and the 'institutionalised counter-elite' felt that in Czechoslovakia things were going too far too fast, and that the party was losing control. East German theorists, the new as well as the old, have always emphasised the element of control rather than participation in their social models. In recent years, particularly since Erich Honecker took over from Ulbricht as first secretary of the party in 1971, the accent has shifted somewhat towards ways of increasing citizens' participation. The aim is to integrate people into the system of social control by increasing their feeling of participating in it. Officials are being told to deal with complaints more rapidly and openly. The press is carrying more critical articles on mismanagement and bureaucratic red tape. Government ministries must take more account of elected representatives. Factory managers must give workers more information.[10] The question to which one must now turn is this: How much participation already exists?

How much 'People's Democracy'?

Not long ago the GDR's trade union newspaper *Die Tribüne* carried a revealing letter from a reader.[1] 'At many of the meetings in our factory,' wrote Kurt Löser from the town of Rothenkirchen, 'when it comes to discussions people say little or nothing. Many of them are shy or afraid to speak up for fear of saying the wrong thing. Others keep quiet, or stop speaking because their criticisms are played down or ignored and they just feel it's pointless saying anything since nothing is going to be improved anyway.' The letter was not an isolated complaint. It appeared beside other readers' letters under the headline 'Silence has many reasons'. Ingeborg Pest, an engineer from Dessau, said she thought the main reason for wasted meetings was that the main speaker dealt with pure theory and failed to relate issues to people's daily work experience. Rolf Witzig from Pretzsch said it was a mistake to have meetings after working hours when people just wanted to go home.

The letters appeared in the two-page pull-out supplement called 'The Shop-steward' which *Die Tribüne* prints roughly every fortnight. They were part of a small campaign running through several issues of the paper in which readers were asked to give their opinions on the way things worked in their factories. In another campaign *Die Tribüne* took up the question of factory discussions on the annual plan. The problem was obvious from a cartoon of a plan discussion going on. Behind a closed door three people, all in suits, were having a confidential meeting.

Clearly things were some way off the proud ideal which

Erich Honecker trumpeted in an article in the *World Marxist Review* in December 1971:

> In elaborating a scientifically grounded policy we never lose sight of the determinative fact that socialism rests on the conscious and planned activity of people, that it arises and develops out of the creative activity of millions of people in which the working class and all working people learn to run their state ... Of cardinal importance for an effective policy is the party's profound confidence in working people, its regular practice of taking counsel with them, of listening to their opinions, criticisms, and suggestions ...

Even without *Die Tribüne*'s letters that statement would deserve to be treated with scepticism. The history of the GDR in the first decade and a half since the war provides plentiful material for doubt. The upheaval of 1953 and the building of the Wall in August 1961 are only the two most dramatic incidents which show that 'the party's profound confidence in working people' was not always as apparent as Erich Honecker suggests.

To be fair his style is not always as inflated as in that theoretical article. At the end of the previous chapter it was pointed out that the SED admits that improvements are necessary. Is it right to conclude from that and from letters like those in *Die Tribüne* that the system needs more than just a few 'improvements'? Should one conclude that the claims for democracy in the GDR's factories and in its society at large are all bogus, and that the system is irredeemably undemocratic? Are Western critics right who claim that a 'new class' has taken power in the GDR and that workers there are no more masters of their own destiny than anywhere in the West? Does the Maoist case that the bourgeoisie has been restored to power hold water, or the neo-Trotskyist view that GDR workers live in a system of state capitalism where the dominant force is the drive for competitive accumulation and where planners expropriate the surplus value from workers' labour without any consultation?

These theories are held tenaciously, partly because statistics are hard to come by which could prove or disprove them. Empirical evidence on industrial democracy is rarely published in the GDR. For many years the party did not seek it. Nowadays the Central Committee Institute for Social Studies and other academic bodies conduct surveys, but their results are normally kept within the party. Outsiders have to make do with piecemeal items. Letters like those in *Die Tribüne* emerge from time to time. The professional journals give occasional glimpses and produce a statistic now and then. And there is the direct evidence which any visitor to the country can pick up in talks with East Germans.

The claim to have instituted a new model of industrial democracy lies at the heart of the GDR's ideological raison d'être. The two key concepts are those of planning and participation. Through planning, the party claims to have replaced the anarchy and spontaneity of the capitalist market with the rationality, security and predictability of scientific decision-making. Planning is described as the most effective mechanism for solving the problems of allocating resources, dividing incomes, and ascertaining the system's potential for extra production. But in order for planning to be efficient and soundly based, the theory continues, people throughout the society must share in it. They must plan, work, and govern together ('mit-planen, mitarbeiten, mitregieren' as the slogan has it).

In East German factories there is a range of some half a dozen institutions whose job is to co-ordinate planning and participation. In charge of the whole enterprise is a single director. The principle of one-man management is paramount, and the director is appointed by the state and is answerable to it. (In most cases he is an employee of the VVB to which the enterprise belongs. In a few cases it is the industrial ministry which makes the appointment.) His authority comes from above. He can only be removed by the state. The director's freedom of manoeuvre is limited by a number of outside controls, including the banks which lend him funds and the various statutory obligations imposed by law. Besides these, the director is bound to take account of several organisations which function in the factory and provide him with information. A factory in the GDR is not only an economic unit. It is also a major element in the country's political and social structure. The main mass organisations which function in society as a whole operate in the country's factories. These groups – the SED, the production committees, the trade unions, and the social organisations for young people and women – do not exist in order to balance out conflicts of interest. The stated assumption is that there is a complete identity of interest between individuals and the whole society. The factory management, the party groups, and the mass organisations work together as a 'unified, social leadership'.

In the huge iron works at Eisenhüttenstadt, known as Eisenhüttenstadt Kombinat Ost, where 9,000 people work, the leadership of the SED party organisation (the Betriebspartei-organisation or BPO) consists of twenty people who meet once a fortnight. They think of themselves as the factory's political conscience, they say. Although they have no right to take a direct part in economic decisions, they act as a form of control and inspection mechanism vis-à-vis the director. The director himself is a member of the BPO and has to answer to his fellow party members at its meetings. In addition, the party secretary in the factory can sit in on all the director's meetings. Through its links 'upwards' with the national party apparatus and 'downwards' with ordinary workers via the various party cells in every branch of the factory, the enterprise party leadership has access to a wealth of information which may not be as readily available to the director through his own channels. It can bring pressure on him for changes. The BPO is in charge of the factory newspaper which gives it control of the most powerful means of communication within the factory. Even without that, the party's presence at every level of the factory makes it a strong, independent force which the director cannot afford to oppose.

The second major organisation is the permanent production council, which groups together leading members of the trade unions, the FDJ (Free German Youth), the DFD (Democratic League of Women) and some members of the technical and economic staff of the factory. They have a purely advisory role. However, since 1971 the director has been obliged to report back to the council on his reaction to their suggestions and give reasons for his decision if he rejects their advice. The permanent production councils oversee the general running of the plant, and give advice on issues such as the closing of one department or the expansion of another, the introduction of a night-shift or the need to install new machinery. They do not have as techni-cal a function as the so-called production committees which were set up with the NES and lasted for a few years after that. Their membership consisted mainly of technocrats who made recommendations on investment decisions, technical changes and ways of rationalising production. Because of its skilled membership, the production committee could act as a kind of substitute management. The Politbüro recognised this draw-back early on. In 1964 Günther Mittag said they should not expand their authority too far, but remain as co-ordinators of existing expertise and not develop into 'separate functional organs'.[2] His fear was that the principle of one-man management might be undermined. In 1971 the production committees began to be disbanded. The permanent production councils which replaced them were meant to act more as a forum for management and unions.

At Eisenhüttenstadt Kombinat Ost the council has 25 members and meets eight to ten times a year. In different branches of the plant there are lower-level committees with a similar role who meet more often, usually twice a month.

The trade union is the largest organisation in the factory with a nearly 100 per cent membership. In the early days of the GDR its role was mainly to organise production drives and help in fulfilling and over-fulfilling the plan. The plan, known as the collective contract, is drawn up jointly by the management and trade unions. In the period of post-war austerity, low pay, and high work norms, the trade union's image for most workers was not favourable. Increasingly the trade unions have been given more responsibility. They have become less like Western trade unions. They are in charge of all social security funds, from sick pay to the allocation of holiday places in trade union hotels. The trade union is in charge of the factory's hospitals and clinics. Under the collective contract the factory is committed to spend money on crèches, kindergartens, new sports facilities, leisure centres and housing. The trade union supervises in-dustrial safety, and ensures that the factory management observes the rules. On this the GDR's record is particularly good. The West German Government's 'Report on the State of the Nation' in 1971 admitted that industrial accidents hit 8·8 per cent of the work force in the Federal Republic but only 4·1 per cent in the GDR. The report commented: 'The low accident quota in the GDR is mainly the result of the system of labour safety which is apparently more efficient and more intensively controlled ... A more comprehensive catalogue of labour safety regulations, coupled with factory instructions, the general factory-based health service, accident research and the trade unions' strong functions in control and participation have produced a system which is superior to that of the Federal Republic.'[3] By 1974 the proportion of the work force affected by accidents had been reduced to 3·5 per cent.

East German trade unions also keep watch over the system of workers' training and further education. With the introduction of the NES in 1963 responsibility for vocational education was delegated to the factories. They must produce long-term and annual plans for training their staff. Under the GDR's 1968 Constitution all young people have the right and the duty to learn a trade or profession. Nowadays part of every collective contract is devoted to 'plans for qualifications', under which a certain proportion of young apprentices, both men and women, are to get training on the job or time off to attend outside courses. In most cases the trade unions pay for the courses. Here too the GDR stands well in comparison with its West German neighbour. In 1968 according to the 'Report on the State of the Nation' 2·4 per cent of the population between the ages of 18 and 45 were attending training courses other than university degree courses in the GDR. In the Federal Republic the proportion was only 1 per cent, and the report added that the GDR figure understated the position as it only included people doing at least a two-year course.[4] The party's emphasis on training undoubtedly falls on fertile soil. Pride in one's work and the desire for self-improvement and status through training are long-recognised German qualities. The SED is on sure ground in encouraging them.

The picture that emerges is of a trade union and factory structure very different from the West. In the West a worker expects from his factory good wages, decent working conditions, and a clean environment. The trade unions' job (where unions are recognised by employers) is to negotiate and fight for them. In the GDR a factory has a more central role. A worker expects it to provide kindergartens, holiday facilities, help with getting a flat, and a range of other services for which private agencies or at most local authorities would be responsible in the West.

In the GDR workers demand more from their factories. In turn more is demanded from them by the factories.

The trade unions are different too. In the GDR they are based on Lenin's model and have a radically changed role from their counterparts in a capitalist system. Instead of a basically negative and defensive approach, trade unions become 'schools of socialism' as part of the process of building a new society. Their three-fold task is to minimise tendencies towards excessive bureaucracy in economic planning, to ensure that the social regulations and the labour code are observed in the factories and to protect their members' immediate interests. There is a rich field for potential conflict here. The trade unions are expected simultaneously to help with achieving production targets and also to defend members' interests. In looking after the latter, trade unions have certain rights. No one may be dismissed without trade union approval. Inevitably this works less well in practice. An official of the central council of the FDGB, the central trade union organisation, conceded in an interview in Berlin that 'sometimes the unions are only consulted afterwards. This must be improved.' Unions deal with workers' complaints about unjust punishments or unfair treatment in the payment of bonuses. In a case at Eisenhüttenstadt a worker who had been absent for two days one September, and was mildly reprimanded at the time, was told at the end of the year that he could not share in the factory's bonus. He complained to the union that he had had no warning of this. They won the case for him.

Generally in disputes unions seem to act more readily for an individual worker than for workers as a group. The original union function of combining workers' strength and solidarity together has given way to more of a welfare role. There is no right to strike. Occasionally workers act on a large scale. At the beginning of 1971, according to the Berlin official mentioned above, massive criticism by workers at a Berlin factory forced the replacement of the director. This incident, and my interview, took place soon after the riots in nearby Poland which caused the overthrow of the Gomulka regime. Could this happen in the GDR? 'We react earlier than the Poles do,' said the official. 'The Poles did not listen to the complaints. They took no notice. We have a system of regular reports from the factories.'

Trade union work is helped by the fact that there is no unemployment. Sudden announcements of mass redundancies and the understandable militancy which it usually provokes, do not occur in the GDR. Herbert Geidel, manager of the VEB Eisengiesserei und Maschinenbau in Zeitz, told me that at the end of the 1960s they had closed the 120-year-old iron foundry in order to concentrate on a new machine-building enterprise. He had originally proposed the closure in 1966. 'At first the workers were against it. I had to explain it. The closure would not take place for two years. Everyone would be guaranteed the same wages afterwards, some by being retained, and some through early retirement on pension.' In the end the factory went on for three more years, and only a few men left early, he claimed. As a result of the bitter experiences of 1953 the trade unions now have a better and more sensitive system of communications and a wide range of social and cultural functions under their responsibility. With the extra and important advantage of a period of steadily increasing prosperity and no political upheavals, such as the GDR has now known for more than ten years, the trade unions seem to have achieved a broadly positive image in people's eyes.

It does not add up to workers' control, but does it give workers any significant participation? Several limitations have already been touched on. One is the leading role of the party which takes precedence over the power of the trade unions. The second is the principle of one-man management. Whatever the trade union recommends, the director and department heads have the last word. Then there is the general principle of democratic centralism which runs throughout the country's political structure and affects trade unions like all other organisations. The simple definition is that whatever the top level of an organisation decides, lower ranks have to obey. Although in practice things are more complicated and the central council of the trade union has to listen to some extent to the rank and file, it has the right and the power in the last analysis to prevent any dissidence or opposition. Finally there is the role of the central planners and the VVBs which effectively circumscribe the actions of trade unions. In their discussions on the collective contract neither the factory manager nor the unions are able to decide what to produce, but only how to produce it.

The unions' power is more limited than that of factory managers. Apart from the top two or three posts in major enterprises, trade union officials are full-time workers who do their union business during their time off. The unions have neither the apparatus nor the expert staff to make an independent audit of management proposals for the plan. Nor are more than two or three weeks normally available for discussion before a highly complex series of plan targets has to be approved. As was clear from one of the letters in *Die Tribüne*, which was mentioned at the beginning of this chapter, trade union meetings do not take place during working hours. The incentive for workers to take part is not high. Dr Hartmut Zimmermann, of the Institute for Political Science at West Berlin's Free University, who has conducted some of the most intensive research into the East German trade unions, believes that the significance of the collective contract is two-fold. It provides for worker-participation in the factory's social policy. It also gives workers a comprehensive supply of information on what is going on in the factory. 'Unlike the situation in capitalist enterprises this makes it possible for him to understand and fit his own work into the context of the factory and the whole economy.'[5] Under new regulations the director is now obliged to give unions monthly reports on the way the plan is being fulfilled. Zimmermann says that the chances of workers identifying with society's overall goals are weakened by the constant changes in the plan during the plan year. These can happen because of unexpected difficulties in the supply of raw materials, in shifts of priorities by the central planners, or by sudden curbs on investment. The effect can often be 'to encourage resignation and disinterest on the part of the individual worker who can no longer take seriously what "they up top" seem to think is important.'

The party is trying to get over this by demanding that plans be made more realistic in the beginning. Some evidence for workers' apathy can be gleaned from the few empirical studies which have been published in the GDR. A study at the chemical plant in Guben showed that workers knew little of what the director's role and powers were.[6] A feeling of distance between director and workers was evident in other research showing that disturbances in the plan that were caused by events beyond his control were still seen by workers as 'his fault' or due to 'his incompetence'. Evidence points to the existence of 'passive work-crews' who are contrasted with 'active work-crews' by their willingness to make suggestions for production improvements. There is sometimes a latent tension between blue-collar workers and the technical intelligentsia, and between apprentices and foremen. Group psychological research suggests that the workers who work hardest are not always the most popular ones among their mates.[7]

The problem with these findings is that they have no statistical weight. They reveal phenomena which one would have expected to discover, but leave open the question of their frequency. The danger in looking at empirical evidence 'admitted' by GDR sources is to assume that it must be 'the tip of the iceberg'. If the problem were not serious the authorities would not mention it at all. So the argument goes. In fact the tentative increase in official discussion of uncomfortable issues is a step forward. All it shows for sure is that the SED is now looking for improvements.

Besides expanding the role of the trade unions, the SED has been developing other techniques of creating a collective consciousness in the factories. The idea of 'socialist competition' in which groups of workers contest each other to overfulfil the plan is old. In the days when there was little feeling of consensus in the society, it was seen by workers as a device for getting extra work for no extra pay. With the GDR's increased stability that feeling has lessened. In the last ten years the formation of 'collectives of socialist labour' has been growing. The slogan for judging these collectives is whether or not they encourage their members 'to work, learn, and live as a socialist'. From this principle, laid down at the Eighth party congress, it is clear that the aim is to go well beyond the notion of simply producing more. The title 'collective of socialist labour' goes to groups whose members are attending night school, or getting further training, who are doing voluntary weekend work at the factory's summer camp or who put on cultural events together. 'Recognition as a "collective of socialist labour" is a mark of social approval', says the trade union resolution, 'for sustained and exemplary performance by a collective and every one of its members in socialist competition for achieving high work results, a high political, cultural, and expert level and the maintenance of the rules of social ethics and morality.'

All this sounds more pompous than it often is. In some cases the 'maintenance of socialist ethics' and 'a high cultural level' may mean little more than decorating a factory work room with flowers or posters. Every brigade or collective keeps a scrapbook. It may contain everything from pictures of its members' children and a record of people's illnesses to snapshots of outings and brief reports of meetings attended. Everybody is made to feel he belongs. In 1965 just over 1,600,000 people were members of these collectives. By 1974 it was close to four million or about half the entire work force. Members of these collectives are 'activists of socialist labour'. The title is also awarded to collectives outside the production environment – in offices, institutes and universities. It is not a permanent title but has to be defended every year. One 'danger' in this system which the party has identified is that the collectives could try to take aspects of workers' control and function as a unit in demanding better holiday arrangements, favourable shift hours, and so on. This trend has been condemned as 'syndicalism'.

The SED wants to foster group solidarity on what it considers the right terms. Collectives which try to defend their weaker members are not encouraged. Apart from the 'collectives of socialist labour' who receive a financial reward besides their title, ordinary collectives in factories receive a bonus at the end of the year. The normal amount is about one-twelfth of their annual earnings, and is called the thirteenth month's pay. The unions are responsible for dividing the bonus, but the party is against the collectives sharing it out equally among their members. Some collectives like to do this partly out of genuine solidarity and partly because it avoids grumbling and bickering if one member gets more than others. But the party criticises this as artificial levelling. In recent years it has tried to build up the role of the individual worker, and to call on people to set themselves their own personal plans.

The search for the right balance between encouraging individual and collective performance is matched by similar shifts of view on the respective advantages of moral or material incentives. The two are obviously linked. The tendency recently has been to increase both, as part of the drive to foster greater productivity and 'discover new reserves'. Titles and decorations are coming back into use after a lull in the 1950s. The prizes that go with them are worth more. Instead of 500 Marks annually for ten years, which amounted to a kind of pension, a winner now gets 5,000 Marks in one go. Some titles are given for life, like the Hero of Socialist Labour, the Order of the 'Banner of Labour', or the 'Activist Emeritus'. Besides these national titles, there are individual awards in different fields. Forty years' work as a miner brings a man a gold decoration 'for services to the coal industry'. Good work on the railways earns the title 'railwayman emeritus'. There is an honour pin for special services in hunting and special awards for firemen, customs officers and frontier guards. The awards are meant to recognise the distinction given to manual work.

Less socialist, and apparently more petty-bourgeois in concept, is the increasing use of status titles in the professions. Teaching and medicine in particular are reverting to the old gradations of German hierarchy. 'Studienrat', 'Oberstudiendirektor' and 'Medizinalrat' are back in usage and the phenomenon is spreading via titles like 'Diplomchemiker' to the technical professions.

Another way of increasing people's 'shared consciousness' in production is the so-called 'innovators' movement'. This is designed to encourage workers to make suggestions for technical labour-saving or cost-cutting improvements. In 1963 some 14·9 per cent of the total workforce was enrolled in the movement and eligible for bonuses as people who had made at least one innovative suggestion. By 1974 the figure was up to 27·9 per cent.[8] In industry the proportion is higher. In metal-working 46 per cent of the work force takes part; in the chemical industry 37 per cent.[9] Sometimes the suggestions may have been of limited value. In 1971, for example, only 6 per cent of the innovations introduced came from 'innovators'.[10] The rest came from the introduction of more advanced technology. Studies also show that the better qualified a worker is, the more likely he is to take part in the innovators' movement. Among unskilled workers only 20 per cent were in the movement in 1974 compared with 64 per cent and 51 per cent among foremen and university graduates. These figures were probably to be expected. It is impossible to know whether they reflect apathy and lack of interest among the working class, or simply the fact that they have fewer opportunities for making significant suggestions.

Outside the production field, factories try to give workers a number of social roles. Sanctions against petty offenders and minor forms of delinquency are handled by 'conflict commissions', elected by trade union members. Here again the GDR prefers to handle within the work context issues which Western societies leave exclusively to local civic institutions like magistrates' courts. The idea is that a person's work collective can produce the best form of discipline, control, help, and re-education since colleagues are in closer and longer contact with him or her than anyone else. In 1973 the GDR had 23,055 conflict commissions.[11] Each one usually has a panel of between eight and ten members. In Eisenhüttenstadt for example with a population in 1974 of 46,500 people there were 86 commissions with 807 members, that is roughly one commission for every 500 people. The Penal Code defines the kinds of punishment which the commissions may impose. A citizen may be ordered to apologise to the aggrieved party or in front of a collective body. He may have to repair the damage he caused, or else pay damages if he is unable to do the repairs himself. He may have to withdraw an insult in public, get a public reprimand or pay a fine of up to three times the value of the damage caused up to a maximum of 150 Marks. If a case is regarded as so serious that a prison sentence or probation is likely, the commission must refer it to a normal court. The conflict commissions handle about 40 per cent of all penal cases. Most sentences imposed by the commissions are upheld on appeal. Only 1 per cent has to be changed or quashed.[12] Very few people – barely 5 per cent – ever commit another offence after appearing before a conflict commission.

These results are impressive even though it is unclear whether most commissions see their role as mainly punitive or reforming. Do they go into a defendant's background and treat the causes rather than the symptoms of the offence? Western observers have not been able to visit commissions on any scale. But once a week the trade union paper, *Die Tribüne*, publishes a supplement called 'The conflict commission'. It is a useful publication, designed for the general reader as well as for members of the commissions. Here they can read brief popularisations of the law and the views of criminologists. Every week the supplement discusses one case study. Typical cases in the first half of 1975 were a young worker who contested his dismissal for repeatedly coming drunk to work and allegedly breaking industrial safety regulations; a 17-year-old girl who started a small fire in the factory's packing-room; a canteen director who failed to supervise his staff and let them get away with pilfering; and a 34-year-old man who stole sausages from the cold store where he worked as a lorry driver.

The write-up in this last case said that 'Ronny' was divorced and paying an allowance for his son.[13] 'He is one of those people who prefer to take rather than give, a selfish type whose nice name goes with a bad character.' He was irregular with his son's payments, and a court order was made to have them deducted from his pay. 'When he joined the Berlin cold store as a driver he was instructed in the meaning of nationalised property and the need to look after it. Ronny listened to the warning and did the opposite.' He regularly hid a sausage and took it home. In a month he had taken eleven sausages worth 268 Marks 95 Pfennigs. He was discovered. The public prosecutor referred the case to the conflict commission with the advice that Ronny could be charged under four paragraphs of the penal code but suggesting that a fine was appropriate. In front of the commission Ronny apparently showed no remorse so that 'the commission acted not as it wished but as was necessary to give Ronny a lesson to ensure that in future he should of his own free will obey socialist laws and their conscious discipline'. He was given a reprimand, and a fine of 100 Marks, and had to pay back the 268 Marks 95 Pfennigs which he had stolen in five monthly instalments. Soon afterwards Ronny left the factory, but, the article concluded, he need not think he can get away with non-payment of the fine imposed by the factory's conflict commission. A copy of that decision was sent to the local town hall to whom the fine had to be paid.

In the case of 17-year-old Patricia who started the fire, the court referred the matter to the conflict commission because she had no previous offences and the damage caused was worth only 50 Marks. Patricia's behaviour was partly attention-seeking, the commission decided. She was annoyed with Sylvia, her brigade leader, who frequently skipped work to go out with a lorry driver. The commission found the atmosphere in the collective was poor, and the FDJ was inactive. 'The collective was no collective,' *Die Tribüne* said. The commission told Patricia she would have to make up the damage out of her pocket but they encouraged her to do her last year of school over again in evening classes and get extra qualifications. The factory director and the FDJ leadership were told to take a closer interest in the brigade. The FDJ promised to hold more frequent meetings and the brigade said it would try to 'become a good model collective by the time of the next party congress'. This was written down in the brigade's programme and was to be inspected every quarter.

From the different handling of these two cases it is clear that the commissions sometimes act in a rather pompous, schoolmasterly fashion but at other times are more sensitive. The sanction of public reprimand and shame in front of colleagues is used as a form of deterrent. An education official discussed with me the case of a colleague who had been caught speeding in his car. 'If he had just had his licence endorsed or been fined by a court, he would have escaped with anonymity', since the GDR rarely publishes crime reports for fear of drawing attention to crime. 'As it was, it was left to our disputes commission and he liked it much less.' Even when it does not come to an outright offence, the technique of public shame is often used. On the internal notice board of the Berliner Verlag publishing house I saw a large notice naming three members of one department who had failed to turn up one Saturday afternoon in the spring when everyone was getting the firm's holiday home cleaned up and ready for the summer. These are the shirkers, the notice said in effect. They were allowed to give their reply. On a separate sheet the three men wrote that they had been falsely accused. They were out on office business that day and would be delighted to explain their case in more detail any time to anyone who was still interested.

In summary then one sees that the role of the factory or the office in the GDR is deliberately designed to express the socialist values of the society. Trade unions, and through them their members do not have the scope for decision-making on major industrial and economic issues. They work within closely defined

limits. Professor Rudi Weidig, one of the GDR's leading socio-
logists, wrote recently that research into the development of
collectives showed that 30 per cent of workers did not feel
sufficiently integrated into important aspects of their factory's
work.[14] 'They did not have enough information to share in
decisions,' he wrote. On social matters trade unions have a
greater role. It is safe to say that in the GDR's factories a collective consciousness has been built up on a deeper and wider
scale than in the West. Over the years the values of collective
living and collective work seem to have been internalised by a
substantial number of people.

Beyond the factory gates one meets similar problems of empirical verification in trying to ascertain what power workers have
in East German society, and how far citizens in general accept
collective ideals. The party claims to have set up a government
of working people by working people for working people. As
Articles One and Two of the Amended Constitution of 1974 put
it, 'The German Democratic Republic is a state of workers and
farmers. It is the political organisation of working people in
town and countryside under the leadership of the working class
and its Marxist-Leninist party ... All political power in the
GDR is exercised by working people ...' The ruling power is the
SED with its 1,907,719 members and 46,411 candidate members in July 1974. Of these over 56 per cent were described as
workers. This was a higher percentage than in earlier years (at
the Seventh party congress in 1967 the percentage of workers
was 45·6 per cent), but it reflects the determined push made by
the party to get more workers into its ranks. The leadership was
conscious that it was in danger of looking less and less like a
working-class party. In recent months it has become much
harder for intellectuals to join the party whereas production
workers have little difficulty. Of the 21,858 candidates taken in
during the first six months of 1974, 75·7 per cent were workers.
The party is aware of the problems of defining a person's class
identification. Does it depend on his origin or his present status?
The party tried to keep a watch on both. Its membership figures
are based on people's current position but their origin is taken
into account when they join. Between 1972–4 the party reported
that the number of members of the intelligentsia 'who come
from the working class rose by 32,000 in the party'.[15] The

SED's membership is large. Roughly one out of every six adults belongs to it which makes it more of a mass party than most of its counterparts in Eastern Europe, including the Communist party of the Soviet Union.

A broadly based sociological spread in the party and mass membership may help to produce a better channel of communication from the rank and file to the top. It certainly does not ensure genuine influence from the bottom upwards. On the contrary the Politbüro still follows the tight-lipped conspiratorial traditions of its days in opposition and the underground. All decisions are taken at the top and there is minimal public or press discussion of them. Under the principle of democratic centralism decisions are passed down the line to the central committee and local party organisations for implementation. Top party politicians still live in suburban seclusion in a guarded residential area at Wandlitz outside Berlin. They probably have less contact with ordinary people than most West European politicians do. The GDR's other 'representative bodies' are even less impressive as decision-makers than the SED's lower-level organisations. According to Article 48 of the Constitution 'The People's Chamber is the highest state organ of power in the GDR. In its plenary sessions it decides on the basic questions of state policy.' For such an allegedly powerful body, the People's Chamber meets very rarely – about six times a year for a day at a time. On average the number of laws passed is twelve a year.[16] In practice all draft bills are introduced by either the Council of Ministers (the Government) or the Council of State to whom the People's Chamber has delegated its authority. The Council of State also has the right to check whether draft laws conform to the Constitution which therefore gives it veto power over the People's Chamber. Moreover the SED lays down the guidelines on which all laws must be based.

The People's Chamber has 500 members. Like the SED, it has a careful balance of people from different backgrounds, 57·4 per cent workers, 14·2 per cent office employees, 8·8 per cent farmers, 6·8 per cent intelligentsia, 10.4 per cent craftsmen and traders and 2·4 per cent others. There is a higher proportion of women (31·8 per cent) and young people (12·2 per cent aged between 21 and 30) than in Western Parliaments. To that extent the People's Chamber is a cross-section of the country as a whole. It also has a carefully calculated balance between the parties – SED 127 seats, LDPD 52, NDPD 52, CDU 52, DBD 52, Trade Unions 68, Free German Youth 40, Democratic Women's League and the League of Culture (Kulturbund) 22 each. However, all votes in the People's Chamber were unanimous until 1972. On March 9 that year fourteen deputies voted against a bill to liberalise abortion. Eight others abstained.[17] All were members of the CDU. Since then there have been no further rebellions. But Wolfgang Heyl, the chairman of the CDU group in the People's Chamber, told me the following year that the party had opposed draft bills in committee on earlier occasions. They had criticised a proposed Family Law because of what they felt were its inadequate references to the influence of religion in society. It had then been withdrawn and redrafted. Later on, in the preliminary discussion on the 1968 Constitution, they had made strong criticisms because there was no mention of the right to profess a religion.

Compared with the stormy role of the CDU in the early postwar years, these recent signs of opposition are small, especially when the number of Christians in the whole society was still nominally eleven million according to the 1968 census. Although deputies have little decision-making power they have a role similar to Western MPs within their constituencies. They can take up individual cases. They have regular hours when citizens can bring complaints. They have to explain Government policy.

At the lower levels of local government, party representation is as carefully graded between parties and social groups. There is a single list of candidates, drawn up at selection committees dominated by the SED. In these circumstances it may seem surprising that people bother to join the other parties. Yet they do. At a large co-operative wheat and vegetable farm near Frankfurt on the Oder, the chairman said that out of 329 employees 60 belonged to the SED, his deputy and 25 others were in the DBD, the farmers' party, and 15 were in the CDU, including the man in charge of potato production 'who is very religious and always goes to church, particularly for harvest festival'. The different party memberships are still considered to represent different shades of emphasis and interest within the population. The SED sees its role not as one of suppressing differences but of integrating them into a collective whole. There is no chance of voters exerting any influence against SED policy. But the People's Chamber and the system of deputies from different backgrounds are meant to keep up a certain link between the population and the Government. At the same time the party is conscious that if real and major differences did exist in the society, the People's Chamber would not be able to paper them over. The aim therefore is gradually to merge social differences. With his characteristic impatience Ulbricht described the GDR as a 'human community'—a 'Menschengemeinschaft'. In a short span of years he had moved from the Stalinist position of a sharpening of tensions during the transition to socialism, to the belief that all tensions had evaporated.

His successors abandoned the concept of a 'human community' as premature. They recognised that differences still existed, and wanted to ensure that they were 'non-antagonistic'. Put at its simplest there would always be a division of labour between mental and manual work. But both had to be given roughly equal status and rewards. In schools from the seventh class, that is age thirteen, children have to do practical work for two to three hours once a week in a factory or on a farm. In some cases they work alongside adults; in others there are special departments for schoolchildren. Already when a child goes to pre-school kindergarten he or she will find links with a factory. Every kindergarten is 'adopted' by a local plant whose staff take a special interest in it. They may help to provide it with extra equipment and financial support. Staff from the factory visit the school regularly and take the pre-school children on tours round the plant and its departments. In many other countries of course children are taken round factories and have a look at the machines and see what they do. The GDR's scheme is meant to let children get to know the factory's workers through having a continuing two-way relationship between one school and one factory. Particularly for children from the intelligentsia the hope is that this will prevent any prejudice about manual labour.

A relatively narrow range of incomes is meant to achieve the same result. With the exception of pensioners who receive very low incomes, the gap between the top and bottom groups in the

GDR is roughly three to one. According to a recent study by the Deutsches Institut für Wirtschaftsforschung, based in West Berlin, the average monthly net income per earner in the GDR in 1972 was as shown in Table 1.[18]

Table 1

	Marks
Employees	720
Members of co-operatives	958
Independent people (craftsmen, private shop-keepers, artists etc.)	2025
Pensioners	221

A more detailed breakdown of the two largest categories, employees and members of co-operatives, was available from the same source for 1970. The figures are net. (See Table 2.)

Table 2

	Marks
Members of LPG I and II	878
Members of LPG III	680
Employees of VEBs	
altogether	757
in industry	765
in building	828
in land and forestry	715
in trade	663

These figures do not show differences within each section between white-collar and blue-collar workers. The GDR maintains pay differentials according to skill in order to encourage people to get qualifications. But they are not great. The DIW measured net household incomes in 1970. It found that the bottom 20 per cent of employees' households had 10·4 per cent of total employees' incomes. The top fifth had three times as much, at 30·7 per cent of the total. (Comparable calculations for West Germany showed a wider range of roughly five to one. The respective figures for the bottom and top fifths of all employees' households were 8·3 per cent and 39·9 per cent.)[19]

These statistics can be fleshed out with some random examples from 1971. An ordinary university lecturer grossed between 900 and 1,600 Marks depending on whether he had a Ph.D. A doctor started at 700. A factory manager ranged between 1,200 and 2,500. The top party official in a county (Bezirk) earned between 1,200 and 1,500 and a full professor got up to 3,400 Marks. These figures suggest that in spite of the attempt to blur the status differences between manual and mental labour, the German tradition of paying senior academics exceedingly well lives on. None of these figures measures the value of undeclared perks. As in the West, certain groups have access to official cars, flats and houses. Some party officials can use special shops. They get private rooms in hospitals. A relatively small number of people at the very top, probably not more than a hundred, are in the luxury bracket. Below this level there is not much wealth. Unlike the situation in the West there is no possibility for a citizen to own land on any scale. Each household is allowed two plots, one for their main house and one for a country cottage. No one can own shares, or have a foreign bank account. Any visitor to the GDR can see that there are no major residential differences in East German cities and no wealthy suburbs. Standards are more uniform. In the countryside the large estates have been nationalised and their grand houses are in the hands of institutions, hospitals and trade unions.

To talk of a 'new class' is wrong. Decision-making, it is true, is in the hands of a relatively small elite. But the elite is not closed. It is based on a combination of education (mainly the younger members) and loyalty to the system. The members of this elite work hard, and their position is risky. The history of the party purges is enough to show that the higher you are, the farther you fall. There is no hereditary right to rule. Factory managers probably feel this the most. The legitimisation of private ownership no longer exists. Directors can only justify themselves by their results. The party and the workers expect an enormous amount from them. The earlier part of this chapter described the wide role factories play in East German society. The man at the top of the pyramid has a proportionately harder job. He must be a specialist in his field (two-thirds of GDR managers are economists, the rest engineers[20]). He must understand Marxism-Leninism. He must arouse, initiate, and keep the trust of his staff, and the various social organisations in the factory from the party to the trade unions. He must be ready to work co-operatively but also take risks. Not surprisingly, according to time-budget studies published in the GDR, the average manager spends between sixty and seventy hours a week on the job. The factory's work-rhythm is constantly being disrupted by failures in vital supplies, which makes it hard to fulfil the plan. Too many directors still spend too long on petty details, either because they are reluctant to delegate responsibility or because junior staff are afraid to take it. About 20 per cent of his work the manager does at home. He neglects his family and rarely takes a complete holiday. According to a study by a GDR sociologist, Gunther Reimann, the director of one Berlin factory had five unpaid jobs on local committees which took up an extra twelve hours a week.[21] An apparently typical manager cited in another study got up at 4 in the morning, walked half an hour to work (his only exercise of the day), and started work at 6 reading papers and files. The factory opened at 7.30 am. Ten hours later after a whirlwind day of meetings and conferences, he went home to an evening of reading more papers.

Perhaps this case is exaggerated. But workers presumably know that most directors have to work hard. For their part, with no unemployment and the chance to change jobs easily most workers can get away without too hard a day. In one way or another a genuine feeling has developed that things are relatively evenly shared and that everyone belongs. People who defect to West Germany often miss the feeling of community. They are unsuccessful in the individual rat-race 'where no one takes any notice of you'. Erika, a 29-year-old teacher, who left the GDR in her late teens, spoke of what she missed most in West Germany. 'It was mainly a kind of moral responsibility that I missed. Or rather I thought I had one but I couldn't find anyone to whom I could explain it. It was simply an empty room that I had come into.'[22] The vicar of one of East Berlin's city centre churches whose previous parish had been in a large industrial town summed up his thoughts this way: 'In the factories people criticise a lot. The older generation may be afraid to open their mouths, but not the younger ones. People have the impression that this society is developing. They don't look on it as finished. They also realise that they have a part to play. Through their work and their social duties people are conscious that they are helping themselves. They actually feel "We are the state".'[23]

8

Leisure, Crime and Private Life

Berlin's old pre-war racecourse at the Hoppegarten with its tall red-brick grandstand dated 1922 is back in business. Every Sunday in summer the crowds come out here to watch the horses, have a few drinks and place an enthusiastic bet. For a big race like the 'Derby of the GDR' some five thousand people turn up. Racing is becoming one of the country's most popular sports. A few private race-horse owners are even flourishing again, although most of the horses belong to nationalised stables. Betting is done on a state totalisator, with a maximum stake of only 10 Marks. To help them with judging the form, race-goers can buy the weekly racing paper, the *Rennkurier*, or look at the naps in their own daily paper. Every newspaper except the official party organ *Neues Deutschland* and the youth paper *Junge Welt* has its tipster.

The Hoppegarten is in the thick belt of woodland and lakes which lie to the south-east of Berlin. Dotted among it on summer weekends you find crowded car-parks by the watersides. Bungalows ring the shores of many lakes and on some of them the owners have managed to have a ban put on motorboats and all their noise. Notices saying 'Private Property' sometimes bar the access to the beach. Nearer in to the city and within easy reach of the overground S-Bahn train there are clumps of small allotments and one- or two-room wooden bungalows surrounded by vegetables and fruit trees. The vast majority have gone up within the last decade. Many are still being built. They are not the property of a new elite, since skilled workers and artisans can comfortably afford them. Nor are they confined to Berliners. The local authorities of most big towns in the GDR are now catering for the demand for private bungalows and have set aside land for them which people lease from the city. Werner Viertel, Mayor of Eisenhüttenstadt, says every third or fourth family in the town has a bungalow. The cheapest cost around 2,000 Marks but the average price for a more solid building is 10,000 Marks.

The bungalows, the popularity of racing, and the upsurge in car ownership are new phenomena—what the GDR's theorists call 'privatisation'. It has grown dramatically in recent years. 'Let's build ourselves a nest', the popular magazine *Neue Berliner Illustrierte* recently invited its readers in a series of articles on home-furnishing. House-and-garden magazines are popular. Among young people in particular, the sales of consumer goods, from portable tape recorders to motor-cycles and pop and jazz records, are high. The planners cannot cater for the demand fast enough. All day long in summer the Alexanderplatz in Berlin is full of young people sitting round the garish multi-coloured fountain or passing the time of day by the revolving international clock. When evening falls, there are not enough places for them to go. In the older parts of Berlin some pre-war corner pubs remain. In the new blocks behind the Karl-Marx-Allee (the former Stalinallee) and along the even newer Frankfurterallee they have built a few giant pubs which look like vast mess-halls. They stand half empty. No one seems to like them. People want discothèques, and a certain number of pubs in Berlin are now being asked to lay on dance facilities by law. The city authorities are opening youth clubs as fast as they can. In 1971 only twelve were operating in Berlin. By 1975 it was up to 32.

After all the talk of collective consciousness, the growing 'privatisation' with its accent on leisure, home life and the family might seem like a contradiction. To some of the older ideologists perhaps it does. The present leadership accepts and encourages it. Although Ulbricht was the one who gave the green light to the New Economic System, and even before that had made it his goal for East German consumers to overtake their Western counterparts, there was always a touch of puritanism about it. The emphasis was on giving the working class culture in its broadest sense and not just consumer goods.

Otto Gotsche, his loyal personal secretary, explains how he would sometimes have to persuade parents to keep their children on at school. 'Why should my daughter stay and do maths and physics if she is going to be a hair-dresser?', a mother would ask him. 'She needs a full education,' Gotsche would reply, 'firstly because she is a human being, and secondly because she is a member of the working class and we want to bring up a German working class that is more educated than any ever before.' Under Ulbricht's successors the party is sounding a less high-minded note. The sense of sin has gone and people are not being told it is wrong to want to have some modest private property. It reflects the old Communists' declining influence. By 1967 only 6 per cent of the party had been members of the KPD or SPD in pre-war days. With them has gone some of the missionary idealism as well as the use of excessive pressure and penal sanctions on people, all in the name of a distant ideal.

Even some of the more liberal Utopians are worried by to-day's trend. Robert Havemann, the critical chemist and philosopher who was expelled from the party in 1964 for a series of unorthodox lectures on Marxism, is disturbed by developments. At the end of 1976 he was briefly detained. He feels the first stage of establishing socialism, with the land reform and the expropriation of private farms, was right. But the second stage, the democratisation of the system, has not yet come. He had hoped for a political liberalisation, independence for the courts, and genuine academic freedom. Instead of that, he argues in a recent essay, the GDR is forcing itself into an artificial competition with the West for all the wrong things – a car for every family, giant high-rise flats, and the notion that industrial development on a level with the richest countries in the world is the first priority for a socialist state.[1]

In some ways the trend towards privatisation seems superficially stronger than in the West. By the early evening on weekdays the streets of most East German towns are empty. Cafés close by 8 or 9 p.m. People sit comfortably at home, 'all in slippers', as one young East German scornfully put it. For visitors it can be a strange experience to walk past high-density blocks of flats and meet hardly a soul on the pavements. Where is everybody? And where is the feeling of socialist community? There are several explanations but one of them is definitely not fear of being mugged. The streets of East Berlin are safer than those of most Western capitals. The reasons lie elsewhere. At its simplest, people are just tired. In most families both husband and wife work, and the factory or office day frequently begins at 7 or 7.30. Shopping after work takes time. Then there is television, the great killer of outdoor entertainment. GDR citizens have four possible channels to watch, two of their own and two from West Germany. Many people study at night. An enormous number are seeking extra qualifications and doing correspondence courses from home.

For others the stay-at-home feeling may be simply a retreat. People withdraw into the privacy of their homes after all the collective activity of the day. In the period after the war, a social worker said, the authorities found it suspicious if someone stayed too much at home and declined to take part in communal activities. The party leadership felt threatened and unsure on many grounds. A citizen's refusal to take part was interpreted as a sign of passive resistance. In some cases it was. Now the party accepts that there is a legitimate sphere for private life and a human need for people to recharge their batteries at home. 'Respect and protection for the family' are laid down in the Constitution. Before the war, and particularly in the 1920s German urban society was renowned for its 'Geselligkeit', its clubbiness. Everywhere there were clubs for this and that, for Esperanto, for chess, for amateur dramatics, for hiking and cycling, for collecting stamps. Perhaps the demand for them was a reaction to the impersonality of the industrial scene and the all-pervasive sense of political and economic instability in the Weimar Republic. If so, the opposite may be happening now. People have enough of the collective spirit by day. In the evening they want less of it. The point should not be exaggerated since there are many exceptions to the rule. People go on evening theatre trips or weekend excursions with their workmates from the factory or office. Team sports are popular. Nevertheless the penchant for private life at home is strong. Coupled with it is a remarkable resilience of the institution of the wider family.

The family tradition has always been deep-rooted in Germany. This is one of the points on which East Germany sometimes seems more 'German' than West Germany. In the West, a sociologist at West Berlin's Free University argued, the wider family has lost its economic function. 'In the GDR it still has a role because of the continuing shortages and bottle-necks in the economy. A woman in Rostock phones her sister in Erfurt to ask whether she can get red curtains down there. There are none up in Rostock. What are conditions like with bananas? We have only had them every second day and now they've disappeared from the shops altogether.' Hotel accommodation is tight everywhere in the country and there are few bed and breakfast places. Distant relations who might have long ago lost touch in the West put each other up. The family also serves a psychological function which perhaps is less necessary in the West. It is a safety valve, a place where one can let one's hair down, grouse, and complain uninhibitedly and not worry what others may think of you.

Sceptics may see signs of anti-social attitudes in the apparent clinging to family life. As with so many other phenomena in the GDR it is hard to measure. In general, however, anti-social behaviour in the GDR seems comparatively low by Western standards. The drop-out phenomenon is rare, and crime rates are under control. But in recent years both have become more serious and there is no doubt that the authorities are worried. Drugs were stamped on ruthlessly and quickly as soon as it began to appear that some were seeping in from West Berlin mainly via Turkish immigrants or West German pushers. Long sentences were handed down. The state requires every youth group to have a recognised organiser, and official clearance for its activities. Brigades and collectives in factories are required to keep an eye open for potential delinquents.

But among the younger generation there is a certain admiration for the non-criminal drop-out and the Western-style hippie. This was shown in the success of a remarkable play, *The New Sorrows of Young W*, which appeared like a bombshell on the East German stage in 1973. The hero, Edgar Wibeau, has taken refuge in a shack outside Berlin from the general pressure of industrial life and particularly from the appalling patronisation and bullying he gets from his foreman at work. Long-haired, dressed in jeans, and provocative, he comes across a paperback copy of Goethe's classic *The Sorrows of Young Werther*. The play mirrors Goethe's unrequited love for Charlotte with Edgar Wibeau's hopeless passion for a nearby kindergarten teacher. She is engaged to an insufferably priggish young officer on national service in the army. In the end Edgar kills himself. The play was a wild success, mainly because of its honest criticism and debunking of so many cult themes in German life from Goethe to the self-image of the GDR itself. For the SED leadership which took a bold decision to allow it to be performed, the play's virtue is that it shows Edgar's drop-out life to be a sympathetic but ultimately futile and suicidal operation. Nevertheless *Neues Deutschland* praised its 'consider-able reality'. Ulrich Plenzdorf, the author, comes from a true-red background. Born in the working-class Berlin district of Kreuzberg (now the largely Turkish ghetto in West Berlin) he was the only child of parents who spent time in Nazi camps. 'Young people,' he says, 'have an elementary need to rebel. It is important to do what you feel strongly pushed towards be-cause people who have found themselves are more productive for society than those who have no courage.'[2] A survey taken among young people in Leipzig revealed that most of them felt that dropping-out was not a wise move by Edgar. But they admitted they would like to try it for a while.

Some do. The crime rate is rising again after long years of steady decline. Dr Josef Streit, the GDR's public prosecutor, recently disclosed that between 1945 and 1949 the average annual number of offences was 470,000.[3] Between 1949 and 1959 it was 157,000. In 1968 it had gone down as far as 100,000 but between 1969 and 1973 the average was back up to 128,000. Some party officials interpret the early figures as evidence that under socialism crime diminishes. Get rid of the capitalist slums and over-crowded tenements, abolish unemployment, create a new social morality and crime will disappear. Although these factors may have played a partial role, the big drop in crime in the 1950s almost certainly had other causes. The high figures of 1945 to 1949 were a result of the immediate post-war chaos, minimal law enforcement, severe economic shortages and weak social discipline. As things stabilised, crime fell while many criminals probably went West where the opportunities and re-wards were greater. Put crudely, the GDR exported criminality. Later it did the same as part of a deliberate policy. In October 1972 the authorities announced an extensive amnesty for thousands of prisoners, the biggest in the country's history. Many were allowed to cross the Wall to the West. Some were people who had tried to flee the GDR or who had come over from the West to help others in escape attempts. A significant proportion, to the dismay of the West Germans, turned out to have been non-political criminals from the East. Eleven were escaped West German criminals who had fled East and were immediately rearrested on their return to the West.

In the early 1970s crime rose again. From 1970 onwards the GDR suddenly stopped publishing criminal statistics on a regular basis. Dr Streit said in an interview that the GDR had no professional criminals or organised gangs. Only 5 per cent of offences were 'crimes, that is, serious attacks on socialist society and its citizens or crimes punishable by at least two years' deprivation of liberty'. The public prosecutor added that about half the offences were 'directed against property, with an annual loss of 500 million Marks'.[4] In a statement shortly before that Dr Töplitz, the president of the Supreme Court, said that there had been no increase in crimes of violence, assault, hooliganism, rape or homicide.[5] But there was an extra dimension of brutality in them, which he put down as 'an over-flow from the developments in the capitalist world'. The GDR's new crime wave seems to be a product of affluence. There is more in the shops, and more of the shops are self-service stores with patently lax security. Opportunities for crime are greater, with more consumer goods, more motor-bikes and cars around. And with the recent drive towards more of a private life, people feel the urge 'to keep up with the Joneses' and show off material goods. Stealing from socialist enterprises has always been common. The weekly paper *Für Dich* complained recently that 'on so many country cottages it is obvious that the gates and fences have been illegally acquired. Anyone can see that, but no one says a word, probably because so many people have also helped themselves from society's great pot'.[6] The courts uncover occasional cases of massive corruption, usually by factory managers who inflate their payrolls and pocket non-existent workers' wages, or account for payments for materials that were ordered but never supplied.

The GDR uses a variety of non-custodial sentences against petty criminals. They include suspended sentences assignment to a work gang, and the requirement that an offender stay at a particular address and report regularly to the police. In 1974 and 1975 punishments were increased, apparently as a result of a public outcry. A court in the Berlin suburb of Treptow recently sentenced two young railway vandals who had smashed windows in an S-Bahn train. It gave them four and three months respectively in prison and made them pay for the damage. According to the *Berliner Zeitung*, after protests from local people the sentences were increased by the city court to eleven and ten months plus compulsory supervision on release.[7] The paper also reported that the work collective in which one of the accused worked was refusing to take him back. Normally, as part of the philosophy that workmates take a helping interest in fellow-workers' difficulties, anyone coming out of prison is supposed to get his old job back and be given moral support. The factory-based 'conflict commissions' have been discussed in the previous chapter. In addition, though they are fewer in number there are local 'disputes commissions'. In 1973 some 5,267 of them in the GDR handled almost 30,000 cases, mainly neighbourhood quarrels, involving petty issues like complaints over excessive noise at night, rows between neighbours, unruly children, insults, and so on. Occasionally, as in a case published in the magazine *Wochenpost*, they deal with more serious offences like child-battering.[8] Another magazine tried to find a collective solution after a road crash in the village of Gierstadt near Erfurt. The *Neue Berliner Illustrierte* brought together survivors, local people and the police to a discussion which it then published. The accident had produced one young man's death and injuries to eight others when the Wartburg car they had crammed into crashed. All of them had been drinking. Although the driver who died was the main guilty party, several people thought the eight passengers should lose their licences. Others thought the people in the pub where the young men were drinking should have spotted the potential danger and warned them against driving. The mayor concluded that everyone in the community should feel some responsibility. A pious platitude? A green light to the busybodies in any community to become more active? Or a genuine attempt to awaken more of a collective spirit? Probably it was a mixture of all three.

The GDR authorities are not averse to more traditional methods of controlling anti-social behaviour. On April 1 1975 the Council of Ministers announced new regulations to increase preventive measures against crime. It affected citizens 'who show serious signs of developing a work-shy outlook, who try to obtain a livelihood in an unworthy way, who break work discipline through constant abuse of alcohol, or who show by their social behaviour that they need extra instruction.' Every factory director was obliged to report signs of incipient delinquency to the local authorities who could order a person to avoid frequenting certain places, do up to ten days of compulsory work, and not change his job or address. Some civil rights were cut. Suspended sentences were made longer.

Within the party's general framework of trying to foster a collective consciousness while recognising differences of opinion comes its attitude to the church. In the early days after the war the church was often looked on as a bastion of the middle-class establishment, indeed almost as a delinquent itself. Now it is seen not exactly in opposite terms, but at least as a potential ally in the socialising process. The church in the GDR has an easier time than any other church in Eastern Europe. Every Sunday, Radio GDR broadcasts a religious service with choir and sermon. Unlike any other Warsaw Pact state, the GDR permits a kind of legal conscientious objection to military service. Christians and other objectors can join in army construction units which do not carry weapons. Service in one of these will not help a man's career but it is better than the single alternative of prison which faces protesters elsewhere in Eastern Europe. (Jehovah's Witnesses refuse even this small concession by the GDR. They have gone to prison for outright pacifism.)

There are three church publishing-houses in the GDR which produce one out of every eight books printed. Bibles and prayer-books come out with little difficulty. General religious books go before the censor. Bishops are appointed without any state interference. Although synods have never chosen bishops from among the few uncritical church supporters of the SED but have picked independents, the party (unlike its counterparts in the rest of Eastern Europe) has never arrested or forced any church leader out of office. Some parsons and laymen were gaoled in the 1950s and several young church people were expelled from the universities but the authorities stopped short of arresting any top leaders. The church runs fifty agricultural enterprises on half a million acres of land. It is the only private landowner in the GDR. The main reason for its comparatively favourable position is historical. The major church is Protestant, and has the nominal allegiance of half the population according to the 1968 census. At the end of the war almost all its leaders were people who had resisted the Nazis, men and women who admired that branch of the Lutheran church which had been martyred like Dietrich Bonhöffer in Nazi prisons and camps. In his study for the British Council of Churches, the Christian writer, Trevor Beeson, says that after the war 'There was little danger that they would bow down to some new idol: but neither would they readily fall for the anti-Communist ideology which Hitler had successfully used to bid for a wide measure of Christian support. These Christians had shared prison cells and concentration camp experience with many of the Communists who were now taking over in East Germany. Nor could these Communists tar the Church with a Fascist brush. When it was tried in the GDR the tar would not stick.' Beeson goes on to comment: 'In the light of the Reformation and recent German history it is therefore no surprise to discover that Christians in the GDR have a deep concern for the social and ethical issues that arise in their form of socialist society. In some respects this offers the possibility of close collaboration with the state; in others the possibility of sharp conflict. This position vis-à-vis the new society, sometimes described as critical solidarity, is unique in Eastern Europe.'[9]

Ulbricht apparently came to believe that Marxism and Christianity could and in some cases should co-operate whatever their philosophical differences. In a meeting with church leaders in February 1961 he said: 'It appears to me that capitalism and basic Christianity are really irreconcilably opposed to each other. Socialism on the other hand despite all the imperfections it may still have will bring about the implementation of the Christian, humanist, and social ideals ... I am coming increasingly to the conclusion that socialists, Communists, and Christians ... simply must work together in shaping life and society and in ensuring peace ... What are the simple ideals and aims which unite us? Peace and humanity and mutual respect, happiness and prosperity for honest working people, happy families and happy children, healthy in body and soul – these are the things which we all strive for.'

The greatest fruit of this tolerant attitude is the state's acceptance of a wide role for the church in the social welfare field. The SED sensibly recognises that the church has the staff and the finances to provide a useful supplementary medical and educational service. The state makes substantial grants to church-run institutions. The Evangelische Kirche – the Lutheran church – had in 1973 6,000 parishes with 4,230 parsons, 5,000 catechists and 5,000 social workers. It runs institutions that are staffed by 15,000 officials. These include fifty-four hospitals, and convalescent homes, 300 nursing stations, thirty-six maternity homes and a large number of old people's homes and kindergartens. Most of the work done with mentally handicapped children in the GDR is performed by the church. The staff ratios in church hospitals and kindergartens are often better than in state ones, perhaps because employees feel more sense of dedication. Party members have no shame or compunction, or fear of adverse comment from their colleagues, if they use these church facilities. A young couple in Leipzig – he is party secretary in his university faculty – told me their child went to a Christian kindergarten because they found that at the state one, which incidentally was nearer, the child 'was not being treated gently enough'. An elderly SED loyalist said she wanted to buy a picture Bible for her grandson so that he at least knew the stories that were so important a part of the Western tradition. A senior party journalist, himself a Jew, was shocked, he told me, that on a recent visit to Naumburg cathedral (the site of some splendid medieval stone carvings) his children revealed a deep ignorance of Christian history.

Clashes between church and state in the GDR have of course occurred, and even today there are many points of friction. For many years the main source of conflict was one of symbol rather than substance. Ulbricht was angry that the German Protestant church in East and West remained united. Only in 1969 with the founding of the Federation of Protestant Churches of the GDR, twenty years after the GDR came into existence, did the church accept the reality of two German states and the conflict ended. Although the authorities wanted a formal split between the churches in East and West, they accepted the continuation of financial links between them. Some of the money for keeping up church-run hospitals and church buildings is sent by congregations in the West. The Roman Catholic Church, which has the nominal support of about 8 per cent of the population, has taken a more conservative line than the Protestants on church–state relations. It has reached a compromise under which it maintains a virtually complete silence on political issues, neither criticising nor supporting the state. In return it is allowed to continue running its internal affairs. The Protestants have been more outspoken and have suffered more. In 1976 the Catholic Primate of East Germany, Alfred Cardinal Bengsch was even allowed to buy a West German organ worth almost one million marks for St Hedwig's Cathedral in East Berlin. In a deal which was never mentioned in the East German press the GDR foreign trade ministry released half that amount in hard currency to let the church import it.

Although half the population still called itself Protestant in 1968, and must go on paying tax to the church, few worship regularly. The church is worried at the sharp fall in the number of confirmations. The church still performs more than half the GDR's funerals, but the clergy find little cause for encouragement in that. Baptisms and church weddings are fewer. One reason is the general trend towards secularisation common to most industrial societies. Another is the undoubted element of harassment which the state practises against individual Christians in spite of official tolerance of Christianity in general. The clergy have problems in getting sites for new churches. Practising Christians cannot expect to get leading posts in industry, the state administration, the universities, or schools. Sometimes Christians cannot even get admission to university as students. In reply to this the church has decided not to set itself up in opposition to the Government or 'to retreat into cultic observance and pietism, thus becoming marginal', as Beeson puts it. He goes on to write that its position of 'critical solidarity' with the state means 'accepting responsibility for the proper ordering of society and at the same time retaining its right to evaluate the actions of Governments and individuals in the light of the Gospel'.

This form of critical solidarity is not the same as that of the

CDU, with which very few prominent clergymen identify. Although the CDU has occasionally challenged SED proposals (see the previous chapter for its opposition to abortion law reform) church leaders consider it has identified itself too closely with the state. The CDU's official role is to speak for 'socialist citizens of the Christian faith', a formulation which the SED only conceded in the early 1970s. In practice, as Wolfgang Heyl, the chairman of its parliamentary group, told me, it is 'to bring Christians into line with socialism'. Many of the clergy feel this is one-sided. They would like the SED to come some way to meet the church.

One of the smallest religious communities must be mentioned. Its symbolic importance far outweighs its numbers. The practising Jewish community of 1,100 people is all that remains of a group that was once the most assimilated in Europe. Buchenwald, Ravensbrück and Sachsenhausen are on the soil of what is now the GDR and they did their horrifying work all too efficiently. East Berlin now has a community of only 650 Jews. Leipzig, once a centre for 18,000 Jews, has 100, Dresden 45, Schwerin 6. Nine out of every ten members is more than 55 years old. The community may soon die away. The last Chief Rabbi Dr Martin Riesenburger was awarded the GDR's Order of Merit. Since his death in 1965 the community has had no rabbi of its own, but is served by one who occasionally comes from Budapest. The state can afford to be generous to these few pathetic survivors. It has paid for the rebuilding of eight synagogues in Berlin, Dresden, Erfurt, Halle, Karl-Marx-Stadt, Leipzig, Magdeburg and Schwerin. It has repaired the Jewish cemeteries. The state pays Jewish survivors the same special pensions which all victims of Nazi persecution get, regardless of race or ethnic origin. This is worth 600 Marks a month.

The GDR's subsidies to the Jewish community are not conscience money paid out quietly on the side. They form an integral part of the SED's ideology and are designed to reinforce the point that the GDR has eradicated Fascism. Government representatives appear regularly at Jewish memorial services and there are frequent exchanges of greetings telegrams between the Jewish community and the Government. Some religious Jews are unhappy about the SED's foreign policy of strong opposition to Zionism. They were upset that private citizens who offered the Jewish community clothes and other help during the Six-Day war in 1967 had to be discouraged officially at the party's insistence. They would like a more varied discussion of Israel in the media. But for every practising Jew there are two Jewish anti-Zionists in the GDR, mostly in senior positions, who support the current party line. Some of them were briefly threatened by a rash of anti-Semitism in the early 1950s during the last days of Stalin (see Ch. 5) but in general the SED has been much more careful in drawing the line between anti-Semitism and anti-Zionism than anywhere else in Eastern Europe. The German Jewish Communists now feel totally integrated. Kurt Kohn, a former deputy public prosecutor, was a member of the Czechoslovak Communist party who spent the war in England. He recalls that when he returned to his native town in the Sudetenland, no one, not even the local Czech Communists, wanted to give him a job. To them he was a German. He moved to Dresden and made a successful career in the GDR.

The GDR has published several best-selling books on anti-Semitism. It has produced records of folk-songs in Hebrew and Yiddish. Some of the first post-war films dealt with Jewish issues, and the GDR is still making new ones on the same subject for a new generation. The latest film 'Jacob the Liar' came out in 1975 and achieved critical acclaim at the West Berlin Film Festival. Admittedly, this film was only produced at the second attempt. Its author Jurek Becker, himself a survivor of the Lodz ghetto, first wrote the script in 1965. After three years of fruitless waiting he decided to make a book of the non-film. The Aufbau Verlag published it. Five years later Becker felt the time was ripe for another try. His success with the film in 1975 was another sign of the gradual thaw in the cultural field which became evident from the end of 1971.

Ever since the great clashes over de-Stalinisation in 1956 the cultural intelligentsia had been held back. It did not matter that most of them wanted nothing more than the kind of 'critical solidarity' with the party which the church had achieved in a different context. Ulbricht wanted uncritical solidarity pure and simple. With his advent to power in 1971 Honecker seemed to be foreshadowing a new policy. He told the central committee in December that year that provided works were based on socialism there would be 'no taboos' in the field of art and literature, either in style or content. It was appropriate that Honecker should be the one to say this. In 1965 as Ulbricht's deputy, Honecker had made a sharp personal attack on the writer Stefan Heym at a central committee plenum which criticised the entire intelligentsia. Eight years later true to his new line Honecker allowed Heym to bring out of his desk drawer and publish a witty anti-Stalinist novel, *The King David Report*. In the same year the poet Reiner Kunze emerged from silence and Hermann Kant had a new novel on sale. The literary magazine, *Sinn und Form*, began to promote livelier discussions than had been allowed for a decade and a half. Plenzdorf's play *The New Sorrows of Young W* came out and there were a number of new and unconventional films. *The Third One* in 1972 and *The Legend of Paul and Paula* in 1973 had the common feature that they both dealt with contemporary themes of love, marriage, and extra-marital sex, and concentrated on an individual's search for private happiness.

Earlier the party had gradually allowed the Berlin cabaret *The Thistle* (*Die Distel*) more room for manoeuvre. It has long been standard East European practice to have one recognised humorous outlet, usually in the form of a weekly satirical journal. The model is Moscow's *Krokodil* which is allowed to poke fun at certain social excesses – the mindless bureaucrat, the clumsy planner, the computer whizz-kid, the boring public speaker and so on. East Germany's version is *Eulenspiegel* which has branched out in recent years into some genuine local muck-raking, uncovering poor amenities, social problems, or bureaucratic incompetence in this town or that. There are well-defined limits on what is out of bounds. Foreign policy, the inadequacy of internal debate, and hypocrisy at the top level of the party leadership are not touched on. But perhaps because it deals with the spoken word *Die Distel* has pushed further at the margins. The 1975 summer show included a number criticising the dreary style of political reporting in which meetings are obscured behind opaque jargon-ridden communiqués telling you everything from who was there to how long the meeting lasted and not forgetting to describe the atmosphere of the talks (frank, comradely, marked by complete unanimity, or whatever). The only thing the reader does not learn is what each side said. Another sketch raised the previously closed subject of travel to the West. A football team was being chosen for a match in West Germany. 'Why is everyone in the team over 65? How can they hope to win?' someone innocently asks. 'They can't but no one younger can get a passport.' It is hard to get tickets to *Die Distel*. The audience that roars at this and other quips is in many ways an in-group in GDR society, though a cross-section of all ages. Their laughter and the tone of the whole show are marked by a feeling of affectionate self-ridicule. It is neither hostile nor bitter. This is the GDR laughing at itself—and a big step forward from the 1950s.

If *Eulenspiegel* and *Die Distel* are in some ways court jesters, licensed to entertain within the system for 95 per cent of the time, though given a fleeting chance for heterodoxy, the party is more nervous about lone intellectuals. It is afraid that one of them may go further than the court jesters and suddenly call out in simulated innocence that the Emperor has no clothes. One who did so was Wolf Biermann. Since 1965 this poet, guitarist, and cabaret singer has been banned from publishing or performing in the GDR. A convinced Marxist, he felt that many of his convictions and principles had been betrayed. About the Wall he wrote: 'I don't want the GDR just to disappear, and I certainly don't want discontented young people to clear out, for they are valuable for any society. We shouldn't pull the wall down just as soon as the GDR has as many cheap cars as the West, but when there's something here in which people can drive a whole lot better—socialist democracy.'[10] Biting, ironic and full of insight into hypocrisy and cant Biermann's poems express a similar disappointment in sharper style. His position in the GDR was fraught with irony. His Berlin flat on the corner of the Chausseestrasse was less than fifty yards from the grave of his hero Brecht and little more than twice that distance from the Wall which for a long time he dared not cross but which the authorities wanted him to cross for ever. He would not go. After 1974 the irony thickened. Right across the street from his flat the Federal Republic built its permanent mission in the GDR, the diplomatic representation of a nation whose people are the only Germans able to buy and hear on record Biermann's energetic and plaintive songs.

The SED still draws the line at Biermann. And it still draws it at Stefan Heym's latest book *Five Days in June*. For twenty years Heym wrote and re-wrote the book, a kind of document with actors about the events of June 1953. Set against the mass wave of strikes, Heym tries to piece together the true story of what happened through the lives of fictional characters. His conclusion conforms to the received wisdom of neither East nor West – a worker's revolt, yes, but with strong elements of provocation from the West as well. Heym's book was finally published in West Germany in 1975. The GDR authorities rejected it. As for Wolf Biermann, in November 1976 they took their chance when he went to West Germany for a concert tour, leaving his wife and child behind. The GDR Government stripped him of his citizenship and refused him readmission. It was an opportunity for which they had been waiting for years, and which Biermann sensed. For a long time he refused all invitations to visit the West just in case he was not allowed to return. Why he accepted this invitation is not clear. In any event the authorities probably did not anticipate the reaction from his friends. Thirteen of the country's most prominent writers protested publicly, including Stefan Heym and Jurek Becker. They chose conciliatory language. Biermann might have been an 'uncomfortable poet' but a socialist society ought to be able to accommodate him better than more anarchic societies, they argued. It was no use. Becker was expelled from the SED and along with Ulrich Plenzdorf and several others, was removed from the board of the Writers' Union. The sudden clampdown marked the end of the modest cultural thaw in which writers had been basking since Ulbricht's retirement. The party leadership made it clear that it likes criticism least when it comes from disappointed loyalists, from the Left rather than the Right, from those whose solidarity has become too critical. Other forms of 'privatisation' are now acceptable. The 'privatisation' of independent criticism is the most anti-social activity of all.

9

Social Services from Cradle to Grave

In spite of grave official concern at the continual fall in the birth-rate, the GDR brought in one of the world's most liberal abortion laws in 1972. At the same time it made the pill available free of charge to any woman of sixteen or over. With these two moves the GDR can justifiably claim to have adopted an outstandingly progressive policy on motherhood. It is also one of the safest places to be born. The infant mortality rate has plummeted from 72 per 1,000 live births in 1950 to 18 per 1,000 in 1973 (in West Germany it is 23 per 1,000). The authorities decided that safety, proper hygiene, and genuinely planned families overrode their fears that the birth-rate might fall even lower. The crude argument that a high birth-rate can be encouraged by limiting women's rights was unacceptable. From 1965 onwards the GDR had already had a moderately liberal policy on abortion. Pregnant women under sixteen, or over forty, or with more than four children could go before commissions of social workers and doctors for permission to have an abortion on social or psychological grounds. Under the new law abortion is available on demand. Not only is it free but patients stay for five days in hospital, get sick leave for another ten to fifteen days thereafter, and are on sick pay the whole time.

Dr Helga Rayner, the head of the Ministry of Health's family planning department, has said that the main reason for liberalised abortion was the high number of illegal operations.[1] Before 1972 hospitals dealt with 55,000 cases a year, including women who rushed bleeding to doctors for emergency treatment after getting a botched-up back-street job. The Ministry estimated that more than 100,000 abortions took place illegally a year. In the first year of the new law hospitals dealt with 119,000 cases and by 1974 it had dropped to 99,000. Previously around 30 women died every year. In 1973 it was only four.[2] The new law met opposition from some religious circles (see Ch. 7), and from a few doctors who considered it was an invasion of their professional competence if women were to have the last word on whether or not to have an abortion. Doctors with reasons of conscience for not themselves performing an abortion can withdraw but they are obliged by law to pass the patient on to another doctor. Dr Rayner says that about 4 per cent of all abortions are performed on girls between 15 and 18. 'This is not a high proportion and is the answer to those who predicted that the abortion law would lead to a "collapse of morals".'[3]

The new provisions for free contraceptive pills were meant to discourage people from looking on abortion as a form of contraception of last resort. The pill had an enormous boom – from 4·4 million packets distributed in 1970 to eleven million four years later. Almost as though it was a reward for their liberalism, a year and a half after the change in the law officials had the welcome surprise of the first rise in the birth-rate for several years. It was only slight, and it is still not clear whether the trend it reflects has become established. The main reason for the decline since 1964 had been purely demographic. The effects of Hitler's war were being visited on the next generation. The small number of babies born in the last years of the war meant a correspondingly small number of parents twenty years later. For the GDR it is a serious matter since in 1973 only 53 per cent of the population were of working age. Every worker had to feed one extra person, and pay for his or her social security. For the industrialised world the GDR's demographic structure is unusually unfavourable. The prospect is that it will go on getting worse before it gets better. Other reasons for the low birth-rate were the increasing proportion of working women with careers which they were unwilling to interrupt. Cramped housing conditions may also have been a factor that deterred couples from having more than one child.

In 1972 soon after the abortion law the GDR brought in a series of welfare measures to help to encourage parenthood. It was these no doubt which must have caused a slight increase in the birth-rate from its low point of 10·6 births per 1,000 inhabitants in 1972. Working mothers with two children or more got longer paid holidays. Universities and colleges were required to make special arrangements for student mothers to extend their courses and take examinations later. Paid pregnancy leave was lengthened from twelve to eighteen weeks, and the grant for the birth of a child was increased to 1,000 Marks. (In order to persuade people to have regular check-ups it was made conditional on mothers making at least two visits before the birth and four afterwards to a local mother-and-baby clinic.) Single women with children who for any reason cannot find a place for their baby in a crèche or kindergarten get the right to a benefit of at least 250 Marks a month.

It was unlikely that many single mothers would need this. They have priority in the queue, and the GDR is in the forefront of European countries in the supply of pre-school facilities for children. As the East German child grows up and goes through life he will find that the standard of public services gradually declines. On maturity the problem of housing will hit him. When he becomes a pensioner he will be in a very poor position indeed. In the first few years of his life he can have few complaints against an unusually generous welfare state. Almost half the country's children under three go to crèches during the day. In 1974 there were 403 places for every 1,000 children. The availability of kindergarten places for the 3-, 4-, and 5-year-olds was more than 800 per 1,000. This means that almost every family which wants a kindergarten place for its child can find one. It costs 35 Pfennigs a day, including lunch. The crèche costs between 60 and 90 Pfennigs a day.

The practical explanation for this very full pre-school provision is that the GDR authorities desperately want as many women as possible to work. With its static population the country needs as big a labour force as possible if its output is to grow. There are educational and ideological motives too. The party believes that children should become accustomed to collective living as early as possible. This is thought to be particularly important in one-child families where there are dangers of parental over-protection and which are common in the GDR. Crèches and kindergartens are also considered better for a child's physical health. Not all parents agree. Some have marked preferences for one kindergarten over another, and move their children around. Every mother has the right to stay at home for the child's first year and still retain her job. Some mothers take advantage of this right out of anxiety about the staff ration in the crèches. When I put this point to Heidi Bieske, director of 'Kombinat Fischer-Insel I' in Berlin, she said she knew the feeling and could understand it. But it was a prejudice, particularly common among mothers who have just had their first child. In her crèche, there were 100 infants, aged from three months to three years. They were divided into groups of twenty each with two rooms, a playroom and an airy dormitory crammed with white-painted cots. Three women looked after each group, making a ratio of roughly six or seven babies for each adult. Although the crèche is open from six in the morning until seven at night for the convenience of parents, depending on their working hours, by law no child can stay more than ten hours a day in the crèche.

Frau Bieske believes her staff ratio is adequate, especially as she says that the idea is not that the staff should develop so full a relationship with the child that they become mother-substitutes. Parents see their children in the evening and at weekends. (For a very small proportion of children whose parents have awkward shift times or whose work takes them out of town, there are dormitory crèches where children sleep over at night during the week. The authorities discourage it. Central Berlin has only one such dormitory.) Frau Bieske does point out, perhaps in implicit answer to critics, that there has been a shift in crèche staff in recent years. They used to be mainly nurses. Now they have to have at least three years' training in education and child psychology.

At the age of three children go on to the kindergarten. The 'Kombinat', as its name implies, has both departments under one roof. The kindergarten teachers make regular visits to the 2-year-olds in the crèche section so that the transition when it comes is as smooth as possible. The Kombinat idea is new and they are still rare. In Berlin's central school district there are sixty kindergartens, about thirty crèches and seven combined units. In the kindergartens the staff ratio rises. In Frau Bieske's there are ten women for 210 children.

School proper begins at six, and lasts in general for ten years. With its system of free, comprehensive, and mixed-sex schools where children stay without any intervening selection or segregation until they leave as adolescents, the SED believes it has fulfilled the dream of generations of progressive German educationalists. The 1965 Education Act proudly boasts: 'The socialist education system is a whole historical era in advance of that of West Germany.' The GDR's lead, the West German magazine *Der Spiegel* conceded in April 1974,

> can be measured. In proportion to the population the GDR has 70 per cent more teachers than the Federal Republic. Eighty-five per cent of the pupils complete a tenth year at the general polytechnic school, the GDR's standard type (which is still a long range target in the FRG). Ninety-nine per cent of all GDR school-leavers learn a profession or trade; in the Federal Republic 10 per cent stay without training. The GDR invests more than 7 per cent of its GNP in education, a sum which is only a target for the 1980s in the FRG (today it is 5 per cent). Out of every thousand people between 18 and 45, seventeen were attending a polytechnical college or university compared with four-teen in West Germany. Student numbers in the GDR jumped from 280,000 in 1965 to 390,000 in 1972. People already in jobs can go on learning. About 168,000 GDR citizens are taking correspondence courses at training colleges or universities or are in evening classes. The statistics of success also make clear the increasing equality of women. In 1972 more than half the students at technical colleges were women, and at universities more than a third. In the Federal Republic only about 25 per cent of the students are women.[4]

The GDR's school system is a combination of the model advocated by many German reformers plus later Soviet additions. The first stage after the war was the abolition of all private schools and church schools. Success was meant to be ensured for the comprehensives by getting rid of all other schools which might 'cream off' the best pupils. The working class was to have complete equality of opportunity. Former Nazis were purged from the teaching profession and the schools came under complete state control. 'The old teachers were buttoned-up, stiff, and middle class, with no understanding of workers' children', according to Dr Alfred Bornkamp, the information spokesman of the teachers' association 'House of the Teacher'. 'We wanted to extend the humanistic and democratic traditions of German education to all children', he told me. The old Volksschule and the fee-paying Mittelschule were combined into an eight-year elementary school, the Grundschule. In 1958 the GDR followed Khrushchev's introduction of the Poly-technical school in the Soviet Union. The idea here was to educate children 'for life itself' by acquainting them with the practicalities of the socialist economy, and with production work. It was to be done 'by linking learning with doing'. Gradually too, the school-leaving age was raised until in 1965 the new Education Act made ten-year schooling compulsory.

Every East German child now attends the same kind of school for ten years. Only in the last two years is there any streaming according to ability. From the fifth year the first foreign language training begins with Russian. From the seventh year poly-technic instruction starts although even before that children have had one hour a week in the garden which is attached to every school. Once a week, children of thirteen and over have a 'day of instruction in production'. Each school is linked either to a nearby agricultural co-operative or to a factory. The 13- and 14-year-olds have three hours there, and the older children five hours. It is a combination of theoretical teaching, experi-ments, and actual productive work. The work done in the factories or on the farms is meant to be instructive. To avoid abuse of children as simply cheap labour, there is no provision for it in the plant's annual plan. In fact where there have been complaints about it, they have been on the grounds that factory managers do not integrate the children into the plant enough but sometimes tend to see the whole exercise of a 'day of instruc-tion in production' as an irritating diversion of time and resources. Children learn simple mechanical processes and basic applications of chemistry, electronics and physics. Polytechnic education is geared to helping the state with planning its future labour requirements. The state guarantees every school-leaver either a place in further education or a job, and wants to ensure that the demand for jobs matches the supply. Even without the 'day of instruction in production' it is remarkable how much of the GDR schoolchild's week is taken up with technical subjects, certainly much more than most Western children have. The GDR's planners have decided that the economy needs technically trained people. The 36-hour week for final-year pupils consists of five hours of history, geography and civics, four of German, three of Russian, two of physical training, one of music and an astonishing sixteen hours of science and mathematics in addition to the five hours of polytechnical instruction.

'The educational value of work was discovered long before our day', one East German publication put it.[5] 'It was put forward, for example, by the great Swiss educationalist Pestalozzi who lived from 1746 to 1827. In the GDR work is brought into the educational process as part of the contemporary technical, economic, and social complex ... Through direct participation in productive work the pupil becomes conscious of reality and of the value of what he has learned and what he has still to learn. He then finds that school and work as an occupation are no longer separate categories or areas of life that simply follow one another in time but that the relationship between them makes learning an authentic task in life from the very beginning. He does not suddenly "end" school and enter something beyond and outside school called "life". If the pupil has taken concrete responsibility in the work process – no matter how simple at the outset – and has had the opportunity to perfect himself in it, he grows into the future more gradually and without a break, and with a full sense of responsibility as a co-owner of his plant and co-ruler of his state.'

Like most educational theories the polytechnic idea works somewhat less well in practice. Some children probably see it as just a break from class work, others as a waste of time. But it cannot help having some effect in teaching children the value of possessing skills in an industrial world. Those children who are going to end up in white-collar jobs at least have a chance to see that factory workers are people.

Outside school, children have an extra dimension of ideological education through membership in the Pioneers. Around two million children belong to the organisation. From six to eight they are 'Young Pioneers' and after that 'Thälmann

Pioneers'. The organisation is the successor of the pre-war KPD youth groups and now embraces 80 per cent of the age group from eight to fourteen. The SED sees the Pioneers as a vital socialising influence, and does not allow even the controlled forms of pluralism which are tolerated for adult society. None of the other parties has any youth organisation nor do the churches. From their motto 'Always Prepared' to many of their activities the Pioneers look and sound like a co-educational version of Boy Scouts or Girl Guides. But they have a more political role. A steady flow of Pioneer groups makes the pilgrimage to Buchenwald to the memorial place for their murdered patron, Ernst Thälmann. A favoured few travel abroad. On a recent summer Sunday among the handwritten notes and tributes at the foot of Karl Marx's grave in Highgate Cemetery in London there was a large and official-looking wreath from a 'Pioneer delegation from the German Democratic Republic'.

The SED wants to project rival heroes for East German children as a substitute for the cowboy or detective idols of Western children. Besides 'fathers' of German Communism there are more easily identifiable figures like Fritz Weineck, the 'little red trumpeter' shot by an anti-Communist policeman in Halle in 1925. The Pioneers prepare children for entry into the FDJ and then for the party itself. The SED's resolution for the 1975/76 school-year imposed several 'tasks' on the Pioneers and the FDJ. It was the year of the Ninth party congress. In its honour and in preparation for the imminent 100th anniversary of Wilhelm Pieck's birth and the 90th anniversary of Ernst Thälmann's, 'every boy and girl must be given deep impressions of the lives and struggles of past and present Communists and be taught to shape their own lives in the image of Communists'. Pioneers and FDJ members needed to be made more conscious that the FDJ 'always stood on the side of the party comrades as a faithful helper'. Pioneers must be given 'pride in our socialist fatherland and eagerness to perform useful service for socialism'. One of the main places for teaching these lessons is the annual Pioneer camp. Thousands of children spend three weeks every summer at one of the organisation's fifty holiday camps. They have a busy programme, concentrating heavily on collective activities and competitions between different grades for the best nature study programmes, the best wall newspaper, the tidiest dormitory and so on. Back home again, Pioneers are meant to learn the same virtues in collective civic projects. They tidy the grounds of blocks of flats, organise drives to collect up waste-paper, and visit old people.

At the age of fourteen nearly every child in the GDR prepares for 'Jugendweihe', the youth dedication ceremony. It is an old ceremony which goes back to the turn of the century when the SPD started the idea of a non-religious initiation rite to replace Christian confirmation or the Jewish Bar Mitzvah. Revived in 1954, it was attended in 1975 by 279,000 children or more than 90 per cent of the age group. The ceremony is as 'voluntary' as pre-war confirmation. The churches originally tried to oppose it by refusing to confirm children who had gone through a Jugendweihe, but they soon had to surrender. In a parish of 35,000 people in the northern part of Berlin, only 21 children were confirmed in 1974 and all but one of them had also had a Jugendweihe. It is preceded by ten special classes, which include political discussions as well as several visits to factories, farms, museums and theatres. The ceremony itself takes place in cinemas, school halls or factories. It consists of a solemn processional entry, a formal address, and the presentation of a document and a book. As with traditional initiation ceremonies, parents of the children coming out give parties afterwards for friends and relations. Old habits die hard, and these are often little more than status symbols. To considerable teasing by his colleagues, one journalist admitted to me that he had spent 600 Marks for a reception at the GDR capital's luxury hotel, the Stadt Berlin, for his son's Jugendweihe.

Far more important for most adolescents is the decision two years later on whether to go to university, and how to get in. The party's constant campaign to encourage people to gain extra qualifications has combined with the deep German respect for education. It produces tremendous pressure on scarce university places and undermines the party's other ideological goal of creating equal respect for manual work. The newspaper *Berliner Zeitung* recently asked its readers 'How does one instil the desire to be a production worker?.' A reader replied that everywhere parents wanted a university education for their children. 'Soon we shall be a poor nation of professors.'[6] It is not that production workers are paid much worse than white-collar people or that they have no social status. The East German media are always praising individual workers who have done well. The problem goes deeper. The GDR's social revolution has eliminated the property-owning bourgeoisie but created a meritocracy in which an individual's performance is the criterion by which he or she is judged. It is easier to satisfy that criterion for oneself and in other people's eyes by getting a paper qualification.

'Over-education' is now officially recognised as a problem. First there is the question of social justice. One of the SED's main boasts early on was that it would provide working-class children with an equal chance for higher education. In the late 1940s quotas and restrictions were imposed on middle-class parents and their children. Special 'Workers' and Peasants' Faculties' were opened in October 1949 for bright young workers who had left school at the age of 14. These faculties gave intensive courses to enable workers to get into university and gradually raised the percentage of students from working-class and peasant backgrounds. By 1950 the proportion had crept up from its pre-war figure of 3 per cent to 38 per cent. In 1960 it reached 50·3 per cent. But all except two of the Workers' and Peasants' Faculties were closed in the early 1960s. After that the proportion of working-class children began to drop again. In 1967 it was down to 38·2 per cent. And even that figure may overstate the number of working-class children now that a new generation of the intelligentsia has emerged which likes to describe its children as working-class even though they now live in white-collar households. (Even taking a conservative estimate of the true number of working-class children, the chances in the GDR were at least as good as, and probably better than, those in the best countries in Western Europe. The Organisation for Economic Co-operation and Development attempted to measure the wide differences in various Western countries. They concluded that the relative chances of what they called 'upper stratum' and 'lower stratum' youth studying in a university were five to one in England and Wales in 1970, twenty-eight to one in France in 1968, and forty-eight to one in West Germany.[7])

The other problem with the drive for higher education is that the GDR is training too many people for highly skilled work. Graduates find that they cannot all get jobs which meet their qualifications, and they get resentful. The economy is already short of labour and cannot afford to over-educate its citizens. Since the late 1960s the authorities have put a ceiling on student numbers. They abandoned plans for an advanced chemical research centre. One result of the cutback is that university entrance has become even more tense for the individual, and harder for working-class children. Better off families can afford private tutoring for their children to give them a headstart in the entrance examinations. At the 'House of the Teacher', the teachers' headquarters, officials put some of the blame on the extra two years of optional schooling available when a boy or girl is sixteen. Although the GDR has no selection of pupils before that age, it comes in when the adolescent is sixteen. Until recently it came in at fourteen. After the eighth grade some pupils went into special preparatory classes which qualified them two years later for two more years at an 'extended secondary school'. This was the vital hurdle for university. Nowadays selection at 13 plus has largely given way but it still remains at 15 plus with the decision on which pupils are to go on to the 'extended school'. Those who leave school still have the chance of university entrance if they take a three-year course of 'professional training plus matriculation', that is, technical training leading to the 'Abitur', the examination which university applicants have to take. This method is harder and requires more concentration than the two-year course at school.

School-leavers who are forced or opt out of the race for university have two years of vocational training as apprentices. The GDR has been wisely cutting down the number of available trades in order to prepare people for a rapidly changing economy in which one skill may become obsolete during a person's working life. From 972 highly specialised craft vocations registered in 1957, the number was reduced to 306 by 1972. Roughly thirty basic vocations, such as cutting-machine operator, electronic technician, and chemical worker, have been established. Apprentices spend eighteen months on these before specialising for the last six months. This period is short (a year less than the norm in West Germany) but the GDR authorities argue that teenagers have already had a good grounding through polytechnical training in school.

The East German teenager who manages to get to university has no easy time of it there. Students are subjected to many of the same pressures which have brought student radicals in the West out on to the streets in protest. Universities in the GDR make no apology for serving the interests of an industrial society, and closely following employers' wishes. Many of the courses are linked to local industry. Eighty per cent of research at the university of Jena, for example, is done for the optical firm, Carl Zeiss. The technical university at Magdeburg has a dozen contracts with local firms. University courses are highly exam-orientated and attendance at lectures is compulsory. During the vacations students have periods of practical work in factories, or help out on building sites. Student life is a long way from the old German idyll of leisurely academic inquiry often lasting for six or seven years before the necessity of taking an exam. The Alma Mater is now unashamedly a learning factory with close links to the demands of the economy. Many students find it tough going, but the authorities argue that it is acceptable for universities to be subordinate to society's immediate needs if that society has become integrated and serves socialist goals.

Whether as students or apprentices young East Germans face a difficult housing problem. About a quarter of all apprentices live in hostels; a few are at the financial mercy of private landlords as lodgers, but most live with their parents. Students usually live four to a room in hostels or else with their parents. The housing stock has almost no provision for self-contained bedsitters or flats shared by several young people. Married couples can at least apply for their own flat and have a chance of getting one within a few years, depending on the city where they live. In Eisenhüttenstadt, which is in many ways one of the GDR's model cities, the wait is between two and three years. As students, however, married couples have the right to get a single room at once.

The chance of escaping the worst of the housing shortage may explain an interesting paradox in the GDR. In spite of the great drive for further education, and the stress on women having careers, people in the GDR are getting married at a younger age than Germans ever have, on average at 21·3 years old for women and 23·3 for men (according to figures for 1971).[8] This is roughly two years younger than the figures for first marriages in 1951 and a year and a half younger than the comparable figure for West Germany. In almost all young households in the GDR the wife also works. Society takes a dim view of non-working wives and mothers. Even where the husband has a relatively high income, the wife is expected to take a job. An 18-year-old girl recently wrote to the advice column of the young people's paper *Junge Welt* asking if she should 'drop out' of her apprenticeship for the next two years until the baby she was expecting from her fiancé was older. She was given a forthright reply: 'We expect more today from an 18-year-old girl than taking refuge in having babies and being "married comfortably" with a husband who makes enough money. Personal and social thoughtlessness coincide here ... If a girl of your age, and your stage of training and economic dependence wants to have a baby with all her might then this shows that she has either been seduced by a family idyll which no longer accords with the social atmosphere, or she has simply not thought things out enough. Your husband's salary may provide a guarantee for your marriage and your personal life, but as you know money alone does not make people happy, and even less so if you earn not a penny of it yourself. Training and a job are not only a means to obtain financial security but also foster the equality of wife and husband, mutual recognition and respect and the intellectual atmosphere of a marriage. The best way to prepare for your baby and your marriage is to take a clear decision on your future. You should discuss this with your parents, your fiancé, and your teachers. But you can only expect understanding and help from them if you make proposals that show you do not simply want to lead a comfortable life.'[9]

Although that reply represented the official point of view on working wives, there is little doubt that it is widely shared by ordinary people. The old German principle that the woman should attend to the three Ks – Kinder, Kirche, Küche (children, church and kitchen) – is dead. In the early post-war years many women may have gone out to work mainly to increase the family's income. Over the years attitudes have changed. The vast majority of women in the GDR work because they want the satisfaction of a job outside the home. In 1960 two out of every three women of working age had jobs. By 1973 it was 84 per cent. Put another way, nearly half the total workforce were women (whereas in West Germany they formed only 37 per cent of the workforce in 1971). Women frequently do jobs which in Britain and the United States are almost invariably done by men. They drive buses and cranes. They are judges and surgeons. On a collective farm near the Polish frontier I saw two huge combine harvesters in the same field, one driven by a man, the other by his wife. Increasingly East German women expect and are getting opportunities for promotion on a level with men. There are still problems. The party leader Erich Honecker has admitted that it is easier to decree equality than implement it. 'It is one of the great achievements of socialism', he has said, 'to have brought about the equality of women in our state both legally and to a great extent in practice.'[10]

Women are most nearly on a par with men in the judiciary. In 1973 45 per cent of lay judges were women, and 36 per cent were professional judges. Among trade union officials 44 per cent were women. In local Government and the People's Chamber roughly one out of every three deputies is a woman. Women are less well represented at the top. Although they provided almost half the party's membership, only one woman, Inge Lange, is among the twenty-three members and candidate members of the Politbüro. The Minister of Education, Dr Margot Honecker, wife of the party secretary, is the only female member of the Government. Roughly 60 per cent of the country's teachers are women, but they fill only a quarter of the headships in schools. These statistics show that full equality is some way off. However, they are still on a rising trend, and are better than most countries in the West. They probably reflect not so much continuing discrimination as the fact that women have so far had a harder time getting further education and specialisation. In 1967 the Government brought in special courses for working women, and a scheme whereby factories will supplement a woman's scholarship by up to 80 per cent of her previous net salary while she studies.

Old habits die hardest in the home. The young East German couple may divide the household chores no differently from its parents even though the wife now has a job. An East German survey showed that women now have the problem of the 'second shift'.[11] They come home from work as tired as the man, but then have to take the major responsibility for shopping, cooking, cleaning and the laundry. According to the survey which came out in 1968 women spent an average of 47·6 hours a week on housework while men spent about seven hours. The full breakdown of the division of labour was as shown in Table 3.

Table 3

Type of work	in % of time		
	Wife	Husband	Miscellaneous*
Meal preparation	84·2	6·8	12·0
House cleaning	78·8	12·5	9·0
Laundry	89·7	2·9	7·4
Shopping	76·5	11·8	11·7

* 'Miscellaneous' is work performed by some other person.

Facts like these help to account for the unusually high divorce rate in the GDR. Women are conscious of their increasing social role outside the home and are not prepared to tolerate inequality within it. Similarly some men feel threatened by their wives' careers, especially when the wife has a better job than the man. With tensions on both sides it is a tribute to the extent of women's liberation that women have enough economic independence to be ready to seek a divorce. An important study of divorce in the GDR published in the legal journal *Neue Justiz* in 1974 disclosed that the percentage of women initiating divorces was rising.[12] In 1964 they took the initiative in 58·3 of the cases. By 1972 it was up to 64·8 per cent which means that two out of every three divorces were demanded by wives. Divorce is easy. If both sides agree, it takes only three weeks after a joint application. For a student couple the divorce costs seventy Marks each. For a working couple the costs are a proportion of each person's earnings. After the applications have been made, a couple's workmates often attempt to effect a reconciliation. In a third of the applications filed, the marriage is repaired. But the

East German authorities believe that if reconciliation fails, there is no point in delaying divorce. The article in *Neue Justiz*, by Professor Richard Halgasch of the department of law at Jena University and Dr Kurt Lungwitz of the bureau of state statistics, gave an interesting list of reasons for the breakdown of marriages. According to figures supplied by the courts in 1972 extra-marital sex was the cause in 22 per cent of cases, incompatibility in 14·4 per cent, drinking in 10·4 per cent, sexual disharmony in 10 per cent, violence in 9·3 per cent, and over-hasty marriage in 6·5 per cent. Other reasons named with some regularity included the negative influence of third parties (usually the in-laws), disagreement about the education of the children and financial difficulties. Halgasch and Lungwitz conclude that increasing sexual equality is behind many divorces. 'Cases are relatively frequent in which extra-marital relations are established at the place of work.' Women are increasingly responsible. In 1958 the courts ruled that 65 per cent of marriages which broke down through infidelity were due to the husband, 19 per cent to the wife and 16 per cent to both. Ten years later there had been a noticeable change: in 56 per cent of the cases the husband's infidelity was the cause, in 31 per cent the wife's and in 13 per cent both. Halgasch and Lungwitz claim that the factor of sexual disharmony is growing because women too demand their right to sexual fulfilment now. 'It is probable that sexual relations will continue to play a growing part in divorce applications. Very often the basis for sexual disharmony lies in outdated views which disregard the woman's personality and sexual needs.'

A very high proportion of divorces occur in marriages which have not lasted long. The highest rate is in the second, third and fourth years of the marriages. Where divorces involve children, the court gives custody in the vast majority of cases (93·2 per cent in 1972) to the mother. The comparatively young age of many married couples also plays a part. 'Premature and unconsidered marriage on the part of young people is often the result of insufficient preparation for marriage and family', the two academics state. 'Parents, state bodies, and social organisations have the responsibility of helping young people to develop into socialist personalities and prepare themselves for marriage and raising a family.'

Earlier in this chapter it was suggested that cramped housing conditions may push some young people into hasty marriages, either as a way of allowing them to apply for a flat or to get parental approval for their living together. As in other countries East German parents are not always willing to let their unmarried children sleep with friends. The family advice column in the young people's paper *Junge Welt* recently took the liberal step of persuading parents to accept 'trial marriage'. 'It is quite proper and in line with our morality for parents to allow teenage children who are living at home to bring back a boy-friend or girl-friend and let them sleep together. One pre-condition though is that it should be a fairly stable relationship already. By that I do not mean couples who are definitely getting married in the foreseeable future. Sometimes too narrow a view of a relationship among young people can be used as a subliminal form of pressure on them to get married too soon. I mean that the couple should have known each other for rather more than three days, should be in love and not just be fulfilling basic sexual needs, and should hope like all lovers to stay together as long as possible.'[13] To many people even this advice may seem prim. At all events it shows an interesting contrast with public practice in the West. In most Western countries the commercial entertainment media encourage promiscuity while the advice columns in newspapers or family magazines preserve a hypocritical taboo against pre-marital sex. In the GDR in films and magazines promiscuity is discouraged (though not ignored) but in the advice columns pre-marital sex is given mature support.

If cramped housing conditions often cause hasty marriages they also contribute directly to divorce. In their survey Halgasch and Lungwitz discovered that 30 per cent of couples getting divorced after less than two years of marriage had not yet got a flat or home of their own. Since the Eighth party congress in 1971 the authorities have made a big push to improve housing conditions in general and for families with several children in particular. They are first on the list of priorities. Then come shift workers, to whom the authorities feel they must offer immediate flats as an extra inducement. Newly weds come third. For young graduates the problem is partially solved in as much as for the first three years they have to take a job assigned to them by the state anywhere in the GDR. Only after that can they return to their home towns if they want to. In most cases enterprises have a quota of flats available for specialists, so that graduates will have the consolation of a home of their own in return for having to go to a possibly distant part of the country. Other newly weds must look after themselves. Usually they will live with one set of their in-laws while waiting for their own place. The commonest type of housing is still the state flat. After the war this was virtually the only kind of property at all. The authorities requisitioned everything in order to house the thousands of homeless, including families resettled from the East. Owner occupiers could still live in their own property but had to give up part of it at a controlled rent to lodgers and tenants. In comparison with West Germany, the area which now forms the GDR had suffered slightly less destruction in the war. Subsequent emigration to the West caused a fall in the GDR's population from the immediate post-war peak. For several years overcrowding was less severe than in the West. Possibly this produced a sense of complacency on the part of the authorities. Massive investments were pumped into industrial projects in order to develop the GDR's economy. House-building suffered a comparative neglect. In the 1950s the GDR's *per capita* house-building production was only a fifth of the Federal Republic's. By 1960 it had only risen to 40 per cent. By 1961 the GDR had built just half a million homes since the war, an average of some 30,000 a year.

The results of this neglect are visible to any visitor. Far too many of the old pre-war tenements, their brickwork unpointed for a generation, still stand in the centre of East German cities. The GDR has one of the oldest housing stocks in Europe. Their amenities are poor. In 1971 only 11 per cent of all flats had central heating, 58 per cent had no inside lavatory, and 61 per cent no bath. Whereas in West Germany more than half the homes were built after the war, in 1971 four out of five in the GDR were not. Half of the GDR's homes were more than fifty years old. East German flats are smaller than those in the Federal Republic. The commonest form of flat has only two rooms. But because East Germany's population size has remained almost static, the country at least has more space per person than other East European nations. Comparative figures for 1970 show that East Germans had 19.4 square metres,

Poles 13.5, Czechs 11.6, and Soviet citizens 11.2. West Germans had 24 square metres each.

To make up for their neglect the GDR authorities began to build faster in the 1960s. By then it was too late to think much about quality, it seems. They used industrialised building methods which produced flats fast, but with minimal aesthetic distinction. From Halle Neustadt to Lütten Klein in Rostock vast concrete complexes appeared all over the GDR. In 1960 only a quarter of the new flats were assembly line prefabricated buildings. Six years later they formed an astonishing 93 per cent of the annual housing increase. They had many critics. People asked why it was necessary under socialism where land was state owned and cheap and where local authorities could not defy the central Government to build high-rise blocks. Why build the 1960s equivalent of the capitalist tenement when it would have been possible for a socialist state to build extensively, and experiment with designs that are more suitable for a community? Families complained of the uniformity, and the lack of green space. By contrast the few brand-new buildings of the 1950s even started to look attractive. The model town of Eisenhüttenstadt has five-storey blocks built around a central grassy courtyard, with trees, benches, and children's swings. Even the Karl-Marx-Allee in Berlin almost takes on an air of comfort when set against the taller, more densely populated buildings near the Wall on the Leipzigerstrasse, which were designed all too successfully as the East's reply to the skyline of West Berlin.

The planners' answer to the critics was that time and cost were the dictating factors. They still are. By the mid-1970s the building-time had been reduced to nine months for a complete flat. Costs were lowered. At times cost-cutting methods reached the point of absurdity. Karl Kulscher, the deputy editor of the satirical weekly *Eulenspiegel*, tells how he received word of a scheme being proposed for the Frankfurterallee in Berlin. To save money, the water-pump for the twenty-storey blocks was to be put in the basements instead of in a separate out-house. When it was pointed out that the noise of the pump would be so loud that no one would be able to live on the ground floor, the Mayor had an inspiration. 'Well, then let's find deaf and dumb people and give them these flats.' *Eulenspiegel* published the suggestion. The Mayor was not amused. Recently the authorities have said they want to put more variety into the country's architecture. The idea is to have more variations on the same theme, by using more combinations of window-sizes, balconies, facias and other elements on a basic eleven-block type of housing which is said to be quicker and cheaper to produce. The rate of house building and the amount of investment in it have considerably increased since 1971. More money is going into repairs, many of which are done collectively. Local authorities organise 'Join-in' competitions between people in different neighbourhoods to encourage them to make improvements. In Berlin they have now renovated some of the old tenements, which were shaped like square-cornered figures of eight. The central section where the flats were darkest has been torn down, so that the block is now a large hollow square with more light in the inward-facing rooms.

The target for the five-year-plan period ending in 1975 was for 525,000 new or improved homes. In the next five-year-plan up till 1980 the target is an extra 750,000 flats as well as a 6 per cent increase in the investment in each one, which will mean a larger number of three- and four-room flats. There is also to be a 50 per cent increase in the budget for repairs. The 1971 party congress also decided to allow people to build their own homes. Partly in order to overcome the country's shortage of building labour, and partly in response to the demand for smaller and less uniform constructions, the party gave the go-ahead for do-it-yourself building. Nowadays in East German outer suburbs on summer evenings and at weekends alongside the car-washers and garden-waterers the new amateur house builders are hard at work. The man shovelling sand outside a half-finished house is probably the owner. He may have started with no capital of his own at all. According to a family's size a couple can get a credit of up to 80,000 Marks to build one of the 44 different types of house-design supplied by the Building Ministry. The money covers materials and labour. The only problem is that the builder must find his mates. Often these new do-it-yourself homes are in small neighbourhoods where several houses are going up. People from the same factory or office help each other. Factories have to assist in supplying bull-dozers and cement-mixers to their employees at weekends. The local authority offers working drawings and plans, and can send plumbers and electricians if the family gets stuck. The scheme has become very popular and between 10 and 12 per cent of the new houses in the GDR are now built by owner-occupiers themselves. The average loan is 65,000 Marks, of which roughly 40,000 goes for materials. On this sum only 1 per cent interest is paid. On the other 25,000 there is an extra 4 per cent. For a finished house with five rooms, kitchen, bathroom, cellar, and garage the monthly cost would be around 136 Marks a month. The amount is low, but it is officially not allowed to be set higher than the rent for a new state flat of the same size.

Housing in the GDR is cheap. This is the main consolation for the serious housing shortage. Rents for a new state flat were fixed on January 1 1967 and have not been increased since. In Berlin they only cost between 1 and 1·25 Marks per square metre; in the provinces between 80 and 90 Pfennigs. For a three-roomed centrally heated flat this works out at roughly 123·25 Marks a month in Berlin, and 97·50 Marks outside. Rents for pre-war flats have not been increased since the war. Besides state flats and do-it-yourself homes some 40 per cent of East German housing consists of co-operative flats. Started by Ulbricht in 1954 the 'workers' building co-operatives' are a way of using enterprise funds for housing as well as creating residential communities based on the factory or place of work. Any group of workers can come together to form a co-operative. They have to supply a certain amount of capital on joining. It is calculated at 300 Marks per 'living unit'. A two-and-a-half room flat, for example, consists of seven units. On top of that tenants have to help in building the co-operative. Tenants' contributions are expected to total 15 per cent of the building costs with the rest provided interest-free by the state. The advantage for tenants is that they get a flat within three years at a rent which is usually 5 per cent lower than that of state flats.

House-hunting problems do not end when the tenant or owner moves into his first home. House-changing is difficult, as there is no slack in the house market. People who want to move from one part of the GDR to another can apply to their local authority. It sends regular lists of potential vacancies to a central computer and states its own requirements. The computer attempts to match supply and demand. A couple from, say,

187

Dresden can find out what is on offer in Schwerin or Magdeburg, but may well have to sign up quickly without even seeing the new place. Or people can advertise directly in a newspaper. Every week papers like the *Berliner Zeitung* are full of notices on the lines of 'Willing exchange three-bedroom flat, c.h., balcony, Jena for similar, Berlin'. This is the nearest to a housing market that the GDR has. No money is officially allowed to change hands. In fact people moving from a smaller flat to a bigger one or from a low-scarcity area to a major city pay the other family's 'removal expenses'.

Citizens in the GDR have complete freedom to move around. Until 1975, rather on the Soviet pattern, outsiders could not take up permanent residence in Berlin without getting a special permit. That has now been abolished. But the tight housing market still acts as a deterrent. The great advantage for East Germans is that housing costs little. The average family spends only 4 per cent of its monthly income on rent and roughly another $1\frac{1}{2}$ per cent on electricity and gas. This compares favourably with West Germany where rents, gas and electricity took up 20 per cent of the average person's income in 1971. Transport in the GDR is also cheap. For 20 Pfennigs you can travel by tram or bus any distance in any city. But East Germans pay comparatively more for food and consumer goods, and have less choice than West Germans. Prices have been remarkably stable, and most basic foodstuffs have not risen for fifteen years. To that extent inflation is unknown, although some prices creep upwards occasionally by the device of changing the name of the product or making other small adjustments and claiming it is a new product. But in general prices rarely move. Coupled with gradually rising incomes East Germans are given the justifiable feeling that theirs is an economically stable society.

Some prices of basic items are pegged at a high level. In 1971 East Germans spent 48·2 per cent of their income on food and delicacies while these items took up only 37.6 per cent of a West German's income.[14] *Per capita* consumption in the GDR was lower than that of the Federal Republic. Figures from 1973 (see Table 4) show each East German's average consumption in that year (West German figures in brackets).[15] From this it can be seen that the East German diet was roughly equivalent to that of the West in dairy products but more in-

Table 4

66 kilos of meat (70)
249 eggs (293)
8·1 kilos of poultry (9)
101·6 litres of milk (86·5)
26·5 kilos of fats, including butter and cooking oils (25·7)
89·9 kilos of bread (62·1)
143·4 kilos of potatoes (93·8)
70·1 kilos of fresh vegetables (66·6)
58·1 kilos of fresh fruit and oranges (110·3)

clined to bread and potatoes and less to meat and fresh fruit. When it comes to 'luxuries', West Germans outdrank the East in wine and beer but not in spirits, and consumed far more coffee and cigarettes. Three things have to be said about these figures. Firstly, they take no account of Western inflation since 1973. The prices of meat and fresh milk in the West have now become higher than those in the GDR, and this may mean a cut in Western consumption. Secondly, West Germany is one of the most prosperous countries in Europe. The GDR's level may still be somewhat lower than the FRG, but it is equivalent to that of Britain and higher than Italy's. Thirdly, the figures indicate that the GDR's agriculture must now have reached a relatively efficient stage for it to feed its people largely out of home-grown produce.

A brief digression into East German agriculture may be in order here. The normal stereotype of Eastern Europe's farming is that collectivisation has been a failure. The Soviet Union is usually contrasted with Poland's largely private system. The GDR's experience shows that things have been more complex. It started the post-war period with a massive influx of labour into the agricultural sector as a result of the flight of Germans from the former Eastern territories. From then on the numbers fell as people went West and the authorities pushed through various collectivisation measures. But full, forced collectivisation was delayed until the end of the 1950s, later than elsewhere in Eastern Europe. Since then the GDR has invested heavily in agriculture, 18·3 per cent of total investment resources in 1966–70 and 15 per cent in 1971–5. Only Hungary in the first period and Romania in the second surpassed this. Nowadays the GDR has a smaller proportion of the workforce engaged in agriculture than other Eastern European countries – only 12·5 per cent. Each farmworker has on average a larger slice of acres. Kurt Hager, the SED's ideological secretary, has called it a 'highly productive, industrial-type socialist agriculture'. It is very capital-intensive with each farmworker in effect supporting roughly thirty inhabitants in 1975, compared with nine in 1949 when the GDR was founded.

Massive investment has brought about the GDR's high agricultural output and productivity which contrast sharply with the relative failure of Soviet agriculture, and compare favourably with West Germany. By 1965 the GDR's yields in tons per hectare of wheat were 3·67 (USSR 0·66, FRG 3·26), rye 2·32 (USSR 0·9, FRG 2·5) and potatoes 17·7 (USSR 9·2, FRG 23·1).[16] Five years later in 1970 nearly all the main farm tasks had been totally mechanised, from grain- and sugar-beet harvesting to milking. The sight of horse-drawn carts, which is still normal in Poland and common in Hungary, is unknown in the GDR. The country's co-operative farms are huge undertakings with an average size of two thousand acres. In the last decade the authorities have been trying to get the co-operatives to become more specialised. New 'co-operative communities' are being created in which independent LPGs (i.e. co-operatives) concentrate on particular related branches of agriculture, like pig-raising or dairy produce and share common facilities for packing or veterinary advice. This trend towards 'horizontal integration' is the third great transformation in East German agriculture since the war. The idea is to take the benefits of large size a stage further, with enormous field areas for crops, and huge cattle installations with sheds for up to two thousand cows. By 1974 70 per cent of the GDR's arable land was in the hands of these new 'co-operative crop departments' (KAP). The development is the latest step in the 'industrialisation' of East German agriculture.

It also affects the co-operative farm's workforce who are increasingly becoming like factory workers. Grouped into 'labour collectives' they are gradually losing the distinction between wage-earners and members of a co-operative. Both types of people receive the same wages, calculated on a piece-work basis. Typical of the new set-up is the KAZ Frankfurt whose president, Günther Lehmann, exemplifies the change in the GDR's rural life. Born in 1929 into a landless farmhand's family near Frankfurt, Lehmann started as a tractor mechanic. He soon became the manager of a machine and tractor station which supplied local co-operatives. In 1958 he was made chairman of an LPG and moved to his present job in 1973. His wife is the chief accountant in a nearby co-operative, and his 16-year-old son is studying agronomy. 'The only pay difference between the 269 co-operative members and our sixty day-workers is that the former pay no tax. They also get fifty Marks a year for every hectare of land which they contributed to the co-operative in the beginning,' says Lehmann. The day-workers come in by bus from Frankfurt on a two-shift system. Like an East German factory, Lehmann's KAZ is building a central canteen and has a number of holiday places on the Baltic coast for its workers. It has an exchange system with a co-operative farm in Czechoslovakia, and workers swap visits.

Co-operative farm members are allowed to own 1·2 acres of private land. But in order to save work, many of them have this land farmed by the co-operative as a whole in return for a share in the produce. One difference from a factory is that co-operative members elect their own chairman and leadership. This is only a marginal addition to their power since the co-operative's planned targets still come from above. The GDR's agricultural success has been bought at a price. The effect of the massive investments in farming cannot be measured exactly. The West German Institute for Economic Research (Deutsches Institut für Wirtschaftsforschung) points out that whereas consumer prices for food are roughly comparable in East and West Germany, the production price paid by the state to farmers in the GDR is 80 per cent higher than the equivalent in the Federal Republic.[17] This gives some idea of the subsidies paid by the state. Thanks to them, it has been correctly stated that in the Soviet Union with its still under-capitalised collective farms the countryside has subsidised the towns, but in the GDR the reverse is true.

Even so, the average income of farmers in the commonest

type of co-operative, the LPG Type III, is still about 10 per cent less than that of industrial workers. This partly accounts for the continuing drift of labour from the countryside. While one-fifth of the workforce at KAZ Frankfurt consists of urban day-workers coming out to the farm, many of the grown-up children of the co-operative members commute the other way to Frankfurt. Towns still act as a magnet.

Although consumption standards in the GDR have improved considerably since 1961, two items have remained relatively hard to attain. For separate ideological reasons, cars and travel are still the preserve of a minority. The GDR authorities deliberately used to restrict car ownership, partly in order to save economic resources, and also on the grounds that the car was a symbol of bourgeois life-styles. The second argument was never convincing since the leadership itself always maintained their cars. Increasingly with the drive to match the Federal Republic in economic performance, and in line with the trend towards 'privatisation', car ownership has been permitted to grow. Demand is still stemmed by setting the price very high. The supply however cannot keep pace, even at high prices. Customers usually have to wait about five to six years for the most popular GDR car, the 600cc Trabant. It costs 8,050 Marks or almost nine months' salary for the average citizen. A 1,200 cc Soviet-built Zhiguli costs 19,800 Marks and may take two or three years to deliver.

Car ownership in the GDR is higher than in the rest of Eastern Europe. In 1972 there was one private car to every twelve inhabitants, compared to one to thirteen in Czechoslovakia, one to thirty-one in Hungary, one to fifty-three in Poland, and one to ninety-five in the Soviet Union (and one to four in West Germany, one to five in England, and one to two in the United States).[18] The GDR authorities have made it their target for every family to have a car by the end of the 1980s. The average East German citizen is also better supplied with consumer goods than his Comecon neighbours. Only the Czechs are on the same level. Seventy per cent of GDR households have refrigerators and 75 per cent have television sets. Here too, prices are deliberately set high. A medium-sized black and white set cost 1,630 Marks in Berlin in 1975 (almost two months' average pay). The smallest refrigerator in the

Centrum department store was 600 Marks. The quality of East German clothing is the best in Comecon. This was made dramatically clear when the GDR and Poland lifted all frontier restrictions between them in 1972. People could buy as much as they liked in each other's country without paying customs duty. Hundreds of thousands of Poles flooded to the GDR to buy clothing, underwear and consumer goods. (In return East Germans who lived near the border drove to Poland to buy its cheaper petrol. There were few other bargains.) The quality of the GDR's goods is also apparent from the fact that much of it is exported to West German mail order firms. For political reasons and because of alleged consumer resistance if people knew where they came from, the importers usually conceal the products' origin with the vague label 'Made in Germany'. The East Germans are interested in the hard currency they earn from this business, and do not complain in spite of their long years of demanding political and psychological recognition. The result is that hundreds of West Germans whose stereotype of the GDR may still be of a bleak and austere society are using good-quality East German products without even knowing.

When it comes to foreign travel to the West, East Germans are less well-off than their Polish neighbours. Almost no East German can go West as a tourist. The only trips for non-pensioners (men over 65 and women over 60 can go for a month's holiday each year) are for officials on business, a few hand-picked spectators at international matches, sportsmen and women themselves, and people visiting relations in the West for 'urgent family reasons'. The relationship has to be close and the occasion important, a funeral, a wedding, or a serious illness. A man may go to see his dying father. He will not normally be able to take his wife with him. People under 26 will almost certainly not get permission unless they are married and leave their spouse behind.

East Germans like travelling but most of them have to stay within the GDR's borders or else go East and South. Roughly half the population leaves home during the holidays.[19] East Germans need no visa for travel to Poland and Czechoslovakia, and in 1973 five and four million respectively took trips there. Another million went further afield to the High Tatras, the Black Sea and the Caucasus. Eighty per cent of the population spent their holidays in the GDR. The typical GDR couple will go on a subsidised holiday, either to a hotel or lodge run by his or her factory (800,000 people in 1973) or to one provided by the trade unions. It is part of the general East European philosophy that workers under socialism should have the right to a low-cost holiday. Trade union holidays cost 52–120-Marks per person for full board for two weeks, depending on the type of accommodation. The cost for a child is only 30 Marks, which means that a family with two children can have a fortnight's holiday on one person's salary. Price is no problem. The difficulty for most couples is making sure that both husband and wife can get time off together, and finding somewhere to stay. The Baltic coast in the summer and the Thüringian Alps in winter are fully booked. Since 1971 the SED has invested more money in building holiday places. Four-fifths of the beds in the GDR's best hotels at Warnemünde, Dresden and Oberhof which were originally built for Western tourists have been turned over to the trade unions. This has barely reduced the shortage and people are lucky if they can get a trade union holiday more than once every five or six years. Factories are allocated a certain number of holiday vouchers every year from the trade unions' central organisation, which they distribute around the staff. The quota system favours heavy industry which has roughly ten places for every hundred workers. The least favoured enterprises receive ten places for every 140 workers. People can also book privately. All along the coast and in the mountains licensed landladies take in lodgers. The columns of small ads in the papers are full of offers and requests for places most of the year round.

Cheap holidays and regular sport are part of the GDR's strongly canvassed cult of good health. For all his stiffness and difficulty in making contact with people, Ulbricht allowed himself to be photographed rowing boats or playing volley-ball in a white sweatshirt. He was a keen keep-fit man and once produced the formidable slogan 'Everyone everywhere, extra sport every week'. By means of early talent-spotting and fierce training the GDR has boosted its national sports performance to one of the world's best. Prestige was a main target for a country which for years was made to feel an inferiority complex in the international arena. But there is also a deep German respect for physical exercise going back long before Hitler's perverted exploitation of it. The country's Gymnastics and Sports Federation has a membership of 2,660,000, about one-seventh of the entire population. Two or three hours of sport a week are compulsory in every school from the first year onwards. Children who show unusual gifts are likely to be transferred at an early age to one of the GDR's nineteen special sports schools. Most of the children at the schools are boarders. They have a curriculum geared to their training schedules. Kornelia Ender, the swimmer who won four gold medals at the Montreal Olympics in 1976 was 'discovered' when she was only eight. Ulrike Richter, the backstroke champion, went to a special school at the age of six. Besides the schools, the GDR has a network of twenty-one elite sports clubs with outstanding facilities. Membership is reserved for those with special talent, and as a reward for the successful the GDR's top sportspeople can jump to the front of the queue for new cars or apartments.

A GDR citizen pays little for health care, social security insurance, and pension contributions. The charge is 10 per cent of one's gross income up to a maximum of 60 Marks. It was fixed in 1947 and has never been changed. A worker's employer pays an equivalent sum. If he falls ill, the citizen is paid 90 per cent of his normal net wage for the first six weeks, and after that between 50 per cent and 90 per cent according to the number of children in the family. For the last few years people earning more than 600 Marks a month have been encouraged to contribute an extra 10 per cent of their income above 600 Marks and up to 1,200 Marks. This entitles them to extra benefits. Patients pay nothing for medical treatment. The country's health service has been completely remodelled since pre-war days with the aim of breaking down the distinction between in-patient and out-patient treatment. In major towns and in almost a hundred of the country's largest factories the standard unit is the 'polyclinic'. Modelled on Soviet practice, the country's five hundred polyclinics each have five different departments under one roof, including a gynaecologist, a pediatrician, a dentist, a general practitioner and a specialist on intestinal diseases. The idea is that a patient can be seen immediately by a specialist instead of being transferred to a hospital. In smaller places two or three doctors form a group practice. In addition there are about 1,500 doctors working on their own for the state. The new system of state medicine was a radical change after the war, and the authorities trod more carefully with the doctors than with any other professional group in order to try to avoid a mass exodus to the West. Private medicine was not abolished outright. The Government sought to phase it out gradually by not granting new private licences to medical graduates. In 1975 there were still 1,000 private doctors, and as many dentists. The church hospitals which provide about 10 per cent of the country's hospital beds have been allowed to continue. They get Government subsidies.

Even these gentle measures were too much for many doctors who were guaranteed higher earnings in the West. In the 1950s about a quarter of the GDR's doctors left the country. This enormous drain of talent was a prime factor behind the building of the Berlin Wall. Since then the number of doctors has exactly doubled to 29,000 which gives the GDR sixteen doctors for every 10,000 people, just under the Federal Republic's figure. The medical schools try to overcome the profession's traditional elitism by making students do manual work for some time each year in outlying villages or in factories. Doctors' salaries have also been drastically reduced in proportion to others'. Nowadays a doctor in a polyclinic earns an average 1,450 Marks a month. This is still twice as much as an industrial worker but in West Germany the proportion is closer to six to one.

The GDR's medical results are impressive. Infant mortality rates have been brought down to levels lower than in West Germany and Austria. Poliomyelitis and diphtheria have been eradicated. Measles and tuberculosis are almost unknown. The system has its weaknesses. In spite of the massive propaganda emphasis on health, cigarette smoking and the consumption of alcohol have been increasing rapidly since 1960. The care of the mentally ill is not nearly as enlightened as that of the physically ill. Too many are still locked away in old fortress-like institutions. Colditz castle, the fearsome wartime prison for captured Allied officers, is a mental hospital now. The GDR's suicide rate, though secret, is thought to be one of the highest in the world. The continuing shortages in the system lead to long waiting periods for patients and a re-emergence of new forms of privileged treatment. Although private practice has been abolished in general, senior surgeons in the prestige university hospitals take private patients for high fees. They can increase their income from around 4,000 Marks a month to 15,000 or more. Most hospitals have private rooms which cost nothing but are at the disposal of local dignitaries in the party, Government and the professions. The official justification is that while these patients are recuperating, they may have to work part-time, making telephone calls, reading documents or receiving important visits. How serious the problem of privileged medicine is is hard to assess. In the country's new hospitals the general trend is now moving away from large wards towards four- and six-bed rooms. The weaknesses in the system stem from scarcity and do not cancel out the general all-round improvement in the care of people's health.

Far more disturbing is the position of the elderly in the GDR. 'Once you become a pensioner, no one is interested', a woman from Mecklenburg complained. No society has yet adequately solved the psychological problem of retirement and giving up work. In the GDR where production is so strongly valued and stressed the problem is acute. Three and a half million people, one in five of the population, are pensioners. They are the only ones allowed to emigrate to the West, and the authorities make no bones of the fact that they are happy to see them leave. Those who stay face a considerable drop in income. Pensions are made up of a fixed portion of 110 Marks and an extra portion related to earnings. But the maximum pension for working people who have only paid the compulsory contributions is 370 Marks. On average a pensioner receives a third of a worker's income. This is better than a British pensioner who gets only 21 per cent of average earnings, but half as good as West Germany where pensioners get 60 per cent. Some Government officials like policemen, customs officers, postmen and railway workers get extra pensions. Senior members of the intelligentsia from school teachers and artists to doctors and scientists have even higher extra pensions up to a maximum of 90 per cent of their previous salary. Hundreds and thousands of pensioners go on working to earn extra money. With its chronic labour shortage the Government encourages this. It gives pensioners their full pension while at work on top of their wages.

Some attempt is made to integrate pensioners psychologically into the community. 'People's solidarity', a voluntary social work organisation set up in 1945 has neighbourhood committees to look after elderly people. They run veterans' clubs, and arrange for meals-on-wheels and home helps. But they cannot provide a sufficient network. Just as in the West the phenomenon of old people dying alone and not being found by neighbours until days later occurs in the GDR. Their relative poverty makes life hard for old people. If they have to move into an old people's home the prospect is disheartening. There is only room for 100,000 people or 3 per cent of the retired population. Most of the homes have no single rooms. Old people are put three or four to a room in impersonal surroundings. As the GDR itself gets older, the prospects for the elderly may improve somewhat. As the system of extra contributions expands and pensions increase, the next generation may have a better old age. Many of the present generation of old folk, who are leaving for the West, had their formative years long before the GDR was founded. Their children have been born and brought up in the GDR's comprehensive welfare system. It would be an irony if on retirement they too should feel that socialism's blunt message was 'Go West, old man'.

The Self-image of a New Germany

One blustery April morning a group of schoolchildren formed a semi-circle in the derelict parade ground of Buchenwald concentration camp. A short man in a black beret with pronounced cheek-bones that pressed like knuckles through his skin, told them that this was where the prisoners' huts once stood. The brick buildings over there housed the gas ovens. On this side you can see the shower block with the cubicle where they shot hundreds of people in the back of the neck while their height was being measured. Behind that wall is the small shrine for Ernst Thälmann, the first secretary of the KPD, whom the Nazis murdered in 1944.

The guide knew what he was talking about. He was one of the band of former inmates of Buchenwald who are now employed to show visitors round. 'A mile away at the bottom of this hill is Weimar, the Weimar of Goethe and Schiller. We like to think of Germany as a land of poets and thinkers. This place where we are standing now was also part of Germany.' The guide finished, and took the children quickly off to the welcome shelter of the wall. There they laid a wreath on Thälmann's grave.

No one could say that the authorities in the GDR ignore Germany's recent past. They talk about it willingly and often. They know what the country was and what the GDR today is not. The problem comes in defining what it is. Revulsion from Germany's past has been relatively easy to foster. It is a harder task to instil loyalty to the present, and confidence in the future. Ulbricht and his colleagues always insisted that their state was not the successor state to Nazi Germany. They ascribed that dubious honour exclusively to the Federal Republic. This move may have given the GDR leadership a moral certitude which it otherwise would not have had. But it created a psychological and spiritual no-man's-land for ordinary people. The GDR did not have the sanction of history. It was a new state – but nobody's fatherland.

For the authorities the existence of another German state in the West was of course a constant irritant. It was a perpetual yardstick for comparison, a pole of attraction for many East Germans, and the home of at least one relation for almost every East German family. Its television programmes were easily available. Visitors from the West came and went. Families wrote letters and compared notes. The building of the Wall in 1961 changed much of that. From that time on, particularly among the younger generation who never lived in a Western system, a new kind of GDR-consciousness slowly grew up. In the last decade and a half the Wall's undoubted air of permanence convinced most people in East Germany that the GDR was a viable state and willy-nilly 'their' state. In the first years after 1961 for people who were unhappy in the GDR it was more of a sense of *faute de mieux*, a negative feeling that they had to make do with the GDR because they could no longer leave it. In 1966 one Western writer described the GDR as representing 'a sort of marriage of convenience, a make-the-best-of-it relationship between society and its leaders'.[1] But it was obvious as time went on that a new generation would emerge with a substantial stake in the *status quo* and a different set of values.

It was this argument that convinced the Social Democrats in the West that Dr Konrad Adenauer's old policy of refusing to recognise or have any dealings with the GDR was bankrupt. The SPD still kept the old view, shared by the West German Christian Democrats, that Germans in the West had a moral responsibility to help their brothers and sisters in the East. It was the psychological counter-part of the concept of 'Alleinvertretung', the notion that the Government of the FRG had the right to represent all Germans, and that the Government of the GDR had no legitimacy. But the SPD also realised that two German states existed, though it was not yet ready to state that publicly. Confrontation between them had produced few benefits for either side. It was better to abandon it. In its place the Federal Republic should open a dialogue with the authorities in the East on ways of expanding contacts between the two states and creating 'human improvements' for people in the East—more trade, easier postal communications, and more visits from West to East if not vice versa. Willy Brandt, the SPD leader, called it a policy of 'small steps'. The question of visits between East and West Germany was a major political issue in the Federal Republic, and of considerable importance in the East as well although it could never be formulated openly. For three years after the Wall was built no GDR citizen could travel West. In November 1964 Ulbricht began to allow old age pensioners to travel to the West for holidays once a year or to visit close relatives in special circumstances. As for visits in the opposite direction permission was given at Whitsun, Easter and Christmas for a few years after 1963 on an erratic basis which had to be negotiated each time by the Western authorities.

None of the SPD's proposals entailed giving the GDR official diplomatic recognition. The underlying premise was that the previous Western policy of boycotting and isolating the East only strengthened the 'hard-liners' in the regime (personified by Walter Ulbricht). The slogan of the new policy was 'Wandel durch Annäherung'—change through rapprochement. By opening contacts with the East, one might be able to change it. In 1966 the SPD entered the Government of the Federal Republic for the first time as a junior partner in the 'Grand Coalition' with the CDU. Willy Brandt became Foreign Minister. In December of that year the Government announced that it was ready to take up contacts with the East 'to prevent the German people drifting further apart'. In April 1967 it proposed sixteen specific subjects for discussion with the GDR. The SED Politbüro saw the issue in opposite terms. What they wanted above all was the international recognition of the GDR and an end to its diplomatic isolation—and at minimum cost in terms of internal changes. This would strengthen the SED and give it one more facet of the legitimacy which it was struggling to create. Without recognition 'change through rapprochement' sounded like subversion in a subtle new form. They replied to Bonn with a draft treaty for the mutual recognition of the 'two sovereign states of the German nation'.

There the matter rested. No further moves of any significance were made until after the 1969 elections in the Federal Republic when the SPD formed a coalition with the Free Democrats to lead the new Government in Bonn. In his first statement as new Chancellor, Willy Brandt announced that the Federal Government could not consider the international recognition of the GDR. 'Even if two states exist in Germany,' he went on, 'they cannot be foreign countries to each other; their relations can only be of a special kind.'[2] This formulation was new. It was the first time that a West German Chancellor had publicly declared that there were two German states, even though it rejected formal recognition. Six weeks later the Warsaw Pact met, and produced a reply which was also a modification of previous stands. It praised Brandt for 'realism' but said that the GDR must be recognised before any normalisation could take place. The Russians recognised that the Brandt Government was different from its predecessors. They respected Brandt's personal war record as an anti-Fascist in marked contrast to that of ex-Chancellor Georg Kiesinger who had served in Hitler's Foreign Ministry. They gave the green light for Four-Power talks on Berlin, began bilateral discussion with Brandt for a Soviet–West German treaty renouncing the use of force, and authorised the Poles to go ahead with a similar pact.

Ulbricht could see all this movement going on around him. But for the time being he was able to mark time since the Warsaw Pact had publicly restated the position that the GDR first had to be recognised before any talks between East and West Germany got going. A fortnight after the Warsaw Pact meeting Ulbricht followed up its communiqué by sending Bonn another draft treaty of recognition. The West Germans side-stepped the issue. Instead, they proposed ministerial talks which would be conducted on their side by the Minister for Inner-German Affairs, Egon Franke. The SED reacted with a flash of inspiration. If it accepted the Bonn proposal and met Herr Franke, that would have meant conceding the notion that the talks between the two Germanies had a special character. If it suggested a meeting of Foreign Ministers, that would have been inviting a rejection and would have displeased Moscow which was privately pushing them to be as conciliatory towards Brandt as Poland and the Soviet Union were being. Ulbricht and his colleagues decided to go one rank higher. They proposed a summit meeting between their Prime Minister, Willi Stoph, and Chancellor Brandt to take place in East Berlin.

Even if they could not get formal recognition, to have the West German Chancellor visit them on their home ground would be an enormous symbolic step forward. The plan was spoiled by the Berlin issue. Brandt accepted the summit meeting in principle, but only if he could travel to East Berlin via West Berlin. This would have reinforced the links between West Berlin and the Federal Republic, which ran counter to the GDR's long-term strategy. After more debate the venue was shifted from Berlin altogether to the small town of Erfurt. At least that had the small advantage for the GDR that it was not far from Buchenwald and they could take the Chancellor up to that parade ground where the school parties went. The Erfurt meeting marked the high point of Ulbricht's diplomacy. He had not yet got a treaty, but the West German Chancellor would step on to sovereign GDR soil, and Willi Stoph would then pay a return visit to West Germany. Yet Ulbricht was still in a sense playing for time. Everything so far was symbolic. He still had not committed himself one way or the other on whether to proceed with negotiations. His inclination was not to go on with them.

Ulbricht's doubts were strengthened by what happened at Erfurt on March 19 1970. Willy Brandt arrived by train for the meeting in the Hotel Erfurterhof just across the main square from the railway station. A crowd formed in the square beside the official welcoming party. All went according to plan for the arrival, but during the morning several hundred people broke through a police line and moved up to the front of the hotel, shouting 'Willy, Willy'. Brandt appeared at a window and acknowledged the cheers. As the shouting continued he did his best to quieten them down. It was a small incident which lasted for only a few minutes. But it was enough to arouse new insecurities in Ulbricht's mind. He had not expected such spontaneous interest in Brandt and such a demonstration of his popularity. It was in marked contrast to the sober tone of the official GDR press. Two months later at Kassel in West Germany on the return visit, the GDR Prime Minister Willi Stoph made it clear that the East Germans were not ready for serious negotiations. At the Erfurt meeting both sides had simply laid out their basic points of view. A fuller exposé leading to negotiations was due to take place at the second round. But at Kassel, Stoph made a tough, bitter, and polemical speech, itemising in some detail the 'revanchist' policy of previous West German Governments and their policy of boycotting the GDR. It claimed that the new Government in Bonn had not yet done enough to show that its policies were different from those of its predecessors. The effect of the speech was to propose a 'pause for thought' in the dialogue, and put the blame for the delay on the West Germans by saying that they were obviously not ready.

Meanwhile Bonn was continuing to talk with Moscow and Warsaw. In August Willy Brandt visited Moscow to sign a treaty renouncing the use of force. The Russians were clearly conscious that his Government offered the best chance for a reasonable reconciliation between Bonn and Moscow which would not prejudice the long-term interests of either side. An historic change was taking place in Soviet–American relations too. After years in which confrontation between East and West had been the norm, the Russians and the Americans were groping towards a new concept of strategic balance between each other. In the United States President Nixon and his national security adviser, Dr Henry Kissinger, coined the slogan that the two powers were moving from an era of confrontation to one of negotiation. The new process was described as *détente*. Both superpowers were feeling the psychological and financial burden of the continuing nuclear arms race, and wanted to reach some form of agreed slow-down which would maintain equality of security for each side and recognise a nuclear stale-mate. The West saw Eastern Europe as a potentially valuable market for its consumer goods and a source of plentiful raw materials and comparatively cheap labour. The Russians wanted advanced technology from the West. At the same time they were increasingly becoming a global power with interests beyond Europe. Confrontation with China continued to look as though it would last for years. In order to conserve resources it made sense for Russia to achieve an orderly settlement in Europe and an end to the Cold War. The two historic pieces of unfinished business there were the ambiguous status of Berlin and the West's refusal to recognise formally the post-war frontiers of Eastern Europe. There was the chance of a broad trade-off if the West recognised realities in Eastern Europe and the East recognised the reality of a Western presence in Berlin.

Within this grand design the GDR's perception of things was not identical with Moscow's. As so often before, the GDR's national interest and that of the Soviet Union did not coincide. After twenty-five years of isolation and second-class citizenship within the international community, sovereignty was the sensitive issue for the GDR. The East German leadership, and Ulbricht in particular, felt touchy about anything that implied their state was less legitimate than any other. They still wanted sovereignty over the Western access roads to Berlin which went through their territory. But just as Khrushchev had resisted Ulbricht in 1961 when he made the same demands, the Russians hesitated again. They were aware of the potential for East–West tension which the access routes provided. In the Cold War they themselves had used the roads repeatedly as a pressure point on the West by harassing, blocking, and delaying traffic. They were unwilling to abandon total control to the GDR.

The SED's other concern was the psychological and political impact inside the GDR of *détente* with the West. Would it create instability? Would closer contacts between East and West Germany undermine the population's loyalty to the GDR? It was Ulbricht's oldest fear. During Khrushchev's period of liberalisation in the Soviet Union in 1962 and 1963 Ulbricht had suppressed most of the anti-Stalinist literature that was coming out in Moscow. He was afraid of any intellectual relaxation in the GDR. Solzhenitsyn's *One Day in the Life of Ivan Denisovich* was never published in East Germany. Ulbricht stated flatly in 1963: 'To those artists and writers who instead of grappling with socialist construction demand that in publishing Soviet literature we should give preference to works which describe the suffering of internees under the Stalinist terror, we say frankly that certain works of this kind may well be effective as far as conditions in the Soviet Union are concerned but there is absolutely no reason why they should be published here.'[3] After Khrushchev's overthrow in 1964, Ulbricht reacted warily. He was unsure of the new Soviet leadership. As a way of winning its attention Ulbricht very delicately played the Chinese card, which he had taken up earlier that summer when Khrushchev began to make overtures to Bonn. The SED opposed the idea that China should be expelled from the Communist movement. The Chinese accused the Soviet Union of being prepared to sacrifice the GDR for the sake of an accommodation with the West. Again, at the time of the reform movement in Czechoslovakia, Ulbricht was afraid that liberalisation would spread to the GDR. Now he was afraid once more.

With the signing of the Moscow treaty with Bonn in August 1970, Soviet pressure on the GDR increased. The Russians told Ulbricht and his colleagues to open genuine negotiations with Bonn in advance of any recognition. In September the Russians and the three Western Powers for the first time exchanged written memoranda on a possible settlement for Berlin. Ulbricht still hoped to delay the gathering momentum of *détente*. To counteract any impact inside the country, he started to shore up his internal defences. In direct opposition to the Western slogan of 'change through rapprochement' Stoph declared on October 7 that because of the completely opposed nature of the two systems in the Federal Republic and the GDR 'an objective process of separation or demarcation' ('Abgrenzung') was taking place between them. A fortnight later the GDR reluctantly conceded its willingness to begin a new series of exchanges of view with the West Germans. The policy was a typical Ulbrichtian compromise – a qualified retreat before Soviet pressure, coupled with a determination not to give up what he saw as the GDR's basic national interest.

In the end however Ulbricht moved too slowly. He continued to stall the negotiations, and for six more months almost no progress was made. Several of Ulbricht's colleagues were already unhappy with his grandiose schemes for the economy. They blamed him for the poor economic results of the previous two or three years. Ulbricht's health was waning. In the spring of 1971 the combination of all these factors was enough for the Russians to give the SED the nod. The Politbüro suggested to Ulbricht that he step down. Moscow wanted someone more flexible. On May 3 Ulbricht told the central committee, 'After thorough consideration I have decided to ask you to release me

from my function as First Secretary. The years demand their
tribute and no longer allow me to exercise such a strenuous
post ... To be honest, it was not easy for me to make this
decision after holding this office for two decades, but there is
no cure against the passage of the years ... '[4]

Ulbricht kept the position of chairman of the Council of
State which was effective Head of State. He had first acquired
the post in 1960. It was a dignified departure with little of the
resentment of de Gaulle, the public hesitation of Adenauer, or
the senile stubbornness of Churchill's last months in power. It
was certainly more dignified and 'constitutional' a transfer of
power than any previous changeover in the history of a ruling
Communist party. Ulbricht departed like some retiring head-
master, respected by his colleagues rather than loved. They
were glad to see him go but awed by the vacuum which he left
behind. Erich Honecker, who succeeded him as first secretary,
had for years been Ulbricht's heir-presumptive. In the shadow
of Ulbricht he had always seemed colourless and grey. But he
was known to be slightly more flexible and pragmatic. Like
Ulbricht he too was an old-fashioned working-class German
nationalist. He was born into a miner's family in the Saar in
1912 and lived through its passage to French control after the
First World War. In the first years after the war the KPD resisted moves to scrap the Treaty of Versailles. Honecker, then
a child of seven, sensed that the French were an occupying
power. His father, who was a Communist party activist and a
trade union leader, imbued him also with the traditions of the
Paris Commune and the French Revolution. The family looked
on France with mixed feelings. But in 1922 the KPD in the
Saar called for the Saar's return to Germany. Because of their
close links with ordinary people through their energetic organising work in the mines, and through taking up nationalist
positions, the Saarland Communists effectively prevented the
Nazis ever gaining much strength in the region. In the 1932
elections, for example, the Nazis won less than 7 per cent of the
vote (against the KPD's 23 per cent). Honecker saw that
Communists could deal with the national issue. One of his
biographers and former colleagues, Heinz Lippmann, describes
an incident in 1949 when Honecker, then the ambitious leader
of the FDJ, met some young Saar Communists at the World

Youth Festival in Budapest.[5] He was furious to find them carrying the French tricolor and taking a pro-French line even though the issue was support for the French Communist party against the West German leader Konrad Adenauer.

Honecker spent the war in Brandenburg prison near Berlin. Shortly before the end of the war he escaped, a fact which earned him a reprimand from the party leader on the ground that the escape was uncoordinated and ruined some plans for resistance by the inmates as a whole. In spite of this error and the fact that he was not one of the 'Moscow' group in the party, he rose rapidly in the apparatus. In 1946 he was given the job of building up the FDJ which gave him considerable powers of patronage over his entire generation. Later he spent two years on a political study course in Moscow. In 1958 he was given the Politbüro portfolio in charge of the army and internal security.

A gradual change in GDR policy became evident soon after Ulbricht's retirement and the Eighth party congress which took place a month later in June 1971. The GDR accepted that under the Berlin agreement between the Soviet Union and the United States, Britain, and France, Moscow should once again retain sovereignty over the access routes. It was Moscow rather than East Berlin which promised that traffic would henceforth be unimpeded. The Berlin agreement laid down that the two German states should negotiate the details between themselves. Three months later this was completed, and East and West Germany initialled the first international agreement which they had ever made together. The crowning agreement of the German–German talks followed in December 1972. Shortly after winning a new mandate in the Federal elections Willy Brandt's Government concluded the 'Basic Treaty' recognising the GDR. The treaty fell some way short of Ulbricht's original demands. It kept the two countries' relations in a special category. Bonn's representative in Berlin was not an Ambassador but a High Commissioner. His office was not an embassy, but a 'permanent mission'. At the same time the Four Powers, including the Russians, reaffirmed their rights in Germany as a whole. Above all, the basic treaty came at the end of a process of step-by-step negotiations during which the GDR had promised to allow much freer travel for West Germans into the GDR and made it possible for more East Germans to go West.

Some Western cynics argued that the GDR would have preferred no treaty at all. International recognition was already coming and the best thing from the GDR's point of view would have been for the GDR to be recognised by everyone except the West Germans. It could then have continued to keep aloof from Bonn, the argument went. It was exaggerated. Until Bonn recognised the GDR, other Western countries held back. If the treaty required concessions from the East, it required more from the West. To soften them Bonn tried to maintain the fiction that one day Germany would be re-unified. Before the signing ceremony in East Berlin, the Federal Government sent a letter to the GDR, giving its view that the treaty in no way contradicted the Federal Government's political goal of 'producing in peaceful conditions a situation in which the German people would achieve their unity again by means of self-determination'. But Bonn also admitted that 'no end of Germany's division is in sight'.[6] Public opinion in West Germany was split almost in half. The Bundestag, the West German parliament, had nearly refused to ratify the Moscow and Warsaw treaties. Brandt's re-election in November 1972 reflected a slight majority in favour of his 'Ostpolitik' but nevertheless the margin was narrow.

While the process of diplomatic rapprochement was going on, Honecker did not give up Ulbricht's policy of practical 'Abgrenzung'. In fact he extended it. Any institution whose title suggested that Germany was a single entity was renamed. The East German radio station, the Deutschlandsender, became the Voice of the GDR. The German Union of Journalists became the Union of Journalists of the GDR, and so on. As recently as 1968 the GDR had ratified a new Constitution which described the country as 'a socialist state of the German nation'. It said citizens of the GDR wanted to overcome the division of Germany which imperialism had caused, 'and achieve a gradual rapprochement of the two German states until their unification on the basis of democracy and socialism'. The 'unity of the nation' was an article of faith in West Germany. In 1972 Honecker called the idea 'a fiction'. Two years later the People's Chamber suddenly changed the Constitution and dropped all the paragraphs and clauses which referred to unity.

Gradually too, the SED began to give a more positive theoretical content to the 'Abgrenzung' concept. Its ideologists developed the line that there always were 'two nations' in Germany. In March 1973 Kurt Hager, the chief ideologist, said that the working class in the GDR had 'taken power and constituted itself into a nation. The socialist nation in the GDR stands in unbridgeable conflict to the old capitalist nation which continues to exist in the Federal Republic.' A generation since its foundation, the GDR started looking for its history. A country which, as the title of its main party paper *Neues Deutschland* makes clear, likes to think of itself as a New Germany is now spending more time and energy researching its past than ever before. East Germany's ideologists argue that the formation of today's GDR is the result of a long dialectical process going back to the Middle Ages. 'The GDR is the work of many generations', as Honecker told the central committee in December 1974. 'The GDR', he said on another occasion, 'is now the state which embodies the best traditions of German history such as the peasant insurrections in the Middle Ages, the struggle of revolutionary democrats in 1848, the German Labour Movement founded by Marx and Engels, Bebel and Liebknecht, and the heroic deeds of the anti-Fascist resistance struggles.'[7]

Schoolchildren who tour Buchenwald and the other camps are now also getting more lessons on German history in the Middle Ages and the nineteenth century. In the schools a new impetus is being given to the so-called 'clubs of young historians' who ferret out titbits of local history for their scrapbooks. There are ten applicants for every university place in history. In June 1975 Professor Ludwig Deiters, the director of the GDR's Institute for the Preservation of Monuments, told me that museum visiting had expanded by more than 50 per cent in the previous three years. 'After the war there was a certain radicalism, a kind of "Proletkult" which maintained that nothing was of interest except what happened after the Russian Revolution.' Some aspects of Germany's history still remain taboo. No mention is made of the enormous centuries-long presence of Germans in Poland, Silesia, Pomerania, Gdansk, or the Sudetenland. Visitors going round these places today in the company of Polish or Czech guides would never know that Germans were once influential here. 'The old chauvinistic idea that Germans went everywhere in the East as bringers of culture was exaggerated under the Nazis', says Professor Deiters. 'Perhaps now we underemphasise it – for understandable reasons.' With its stress on history the SED hopes to awaken a new form of national identity, not the old chauvinism of the past. The party now makes a distinction between 'nation' and 'nationality'. According to a key article in *Neues Deutschland* 'nation' is a wide concept, which includes social, economic, historical and ethnic components. 'Nationality' merely describes the ethnic characteristics which hold a people together.[8] In some cases a nation has been formed from several nationalities, the prime example being the United States. In other cases several nations have developed from one nationality. Just as the Swiss, the Austrians, the Dutch and the Germans developed in the German-speaking areas of Europe, so now two German nations have also grown up.

Whatever psychological defences the SED has been raising recently, the passage of the Basic Treaty and the traffic agreements for Berlin have increased contacts with the West. For the first time West Germans can visit the East as tourists even if they have no relatives there. Before that, West Germans could only come in to see relations for one trip of up to four weeks. Now people can make repeated trips, although it is still limited to thirty days in the year. They can bring their cars in if they have small children or are going to remote places. The GDR is still trying to prevent a flood of West German cars from giving East Germans an image of conspicuous Western consumption. More frontier crossing points have been opened. West Berliners can make day trips to East Berlin up to a maximum of thirty days, and have to change at least six Marks fifty Pfennigs at the frontier. Some six million West Germans living in fifty-six areas near the frontier with the GDR can also make thirty day trips into the frontier areas on the other side.

The result of all these measures has been a sudden stream of Western visitors. From a total of $1\frac{1}{2}$ million visitors in 1972 the number went up to about ten million in 1973. By the Friedrichstrasse railway station in East Berlin the authorities built a new glass-walled customs hall known locally as the Crystal Palace. Day and night it is full of people passing through. The old delays when bags were exhaustively searched are over. It now takes little more than ten minutes to cross, depending on the crowd. The East Germans have removed one of the most forbidding images which used to confront passengers travelling under East Berlin by underground. As the trains slowed down to a walking pace in several deserted stations in the East which are now closed, armed guards could be seen patrolling the platforms in the murky half-light on the look-out for stowaways on the outside or roofs of the carriages. Now they have gone and the trains go through faster instead.

Travel has also increased in the other direction, though not by anything like the same amount. Besides old age pensioners, East Germans with relatives in the West can visit them for weddings, funerals, and serious illness. But even in these categories young East Germans rarely get permission, and married couples cannot go together. In the first year after the Basic Treaty was signed the East Germans claim that there were $3\frac{1}{2}$ million crossings by GDR citizens from East to West. The figures do not show how many of these were old people or Government officials making repeated trips. The number of independent young travellers was probably small. But interest in travel remains very high in the GDR. The lack of opportunities for it is perhaps the single most important grievance which young East Germans have. Shortly before the treaty came into force, hopes were high that it would allow a significant increase in travel. Since then there has been some disappointment. One young East German student who recently divorced his wife laughed bitterly that this would put off any chance of Western travel. Other East Germans contrast their limited possibilities with those of Poles who can travel to the West with comparative ease. East Germans constantly see images of the West on television. They want to see the actual places in real life. It is impossible to estimate how many of them would stay in the West once they saw it. East Germans often say that if the Wall were taken down for good, they would want to visit the West just to taste the forbidden fruit. But they would return. Unemployment, inflation, and the economic crisis in the West have taken the glitter away.

It is an experiment that is not going to be put to the test, at least for a long time ahead. The Wall is not about to be removed. In recent years the authorities have been strengthening and re-mining the death-strip that runs along it. Along the entire border with West Germany they have been installing more of the automatic shooting-devices which have killed several would-be escapers. Many East German border guards have themselves crossed the frontier. Others are reluctant to shoot fellow citizens trying to get out. The machines do not hesitate. One right-wing Western group estimated in 1974 that since the Wall went up close to 34,000 East Germans had left, of whom 2,668 were border guards or members of the armed forces.[9] As the Wall has been strengthened, more East Germans have left the GDR via other countries, like Yugoslavia or Hungary. In the first half of 1974 the group claimed that 442 people had crossed the inter-German border, while 1,658 had left via other countries or had not returned from visits abroad. Human smuggling has become big business, with various shady Western operators charging up to 40,000 Marks to get a person out, in false compartments of cars, on forged papers, or by tunnel. The GDR authorities were conscious that the lifting of some travel restrictions could make the escape business easier. In 1974 they gave maximum publicity and severe sentences to several people who were charged with 'trafficking in human beings against the state'. Between mid-July and mid-August East German courts sentenced thirty-two West Berliners and thirteen West Germans to terms of up to fifteen years. In 1975 it was revealed that even the Governments of the two Germanies had been involved in a secret transfer business. The GDR routinely imprisons citizens who illegally try to leave the country. When outside groups like Amnesty International talk of political prisoners in the GDR (an estimate of 6,000 in 1975) the majority are escapers who failed.[10] Since 1961 the Federal Republic has regularly been buying many of them out for hard currency. In one particularly large deal two buses crossed the border in 1975 with 82 people on board. Many of the passengers were doctors, who had been convicted of trying to escape.[11] According to the magazine *Der Spiegel* about 2,000 prisoners were bought in 1974. The money came from the Ministry for Inter-German Relations. The deals were handled by Wolfgang Vogel, an East German lawyer who was also involved in the exchange of the American U-2 pilot, Gary Powers, for the Soviet spy, Colonel Rudolf Abel. In December

1975 a storm broke out in West Germany after *Der Spiegel* reported that in a few cases the East Germans had kept back people's children and had them adopted in the East after their parents fled.[12] The GDR reacted fiercely, claimed the facts had been distorted and expelled the magazine's East Berlin correspondent, Jörg Mettke.

On both sides the Wall remains a highly sensitive issue. In spite of the new treaty between the two countries, Western publicity about the Wall for a time increased. The West argued that East German official attitudes went against the spirit of *détente*. The East argued that the image of the Wall was being artificially spot-lighted in the Western media as a way of preventing more realistic views from emerging on other aspects of the GDR. Certainly for many West Germans the Wall, and the division of families, remain potent symbols of the GDR. They obscure the amount of change that has taken place inside the GDR — the greater relaxation of cultural life, the increased tolerance towards people's private pursuits, the rising standard of living. Other misconceptions live on in the West. The hoariest and most inaccurate is the view of the GDR as a haven for ex-Naxis. Perhaps precisely because the GDR's record on de-Nazification is good, the country's most insistent detractors try hardest to knock it down.

There are two frequently quoted sources for the argument. One is a document put out in 1965 by a secretly funded anti-Communist group in West Berlin called the Investigating Committee of Free Jurists.[13] The other is a list of thirty-nine names of East German journalists and media spokesmen published by Dr Simon Wiesenthal who ran a documentation centre in Vienna.[14] Neither document makes a clear distinction between prominent party members who joined Hitler early on and 'nominal Nazis' who joined the Nazi party at a young age towards the end of the war. Nor do the documents identify people who genuinely switched sides and left the party while Hitler was still in power or soon afterwards. The NDPD in East Germany was set up as a political instrument for re-educating Nazis. In 1965 the 'Free Jurists' named five members of the GDR's Council of Ministers who were former Nazis. One was Hans Reichelt, a deputy chairman of the Agricultural Council, who joined the Nazis as a 19-year-old in 1944.

Another, Heinz Matthes, the chairman of the Workers' and Peasants' Inspectorate, joined when he was 17. Dr Herbert Weiz, a deputy Prime Minister, was an 18-year-old when he became a member in 1942. These men typify the ironic fact that the number of nominal Nazis could be increasing in East German public life. The age group which was in its late teens at the end of the war is now around fifty and at the peak of their careers. Of the other two ministers mentioned by the 'Free Jurists', one Hans Bentzien has been dropped from the Council of Ministers. The other, Professor Ernst Joachim Giessmann, at that time Minister of Higher Education, also joined the Nazis in his teens. But it was relatively early on, in 1937. His case therefore raises some doubts, although the SED was presumably satisfied that he has reformed.

Dr Wiesenthal's list mentions Günther Kertzscher, an assistant editor of *Neues Deutschland*, who was 24 years old when he joined the Nazis, but was subsequently captured on the Eastern front, joined the National Committee for a Free Germany, and was sentenced to death *in absentia* by the Nazis. Similarly Kurt Blecha, the main GDR Government spokesman, joined the Nazis in 1941 when he was eighteen. He also was in the National Committee for a Free Germany before the end of the war. Gerhard Dengler, another former *Neues Deutschland* correspondent on Dr Wiesenthal's list, was sentenced to death *in absentia*, and his mother was taken hostage after he left the Nazi party in captivity. Nor was the changing of sides by many German POWs in Russia simply opportunism. Many of them were sent back behind the German lines on dangerous missions to try and arouse troops to mutiny. Only rarely have Western researchers come up with a former Nazi in a high position in the GDR who was more than a nominal party member or who had not changed sides during the war. In 1958 Major General Arno von Lenski was removed from the GDR army after he was found to have passed death sentences as a judge in a Nazi people's court. Ernst Grossman who became a member of the central committee in 1959 was exposed by Western sources as a former guard in Sachsenhausen concentration camp. In 1963 it was revealed that a new agricultural minister and central committee member Karl-Heinz Bartsch had been in the Waffen SS. The SED immediately dropped both men.

The charges that East Germany harbours prominent former Nazis do not hold water. They were always inherently implausible, because the strongly anti-Fascist views of the Communists who returned to Germany in 1945 did not put them in a very forgiving mood. Even if one or two Nazis slipped through the net, the centralised nature of the GDR's system would have prevented any Nazi views which they might have retained from having much influence. In occasional cases in orphanages and children's homes, areas in most societies which tend to be neglected, I have heard, but not been able to confirm, that authoritarian staff members 'with Nazi views' still survive. In the mainstream of East German society they have gone. The charges against the GDR were revived after the 1967 war in the Middle East when all of Eastern Europe took a strongly anti-Zionist line. In Poland there was a brief but sordid outbreak of anti-Semitism. The GDR had nothing similar. It still has a high proportion of senior Jewish Communists in public life. Alfred Norden is a member of the Politbüro. The head of the state bank, Dr Grete Wittkowski, who died in 1975 was of Jewish origin. Alexander Abusch was a deputy Prime Minister. There have been no scandals in the GDR comparable to the repeated revelations of prominent former Nazis in West Germany and the frequent cases of war criminals who go untried or unpunished. On February 7 1973 the *International Herald Tribune* reported that the International Committee of Survivors of Auschwitz had deplored the fact that four big Nazi criminals were still at large in West Germany. They included Horst Schumann, who allegedly sterilised people in concentration camp experiments, Johannes Thummler, Gestapo chief in Katowice, Albert Ganzenmüller, a state secretary in Hitler's Ministry of Transport, who reputedly arranged for the deportation of future murder victims, and Horst Wagner, liaison man between the Foreign Ministry and Heinrich Himmler's SS. On the same day in two separate cases seven former Nazi police officers were convicted of mass murders of Soviet prisoners of war and Jews in Byelorussia and occupied Poland. They were all immediately released on grounds of ill-health.

Another Western charge against the GDR is that it is a 'militaristic' society. The field-grey uniforms of the National

People's Army (NVA or Nationale Volksarmee), the goose step of its ceremonial marches, the ubiquitous sight of men in uniform, and the fact that the GDR is the last country in Eastern Europe which holds a military parade on May Day, can all give visitors an uncomfortable impression. Much of it is superficial. East Germany is a heavily garrisoned state, but like other countries in Eastern Europe its soldiers are expected to wear their uniforms when on weekend leave in public places like cinemas, parks, or trains. When the NVA was formed in 1956 the authorities decided to keep the traditional German uniforms. In West Germany the army was given American-style uniforms. If the East Germans had chosen Soviet uniforms, they would presumably have been called puppets. More important than its uniforms is an army's officer corps. A West German study made in 1965 concluded that out of fifty top officers in the NVA thirty-three were pre-1933 members of the KPD or SPD, who either fought in Spain or were imprisoned by the Nazis.[15] The head of the NVA and Minister of Defence, General Heinz Hoffmann, escaped from Germany in 1935 and served as a battalion commander in the International Brigade. Another twelve of the top fifty officers were former Wehrmacht men, most of whom had been captured on the Eastern front and went over to the Communist side. Increasingly nowadays the NVA's generals are highly drilled professionals who have been trained since the war. A more recent study by Werner Bauer and Ralf Dahrendorf found that half the East German generals were under 57. In the West German Bundeswehr in the same year only 5 per cent were. Whereas most NVA officers came from backgrounds in the working class or petty bourgeoisie, in the Bundeswehr 16 per cent were aristocrats, and 37 per cent the sons of high-ranking officers. In choosing their new officer corps Ulbricht and his colleagues looked mainly for political reliability. The West Germans ostensibly went for professional competence in the first instance, but ended up with an appropriately conservative anti-Communist elite, many of whom had happily served under Hitler. In the NVA no one can wear medals earned under previous regimes. In the Bundeswehr there is no such ban. East Germany's officers are tough professionals who serve a disciplined and authoritarian state. Its leaders have always been acutely conscious of the GDR's security and have tended to be over-cautious. But to see that as a continuation of the aristocratic chauvinism of the Nazi Wehrmacht or the Kaiser's Prussian officer corps is incorrect. Nor is there much evidence of the aggressive nationalism which was always part of the earlier tradition of German militarism.

Less offensive and probably more widely held in the West is the misconception that the GDR is becoming purely 'a consumer society'. The country's rising standard of living, the new visibility of consumer goods, jazz in Berlin, portable tape-recorders blaring out on Baltic beaches, the developing traffic jams, flashing neon lights, and queues for nylon tights give an impression of a country whose goals are little different from those in the West. It is a comforting illusion which implies the GDR is still 'losing the race'. Since it is much the same as the West except less free and further behind materially. In fact, as Ch. 7 suggested, collective institutions are strong in the East, and have been accepted by a growing number of people. In a book of interviews, published in West Germany in 1970,[16] several refugees from the East talked about their impressions of both societies. Barbara Grunert-Bronnen, the book's author, wrote that although the interviews were not necessarily typical, they were more so than most people thought. One of those interviewed, Christine E. aged 33, a freelance journalist who left the GDR in 1958, described her impressions of the West: 'When I came here I was simply amazed and taken aback, shaken even, by the thought that these people here in the Federal Republic have, based on their Constitution, the possibility of freedom, of self-fulfilment. They can say what they think without having to expect the secret police at five the next morning. This country claims to be democratic — I was amazed that people make absolutely no use of it. That was the biggest shock. This attitude: politics is bad for the character, hold your tongue, otherwise you get into trouble, make yourself unpopular, get left behind — such protecting of oneself from above and below and from all sides, that did rather annoy me.' She found it hard to make friends. 'In East Germany when we spoke of friendship, we really meant friendship. It was not just an empty word, but a word with definite meaning, signifying an obligation. That was not the case here ... One always seems to be doomed. One longs for what one does not have ... when I was in the

GDR I felt amputated, I longed for the freedom of the West And when I had the freedom of the West, I sometimes longed for the collectivity of the GDR.'

Harald M. is a 29-year-old waiter whose family moved from the Sudetenland to East Germany in 1946. He left the GDR in 1960 when he was 20. He found much to criticise in the West and he joined the Communist party. 'In the GDR as a result of the breaking down of class relations, human relations are much more genuine. They are not, as here, stamped by the consumer society ... here one only counts as someone if one has all the things a man has to have, starting with a car ... ' He found Western ambitiousness a divisive factor. 'In the GDR ambition has its limits. Here in the West a worker who has saved two thousand Marks can travel to the Sudan and shoot a wild deer. That is an alienating factor in our society, that the proletarian believes he is no longer a proletarian. Over there, the worker sees himself quite clearly as a worker. The state is constantly saying to him: "It is you who must change society." ... Here they want to split the workers as a social block into individualists. Here they say everyone is free ... Indeed everyone here is an individualist, but a sick individualist.' In the GDR, Harald said, he had girl-friends from all levels of society, the daughter of a teacher, a senior official or a party boss, it did not matter. 'But when I came to the West I immediately noticed there was a clear separation. I realised how, without noticing it, I had been influenced by growing up in the harmony of a socialist society. To my mind it is not for nothing that many of the left wing here come from the GDR.'

Another writer, Manfred G. aged 35, left the GDR when he was 21. 'What annoyed me most of all in the West was that the image of the West which I had when I came over did not fit. I found a situation in which the individual is lost. It was never like this in the GDR. Of course it didn't suit you to be always in a collective, that there were always student groups, that you were always with other people even when you weren't working, that you went to the theatre with other people and then discussed it together. But at least you could never develop such a feeling of being lost and abandoned. Of course it was a bit annoying because it was sometimes simply too much, and always politics ... but all the same you were in a collective, and there was an ideological consistency to it, even when you differed with people. You were always discussing things. There was a chance for communication ... ' Some East Germans return. Between 1950 and 1964 roughly 500,000 people with West German identity papers went to the GDR, up to half of whom were disillusioned East Germans going home again.[17]

East Germany is different from the West. It is not just a less developed consumer society. Its goals are different and the policies adopted on the way to them are different. Every week a minority of people are prepared to risk their lives to get out. Some have political motives in going. Most are skilled workers and professionals who go for economic reasons. They know they will get better pay, more chance for promotion, and a bigger chance to fulfil their personal ambitions. Those who stay behind accept the GDR for what it is. They may grumble at it constantly in private, yet rush to defend it if Westerners criticise too much or poke fun. They envy their Western relations for being able to come in and out at will, but resent being patronised or treated as poor cousins. They will boast of their superior education system but complain that university libraries will not stock the works of critical authors. They praise the orderliness and stability of their society but blame it for being so slow to change. They will tell you how long prices have been fixed, and remember the cost of basic groceries because they have not changed for years. But how is it, they will ask, that this item or that is never in sufficient supply.

For all the politicians' talk in West Germany of reunification, most West Germans have lost interest in the East. A public opinion poll conducted for the Federal Government in 1972 found that 60 per cent of people either said they knew enough about the GDR or were not interested in it.[18] East Germans are probably more curious about the West than vice versa. Their access to Western television puts them in a unique position in Europe, East or West. They are probably better informed and more critical towards the two ideological systems on either side of the great divide in Europe than any other people. They can see their strengths and weaknesses. East Germans seem more aware of international events than people in the West and in the rest of Eastern Europe. The GDR's record in collecting money in factories and offices for Vietnam, and for African liberation movements ranks with the best in Scandinavia. East Germans remain interested in the West. Over the years two nations will continue to develop as Erich Honecker hopes. But there is bound to be a special psychological and cultural relationship for a long time to come.

The two nations' political relationship is likely to be more placid over the next decade than ever before. Most of the major business of the Cold War is now complete, thanks to the string of agreements which the two states signed. West Germany will go its way behind its main goal of strengthening the Common Market. The GDR is busy with Comecon and its own internal economic problems. Minor rows will continue to produce shortlived flare-ups. The status of Berlin still contains ambiguities. The 1971 agreement produced a compromise which satisfied both sides because it was vague. It stated that West Berlin was not a constituent part of the Federal Republic but also said that its ties to the Federal Republic could be expanded. Ever since then there have been minor incidents as East and West each tries to stress their interpretation of that contradictory statement. But Berlin is unlikely to become an issue of major international tension in the predictable future as long as East–West *détente* as a whole continues. The GDR will always be a special emotional issue in West German politics, a political football between the West German left and right. But it will no longer be a central or determining factor in any election.

The economic relationship between the two states will remain close. For years West Germany has been the GDR's best trading partner after the Soviet Union. Since the Treaty of Rome was signed in 1957 setting up the Common Market, the GDR has had a special arrangement which allows its trade with the Federal Republic to be counted as internal German trade. Its goods can enter the Common Market exempt from tariffs. East Germany benefits by having privileged access to the Market which is denied to the rest of Eastern Europe, much to their chagrin. In return West Germany has a competitive head start in the GDR market over other Western countries. This loophole has caused some Common Market members annoyance and resentment. Some 30 per cent of the GDR's trade is with Western countries and of this volume the Federal Republic takes a third. For a time the East Germans seemed hesitant about making co-operative agreements or licensing deals with West German firms. Since recognition that appears to have changed. Giant West German firms like Krupp and Siemens which the GDR used to attack because of their war-time connections with Hitler have recently made long-term deals in the GDR. Like other East European countries which are increasingly looking to the West to buy advanced techno-logy, the GDR is losing some of its earlier inhibitions.

When it comes to its relations with its Eastern neighbours, the GDR has still not completely overcome the terrible legacy of history. Its approaches to the East seem motivated by duty and necessity rather than affection. The SED wants good relations with the Slavs on its borders partly as a way of deflecting the GDR population's interest away from the West and partly in order to make amends for Germany's overweening arrogance in the past. Ulbricht and his colleagues always took care not to let the development of their own country be held back if they could avoid it. For more than a decade the GDR has been the strongest economic power in Comecon after the Soviet Union. When Khrushchev tried to create a supranational planning organisation for Comecon in 1962 Ulbricht reacted not much less tenaciously than the Romanians although he was quieter about it. He was against the idea of a levelling of incomes within Comecon which would have meant the richer countries having to help the poorer. In December 1964 Ulbricht said that co-operation in Comecon must be based 'strictly on economic criteria'. The GDR denounced the original Comecon resolution of 1949 which forced one country to pass on scientific and technical data to a more backward country without any payment.[19] Only in the last ten years has there been a significant increase in economic co-operation between the GDR and its neighbours, Poland, Hungary and Czechoslovakia. Although it would have been logical to create a single integrated Eastern European car industry, the Poles, Czechs and East Germans still each have their own car plants. Plans for a combined East German and Czech car collapsed in the early 1970s. The first joint factory between Poland and the GDR, a textile plant at Zawiercie in Poland, only opened in 1975. In spite of the GDR's chronic shortage of labour and Poland's surplus — at least until the mid-1970s — the two countries were slow to permit

Poles to work in the GDR except in the immediate border areas along the Oder. The fear apparently was that frictions could revive the enmity of the past.

In November 1971 after Ulbricht's retirement Honecker took what looked like a spur-of-the-moment decision to reverse the old policy. He agreed with Edward Gierek's new Polish Government to lift all visa restrictions between Poland and the GDR on January 1 1972. At the same time East Germans were allowed to travel to Czechoslovakia without visas or passports. The experiment was too successful in some ways and a disaster in others. In the first year ten million Poles poured over the frontier, mainly to buy East German consumer goods which could not be obtained in Poland. The sudden invasion produced shortages for East Germans, crowds of Poles in department stores in Berlin, Dresden and Leipzig, and a good deal of German resentment. The move threatened to arouse old prejudices against the Poles. By the end of the year the Poles had to impose a personal exchange allowance of 200 Marks. Six and a half million East Germans travelled to Poland in the same period. On the Czech–German border the boot was on the other foot. There it was the East Germans who were pouring over to buy good-quality Czech textiles and electrical equipment. The Czechs quickly imposed export restrictions.

The episode was a reminder of how slow and impersonal 'socialist integration' had been in Eastern Europe. It took almost twenty-five years from the founding of Comecon for genuine human contacts to be allowed across international frontiers. Countries which were military and political allies, and claimed to be bound by 'fraternal and comradely ties' remained strangers to each other at all but the official level. No wonder that national stereotypes about Germans still live on in Eastern Europe, and that many ordinary people make little distinction between Germans from East or West. They respect the GDR for its economic success but it will take more than one generation to convince them that a new Germany has been born. With the Soviet Union the GDR's relations are also still largely confined to the official level. The two countries have no 'open frontier' between them. Numerous delegations visit each other's countries, but they are mainly made up of party groups, engineers, technicians, army officers, and some young people.

The average member of the working class in each country is not often included. Nevertheless, the strong dose of propaganda, particularly about the Soviet Union's role in the war has had an effect on the younger generation. More than half the GDR's population has been born since 1940. Too young for Hitler's ideology, they accept that the alliance with the Soviet Union is a necessity without which the GDR could not have survived. Unlike most older Germans who were taught to see Russia as barbarian, the young have an image of the Soviet Union as a rapidly industrialising country with impressive achievements in science and space research. The young also acknowledge that the GDR's dependence on the USSR for raw materials and energy is almost total.

At the top level of the party Honecker's relations with the Soviet leadership are undoubtedly better than those of Ulbricht. Ulbricht was in supreme power long enough to carve out a position of incumbency which was only assailed as his health declined. He annoyed the Russians with his didactic tone and his self-appointed role as the guardian of Leninist orthodoxy. At Warsaw Pact meetings he irritated them with his boast that he was the only living Communist leader who had met the great Vladimir Ilyich. Honecker is a new man, more pliant, more modest and less opinionated. He also has an easier task. The original tensions between the Soviet Union and the SED are things of the past. The contradiction between the Russians' early post-war role as a vindictive occupying power and simultaneous mentor for Communism in Germany is long since over. There is no question of the Russians' giving up the GDR in the interests of a wider settlement with West Germany. The 'indissoluble friendship' between the two countries is much less soluble now. The GDR is not a satellite, but a junior partner, economically, politically and diplomatically more powerful than it ever used to be.

Epilogue

They have buried the founders of the GDR in a mildly inconvenient place. It is not like the Kremlin Wall in Moscow, bang in the city centre with Lenin's mausoleum in front and the rest of the Soviet pantheon ranged alongside. To get to the 'Remembrance Place of the Socialists' in Berlin you have to take a tram or underground to the industrial suburb of Lichtenberg. Then follows a ten-minute walk beside a railway cutting.

The journey to the cemetery is worth making. Beyond a large lawn planted with birch and beech trees they have built a redbrick semi-circular wall open at the front. At its foot and in niches round the side the ashes of the lesser figures are preserved. In the centre of the semi-circle stands a tall, granite rock. Its simple atheistic inscription reads 'The dead admonish us'. In pride of place in front of it lie Rosa Luxemburg and Karl Liebknecht. They were originally buried here at Lichtenberg in a much less distinguished part of the cemetery, after Luxemburg's murdered body was dredged by faithful admirers from the Landwehr Kanal and Liebknecht was collected from the morgue. Hitler had their graves razed and the suburban monument torn down. After the war they were given full honours. Walter Ulbricht is in the centre with them, but his grave is round the side.

Only a few strollers come here; a young couple with a child, two elderly ladies, then for another ten minutes the place is empty. The GDR never had a cult of personality for its leaders, and Ulbricht's brief attempt at one for himself in 1953 was called off by the Russians. If anything, it is the opposite now.

'He's the nearest thing to an unperson that we have', said Stefan Heym in the summer of 1975.[1] They renamed the Walter Ulbricht stadium two months after he died in 1973. His former colleagues almost never mention him in speeches or party documents. He is not dishonoured, just quietly forgotten. His successors need time to establish their own image. Ulbricht's shadow was best pushed aside, they thought. There is no advantage for them in invoking his name before a population who never loved him.

To his credit Ulbricht never planned an imposing burial. To find a place for him in the central circle at Lichtenberg they had hurriedly to take out an obscure pre-war Socialist and re-bury him elsewhere. Ulbricht lies between Otto Grotewohl and John Schehr, the KPD Politbüro member whom the Nazis shot in 1934 'while trying to escape'. A mausoleum for Ulbricht on the style of Lenin's would have been inappropriate. He had none of Lenin's intellectual brilliance nor his energy in action. Ulbricht was a functionary rather than a revolutionary. He had no gift for working with people. What he did have was boundless determination and stubbornness. Inevitably the story of the GDR is in large part the story of Ulbricht. In spite of his long service in the Comintern and abroad, he was above all a German nationalist. He wanted to bring his concept of socialism to Germany, because he thought that only under a socialist system could the German people once again lift their heads without shame and retrieve the national honour they had lost by starting Europe's two worst wars.

Ulbricht was always concerned with security. He had a front-line mentality, the feeling that he was socialism's sentinel standing on the wall on guard against the neo-Fascist hordes. Asked once why he did not follow Khrushchev's example and liberalise, he replied 'Back there, they can afford to do anything.'[2] Ulbricht's obsession with security stunted and blocked any sustained development towards political relaxation in his lifetime. His successors have not yet thrown off the feeling themselves. Their excessive caution, and lack of confidence in a population which often seems more loyal than the leadership expects are still major hallmarks of the GDR. After living so long in a cave as international outcasts, they still find the sunlight of diplomatic recognition a little dazzling.

The GDR's first international meeting in Europe was the grand finale to the European Security Conference in Helsinki in July 1975. By an accident of the French diplomatic alphabet Erich Honecker found himself sitting between the Chancellor of West Germany and the President of the United States. Nothing could have been more ironic than that he should be flanked by the leaders of the two countries which had done more than any others to prevent the GDR from coming into being. Honecker was not awed by the occasion. He chatted happily with both his neighbours. In the 1960s Willy Brandt once described West Germany as 'an economic giant but a political dwarf'. The remark fits the GDR even more aptly. The most prosperous country in Eastern Europe, with a higher *per capita* income than Britain, the GDR has been ignored until the last few years. The excesses of its political way of life and the lack of travel possibilities for its people are the product of special conditions, and the continuing confrontation with West Germany. But its overall social and economic system is a presentable model of the kind of authoritarian welfare states which Eastern European nations have now become. Totalitarianism is no longer a useful concept to describe Eastern Europe. Authoritarianism is a better word. Within a centralised pattern of political organisation, Eastern Europe has produced a variant of the welfare state which is different from Scandinavian socialism and English or West German social democracy but which deserves close inspection. For too long it has been fashionable to reject Eastern Europe's post-war experience as an unmitigated disaster. The emergence of the GDR as a viable state against all odds ought to be an intellectual warning that from the most inauspicious beginnings worthwhile results can come. Socialism in the GDR is as much a part of the socialist tradition as any of its other national manifestations elsewhere in the world.

Notes

Introduction

1 *The World Bank Atlas,* The International Bank for Reconstruction and Development, Washington D.C., 1977.
2 Hans Apel, 'Bericht über das Staatsgefühl der DDR-Bevölkerung', *Frankfurter Hefte,* XXII, no. 3, March 1967, p. 171.
3 Deutsches Institut für Wirtschaftsforschung, *DDR-Wirtschaft: eine Bestandsaufnahme,* Fischer Taschenbuch Verlag (hereafter referred to as *DDR-Wirtschaft*), Frankfurt am Main, 1974, p. 36.
4 *New York Times,* March 23 1975.
5 *Guardian,* July 7 1973.

Chapter 1   *Splits and Wounds on the German Left*

1 Erich Matthias and Rudolf Morsey, eds, *Das Ende der Parteien, 1933,* Droste Verlag, Düsseldorf, 1960, p. 662.
2 Ibid., p. 693.
3 Fritz Selbmann, *Die Erste Stunde,* Verlag Neues Leben, Berlin, 1974.
4 Rosa Luxemburg, 'Reform or Revolution', Bombay, 1951, pp. 29–30, quoted in Tony Cliff, *Rosa Luxemburg: a Study,* Socialist Review Publishing Co., London, 1959.
5 Ibid., p. 64.
6 Rosa Luxemburg, *Gesammelte Werke,* Band III, Berlin, p. 366, quoted in Tony Cliff, op. cit.
7 Fritz Selbmann, op. cit., p. 313.
8 Matthias and Morsey, op. cit., p. 677.
9 Ibid., p. 690.
10 Ibid., p. 696.
11 Ibid., p. 694.
12 Paul Merker, 'How German Democracy Collapsed', *Freies*

Deutschland, II, no. 3, February 1943, Mexico City.

13 Karl Mewis, *Im Auftrag der Partei*, Dietz Verlag, Berlin, 1972, p. 52.

14 Matthias and Morsey, op. cit., p. 717.

15 Roy Medvedev, *Let History Judge*, Macmillan, London, 1972, p. 222.

16 Margarete Buber Neumann, *Kriegsschauplätze der Weltrevolution: Ein Bericht aus der Praxis der Komintern, 1919–1943*, Seewald Verlag, Stuttgart, 1967, p. 484.

17 Wolfgang Leonhard, *Child of the Revolution*, Collins, London, 1957, pp. 65–73.

18 Margarete Buber Neumann, op. cit., p. 489.

19 Karl Mewis, op. cit., p. 37.

20 Paul Merker, 'Die Juden und das Neue Deutschland', *Freies Deutschland*, IV, no. 11, October 1945, Mexico City.

21 Fritz Selbmann, op. cit., p. 386.

22 Isaac Deutscher, *Stalin*, Penguin Books, London, 1966, p. 523.

Chapter 2   *A German Road to Socialism*

1 Wolfgang Leonhard, *Child of the Revolution*, Collins, London, 1957, p. 281.

2 Isaac Deutscher, *Stalin*, Penguin Books, London, 1966, p. 525.

3 Quoted in *Freies Deutschland*, IV, no. 12, November–December 1945, Mexico City, p. 3.

4 Wolfgang Leonhard, op. cit., p. 121.

5 Ibid., pp. 257ff.

6 J. W. Stalin, *Über den Kampf um den Frieden: Eine Sammlung ausgewählter Aufsätze und Reden*, Berlin, 1954, p. 243, quoted in *Geschichte der Deutschen Arbeiterbewegung von 1945 bis 1963*, Teil I, 1945–9, Dietz Verlag, Berlin, 1967, p. 27.

7 George Kennan, 'Telegram, March 6 1946', in *Foreign Relations of the United States 1946*, vol. V, *The British Commonwealth; Western and Central Europe*, Washington D.C., 1969.

8 Ibid.

9 Carola Stern, *Ulbricht: a political biography*, Pall Mall Press, London, 1965, p. 79.

10 Wolfgang Leonhard, op. cit., p. 298.

11 Fritz Selbmann, *Die Erste Stunde*, Verlag Neues Leben, Berlin, 1974, p. 9, quoting from 'Situationsbericht von Anton Ackermann' in *Staat und Recht*, XIV, no. 5, 1965.

12 *Difficult Years Bear Fruit*, Verlag Zeit im Bild, Dresden, 1971, p. 19.

13 Ibid.

14 Frederick Ford, 'What happened to Nazi Criminals?', in *Democratic German Report*, March 26 1975, Berlin.
15 Ibid.
16 Gordon Schaffer, *Russian Zone*, George Allen & Unwin, London, 1947, p. 120.
17 Wolfgang Leonhard, op. cit., p. 353.
18 *Geschichte der Deutschen Arbeiterbewegung von 1945 bis 1963*, op. cit., p. 156.
19 Wolfgang Leonhard, op. cit., p. 348.
20 Ibid., p. 356.

Chapter 3   *The Soviet Connection causes Problems*
1 Paul Merker, 'An Meinen Bruder in London', *Freies Deutschland*, IV, no. 6, May 1945, Mexico City, p. 8.
2 *Geschichte der Deutschen Arbeiterbewegung von 1945 bis 1963*, Teil I, 1945–9, Dietz Verlag, Berlin, 1967, p. 56.
3 J. P. Nettl, *The Eastern Zone and Soviet Policy in Germany 1945–50*, Oxford University Press, 1951, p. 58.
4 Quoted in *Der Spiegel*, May 12 1975, p. 70.
5 Quoted in *Der Spiegel*, May 12 1975, p. 76.
6 Heinz Brandt, *The Search for a Third Way — my path between East and West*, Doubleday, New York, 1970, p. 152.
7 Gordon Schaffer, *Russian Zone*, George Allen & Unwin, London, 1947, p. 19.
8 J. P. Nettl, op. cit., ch. 7.
9 Heinz Kohler, *Economic Integration in the Soviet Bloc with an East German Case-Study*, Praeger, New York, 1965, p. 14.
10 Gordon Schaffer, op. cit., p. 22.
11 Interview with author, July 1975.
12 Ibid.
13 Gordon Schaffer, op. cit., p. 69.
14 *Geschichte ...* , op. cit., p. 175.
15 Gabriel Kolko, *The Politics of War*, Random House, New York, 1968, p. 573.
16 Charles Bohlen, *Witness to History*, Weidenfeld & Nicolson, London, 1973, p. 264.
17 *Geschichte ...* , op. cit., p. 226.
18 J. P. Nettl, op. cit., p. 181.
19 Ibid., p. 166.
20 *Geschichte ...* , op. cit., p. 221.
21 John Peet in Democratic German Report, November 6 1974, Berlin.
22 J. P. Nettl, op. cit., p. 253.

23 *Geschichte* ... , op. cit., p. 268.
24 Ibid., p. 309.
25 Ibid., p. 311.
26 Milovan Djilas, *Conversations with Stalin*, Hart-Davies, London, 1962, p. 119.

Chapter 4 *Birthpangs of a Divided Nation*

1 Lucius D. Clay, *Decision in Germany*, Heinemann, London, 1950, p. 439.
2 *Geschichte der Deutschen Arbeiterbewegung von 1945 bis 1963*, Teil II, 1949–55, Dietz Verlag, Berlin, 1967, p. 19.
3 Ibid., p. 20.
4 Ibid., p. 20.
5 Stefan Thomas, 'Beyond the Wall', in *Survey*, October 1960, p. 60, quoted in Jean Edward Smith, *Germany beyond the Wall. People, Politics, and Prosperity*, Little, Brown and Co., Boston and Toronto, 1969, p. 218.
6 *Geschichte* ... , Teil II, p. 23.
7 Ibid., p. 82.
8 Ibid., p. 39.
9 Ibid., p. 33.
10 Joachim Schultz, *Der Funktionär in der Einheitspartei*, Ring Verlag, Stuttgart and Düsseldorf, 1956, p. 137, quoted in Arthur M. Hanhardt Jr, *The German Democratic Republic*, Baltimore, 1968, p. 49.
11 *Geschichte* ... , Teil II, p. 113.
12 Ibid., p. 107.
13 *Neuer Weg*, no. 23, 1952, p. 45, quoted in Arnulf Baring, *Uprising in East Germany: June 17 1953*, Ithaca and London, 1972, p. 67.
14 Baring, op. cit., p. 18.
15 Ibid., p. 13.

Chapter 5 *A New Course after Stalin's Death?*

1 Heinz Lippman, *Honecker and the New Politics of Europe*, Angus & Robertson, London, 1973, p. 151.
2 Martin Janicke, *Der Dritte Weg: die antistalinistische Opposition gegen Ulbricht seit 1953*, Neuer Deutscher Verlag, Köln, 1964, p. 25.
3 Stern, *Ulbricht: a political biography*, Pall Mall Press, London, 1965, p. 139.
4 *Neues Deutschland*, April 16 1953.

5 Baring, *Uprising in East Germany: June 17 1953*, Ithaca and London, p. 85.
6 Heinz Brandt, *The Search for a Third Way — my path between East and West*, Doubleday, New York, 1970, p. 187.
7 Ibid., p. 191.
8 Ibid., p. 194.
9 Ibid., p. 196.
10 *Geschichte der Deutschen Arbeiterbewegung von 1945 bis 1963*, Teil II, 1949–55, Dietz Verlag, Berlin, 1967, p. 232.
11 Stern, op. cit., p. 145.
12 Robert Havemann, *An Alienated Man*, Davis-Poynter, London, 1973, translated by Derek Masters from *Fragen, Antworte, Fragen*, Piper Verlag, Munich, 1960.
13 Baring, op. cit., p. 52.
14 Brandt, op. cit., p. 213.
15 *Der Spiegel*, July 2 1958.
16 Baring, op. cit., pp. 76ff.
17 *Manchester Guardian*, June 22 1953.
18 Baring, op. cit., p. 76.
19 Havemann, op. cit., pp. 93ff.
20 Baring, op. cit., p. 107.
21 *Neues Deutschland*, July 7 1953.
22 Lippmann, op. cit., p. 160.
23 Walter Ulbricht, *Der Weg zu Frieden, Einheit, und Wohlstand*, Dietz Verlag, Berlin, 1953, p. 13.
24 *Geschichte ...* , Teil II, p. 306.
25 Fritz Schenk, *Im Vorzimmer der Diktatur*, Kiepenheuer and Witsch, Köln, 1962, p. 280.
26 *Neue Deutsche Literatur*, no. 8, August 1953.
27 *Neues Deutschland*, July 12 1953.
28 From *The search for a Third Way—My Path Between East and East* by Heinz Brandt, translated from the German by Salvator Attanasio. Translation copyright © 1970 by Doubleday & Company, Inc. Reprinted by permission of Doubleday & Company, Inc.
29 *Neues Deutschland*, August 26 1953.
30 Janicke, op. cit., p. 52.
31 *Pravda*, July 6 1953, quoted in Janicke, op. cit., p. 78.
32 Janicke, op. cit., p. 79.
33 Ibid., p. 105.
34 Ibid., p. 157.
35 Ibid., p. 88.
36 Ibid., p. 90.
37 Ibid., p. 159.

Chapter 6   *Shaping an Economic Miracle*
1 Nikolai Fadeyev, *Der Rat für Gegenseitige Wirtschaftshilfe*, Staatsverlag der DDR, 1965, p. 140.
2 Wolfgang Zapf, 'Wandlungen der deutschen Elite. Ein Zirkulationsmodell deutscher Führungsgruppen, 1919–1961', Munich, 1965, quoted in Peter C. Ludz, *The Changing Party Elite in East Germany*, MIT Press, Cambridge, Mass., 1972, p. 170.
3 Ernst Richert, *Die DDR-Elite oder Unsere Partner von Morgen?*, Rowohlt Taschenbuch Verlag, Hamburg, 1968, p. 64.
4 Thomas Baylis, 'East Germany: in quest of legitimacy', in *Problems of Communism*, United States Information Agency, Washington D.C., March–April 1972, p. 48.
5 Ludz, op. cit., pp. 40ff.
6 Kurt Sontheimer and Wilhelm Bleek, *The Government and Politics of East Germany*, Hutchinson, London, 1975, p. 113.
7 Ludz, op. cit., p. 42.
8 Georg Klaus, 'Schematische und schöpferische geistige Arbeit in kybernetischer Sicht', *Deutsche Zeitschrift für Philosophie*, 9, nos 2–3, February–March 1961 quoted in Ludz, op. cit., p. 352.
9 Richert, op. cit., p. 79.
10 Friedrich Ebert, *Zur weitern Entwicklung derso zialistischen Demokratie in der DDR*, Dietz Verlag, Berlin, 1975. A lecture given to party cadres on April 21 1975.

Chapter 7   *How much 'People's Democracy'?*
1 *Die Tribüne*, January 6 1975.
2 *Die Wirtschaft*, 19, no. 40.
3 Bundesministerium für innerdeutscher Beziehungen, *Bericht und Materialien zur Lage der Nation*, Bonn, 1971, p. 169.
4 Ibid., p. 199.
5 Hartmut Zimmermann, 'Probleme der Mitbestimmung in der DDR', in *Kommunität, Vierteljahreshefte der Evangelischen Akademie*, Berlin, XVII, Heft 65, January 1973, p. 12.
6 Irmhild Rudolph and Erhard Stölting, 'Soziale Beziehungen im VEB im Spiegel betriebssoziologischer Forschung in der DDR', in *Deutschland Archiv Sonderheft, 'Industriebetrieb und Gesellschaft in der DDR'*, Akademie für Politische Bildung Tutzing, III, October 1970, p. 115.
7 Ibid., p. 118.
8 *Die Tribüne*, June 4 1975.
9 Manfred Lötsch, 'Über die soziale Struktur der Arbeiterklasse; einige Schwerpunkte und Probleme der soziologischen For-

schung', in *Soziologische Probleme der Klassenentwicklung in der DDR*, Dietz Verlag, Berlin, 1975, p. 109.

10 Zimmermann, op. cit., p. 13.
11 *Democratic German Report*, June 6 1973.
12 Ibid., June 6 1973.
13 *Die Tribüne*, 'Die Konfliktkommission', June 12 1975.
14 Rudi Weidig, 'Die Entwicklung der Arbeiterklasse und der Persönlichkeit bei der Gestaltung der entwickelter sozialistischen Gesellschaft in der DDR', in *Soziologische Probleme der Klassenentwicklung in der DDR*.
15 *Neues Deutschland*, July 6 1974.
16 Kurt Sontheimer and Wilhelm Bleek, *The Government and Politics of East Germany*, Hutchinson, London, 1975, p. 75.
17 *Le Monde*, March 11 1972.
18 Deutsches Institut für Wirtschaftsforschung, *Wochenbericht*, 5/74, p. 39.
19 DIW, *DDR-Wirtschaft*, op. cit., p. 248.
20 Joachim Nawrocki, 'Für Betrieb und Partei', *Die Zeit*, October 25 1974.
21 Ibid.
22 Barbara Grunert-Bronnen, *Ich bin Bürger der DDR und lebe in der Bundesrepublik*, Piper Verlag, Munich, 1970, p. 13.
23 Interview with the author, June 1975.

Chapter 8   *Leisure, Crime and Private Life*
1 Robert Havemann, 'DDR: im Strudel des kapitalistischen Infernos?' in *Die Sowjetunion, Solschenizyn, und die westliche Linke*, edited by Rudi Dutschke and Manfred Wilke, Rowohlt Taschenbuch Verlag, Hamburg, 1975.
2 *Der Spiegel*, May 14 1973.
3 *Neue Berliner Illustrierte*, 18, 1975.
4 Ibid.
5 *Frankfurter Allgemeine Zeitung*, December 7 1974.
6 *Der Spiegel*, May 5, 1975.
7 *Frankfurter Allgemeine Zeitung*, December 7 1974.
8 *Wochenpost*, July 4 1975.
9 Trevor Beeson, *Discretion and Valour: Religious Conditions in Russia and Eastern Europe*, Fontana Books, Collins, 1974, p. 170.
10 Quoted in Michael Morley, 'Hard Times for Poetry' in *Index on Censorship*, London, no. 2, 1973.

Chapter 9   *Social Services from Cradle to Grave*
1 *Democratic German Report*, March 27 1974.

2 *Frankfurter Rundschau*, April 10 1975.
3 *Democratic German Report*, March 27 1974.
4 *Der Spiegel*, April 22 1974, p. 38.
5 'Education for Today and Tomorrow', Verlag Zeit im Bild, Berlin, 1971.
6 *Der Spiegel*, April 22 1974, p. 49.
7 'The Advent of Mass Higher Education', *OECD Observer*, no. 66, October 1973, p. 27.
8 DIW, *DDR-Wirtschaft*, op. cit., p. 32.
9 *Democratic German Report*, March 13 1974, p. 28.
10 'Women under Socialism', written and published by Panorama-DDR, the foreign press agency of the GDR, Berlin, 1974, p. 15.
11 *Der Morgen*, September 22 1968.
12 *Democratic German Report*, April 10 1974.
13 *Junge Welt*, July 9 1975.
14 DIW, *Wochenbericht*, May 24 1973.
15 DIW, *DDR-Wirtschaft*, op. cit., p. 258.
16 US Department of Agriculture, Economic Research Service, *The Europe and Soviet Union Agricultural Situation: Review of Outlook for 1966 and 1967*, Washington D.C., 1967.
17 DIW, *DDR-Wirtschaft*, op. cit., p. 178.
18 Ibid., p. 267.
19 Ibid., p. 261.

Chapter 10   *The Self-image of a New Germany*
1 Ernst Richert, 'Ulbricht and After', *Survey*, October 1966, p. 156.
2 Willy Brandt, 'Regierungserklärung von Bundeskanzler Willy Brandt, Oktober 28 1969', in *Die Entwicklung der Beziehungen zwischen der Bundesrepublik Deutschlands und der Deutschen Demokratischen Republik: Bericht und Dokumentation* (referred to hereafter as *Dokumentation*), Bundesministerium für innerdeutsche Beziehungen, Bonn, 1973, p. 49.
3 *Neues Deutschland*, March 30 1963.
4 *Neues Deutschland*, May 4 1971.
5 Heinz Lippmann, *Honecker and the New Politics of Europe*, Angus & Robertson, London, 1973, p. 107.
6 *Dokumentation*, op. cit., p. 142.
7 *Democratic German Report*, July 4 1973.
8 Alfred Krossing and Walter Schmidt, 'Nation und Nationalität in der DDR', *Neues Deutschland*, February 15 1975.
9 'The 13th of August Working Group', quoted in *The Times*, August 13 1974.

10 *Amnesty International Annual Report 1974/75*, Amnesty International Publications, London, 1975.
11 *New York Times*, October 6 1975.
12 *Der Spiegel*, December 22 1975.
13 Investigating Committee of Free Jurists, *Ex-Nazis in the Service of the 'German Democratic Republic'*, Berlin, 1965.
14 Simon Wiesenthal, 'Die Gleiche Sprache-Erst für Hitler, Jetzt für Ulbricht', transcript of press conference in Vienna, September 6 1968, provided by the author.
15 Werner Bauer and Ralf Dahrendorf, quoted in John Dornberg, *The Other Germany*, Garden City, New York, 1968, pp. 291ff.
16 Barbara Grunert-Bronnen, *Ich bin Bürger der DDR und lebe in der Bundesrepublik*, Piper Verlag, Munich, 1970.
17 John Dornberg, op. cit., p. 120.
18 Bundesministerium für innerdeutsche Beziehungen, *Materialien zum Bericht zur Lage der Nation 1974*, Bonn, 1974, p. 119.
19 *Einheit*, no. 4, Berlin, 1965.

Epilogue
1 Interview with author, June 1975.
2 Communication from Paul Oestreicher on a meeting with Ulbricht in 1964.

Index